The waterline rose swiftly as the crippled ship began to slide over on its side. Suddenly they were engulfed in a boiling maelstrom, sucked into its vortex along with every other being and the ship's debris. Bodies were first swallowed up, then thrown out into the air as if by a geyser's spume. Furniture, barrels of cargo, chunks of metal—all tossed about while the SS West Lashaway groaned and fought and spun, then disappeared, leaving only a cloud of steam hovering over a massive slick and the acrid stench of explosives to mark its grave. From the first alert to the ship's sinking had been less than two minutes.

IN PERIL ON THE SEA

ROBERT W. BELL
AND D. BRUCE LOCKERBIE

LIVING BOOKS®
Tyndale House Publishers, Inc.
Wheaton, Illinois

*Original hardcover edition published by Doubleday &
Company, Inc., Garden City, New York*

First printing, Living Books edition, April 1989

*Living Books is a registered trademark
of Tyndale House Publishers, Inc.*

Library of Congress Catalog Number 88-51927
ISBN 0-8423-1631-0
*Copyright 1984 by D. Bruce Lockerbie and
Robert W. Bell*

To the memory of ETHEL G. BELL,

whose example gave living proof

that whoever "dwelleth in the secret place

of the Most High

shall abide under the shadow

of the Almighty."

Psalm 91:1

CONTENTS

Wednesday, September 2

Thursday, September 3

Friday, September 4–Saturday, September 5

Sunday, September 6

Monday, September 7–Wednesday, September 9

Thursday, September 10–Saturday, September 12

Sunday, September 13–Thursday, September 17

Friday, September 18

ILLUSTRATIONS

PREFACE

How does a book make a comeback—a shipwrecked book about a shipwreck? How does a book about survival survive and go on to a new life?

In 1984 the original publisher of *In Peril on the Sea,* Doubleday and Company, had the best intentions for this book. But a series of corporate changes, including the sale of the company to a German conglomerate, disrupted the entire publishing house, resulting in major internal uncertainties. *In Peril on the Sea* fell victim to these circumstances and was removed from the active list before its time and sank from view.

But in 1988 two events occurred that helped to bring this book back from the depths. First, the February issue of *The New Yorker* carried a feature article in its "Annals of War and Peace" series, written by E. J. Kahn, Jr., describing a strange reunion between the crews of an American warship, the USS *Buckley,* and a German submarine, the *U-66.* Kahn's story dealt at length with the efforts of one Robert W. Bell to bring about such meetings forty years and more after World War II.

In March 1988, my mother Jeanette Lockerbie Johnston and sister Jeannie Lockerbie had been invited to speak at a British conference of Christian publishers and booksellers. A third travelling companion's plans changed, leaving Mother with a first class railroad ticket to London to offer for someone else's use. As it happened, Bob Bolinder, a Tyndale House representative, availed himself of the offer.

During the train trip from Blackpool to London, Bolinder talked with my mother and sister about the possibility of their writing for his company. At some point, Mother also mentioned my work and asked if Bolinder had ever read *In Peril on the Sea*.

When she returned home, my mother related her conversation, suggesting that I send Bob Bolinder a copy of the book. A month later, Wendell Hawley, editor in chief of Tyndale House Publishers, had issued a contract for this new edition.

Call it coincidence? Or does the same God who brought Bob Bell and his family safely through their peril on the sea still desire to have this story of faith and triumph told in print?

> D. Bruce Lockerbie
> Stony Brook, New York
> Spring 1989

PREFACE TO FIRST EDITION

For most of us, World War II happened a long time ago; in fact, the majority of today's population was not even born when V-E and V-J days were celebrated in the spring and summer of 1945. Yet books and stories, plays and films about World War II continue to fascinate us; perhaps because, unlike subsequent wars in Korea, Vietnam, and elsewhere, the 1939–45 war clearly defined who was Right and who was Wrong. The cruel and inhuman forces of the Swastika and the Rising Sun, we believed, were representatives of consummate evil. So today we see the event called World War II in sweeping, almost cosmic terms, not merely as a struggle pitting the Allies against the Axis Powers but as a moral conflict between Good and Evil.

Every war, however, is also a human tragedy, with individual men and women and children suffering the consequences of human enmity. Sometimes we lose sight of this fact. In the enormity of the Jewish Holocaust, for example, we may miss the fact of suffering by families and by individuals within those families. Conversely, out of every war also comes human triumph by individuals—ordinary people who, after having been tried out in the fires of personal calamity and human disaster, emerge as gold.

Robert W. Bell is such a man, as this book intends to show. Victimized as a boy of eleven by the apparent randomness of war, he survived without bitterness. Indeed, he has come to know and embrace as friends the very men who set him adrift on the Atlantic more than forty years ago—the captain and crew of a German submarine.

I was a boy of eight when I first heard Robert Bell's story, told by his mother soon after their rescue to an audience in a Canadian church. Twenty-five years ago, our mutual friend, Bruce C. Dodd, Jr., introduced me to Bob Bell; since then I have witnessed at firsthand—as neighbor, colleague, and friend—the character and quality of this man. I have heard him recount his experience to listeners of all ages and have always believed that his story is worth writing and worth reading. Not just because of its adventure but also because of the man whose life was shaped by these events, and mostly because of the God in whom Robert Bell trusted then and still trusts.

D. Bruce Lockerbie
Stony Brook, New York

ACKNOWLEDGMENTS

I wish to thank Dr. Jürgen Rohwer, Superintendent, Library of World History, Stuttgart, Federal Republic of Germany; the Historical Scheepvaart Museum, Amsterdam, Netherlands; J. D. Brown, Esq., Naval Historical Branch, Ministry of Defense, London, England; and E. L. V. Ifill, Chief Librarian, Public Library, Bridgetown, Barbados, West Indies, for their generous assistance in making available documents and photographs.

The courtesies extended by Olif Harringer, former Director of Exhibits, Museum of Science and Industry, Chicago, Illinois; Carolyn Ritger, Cataloguer of Photos, Maritime Museum, Newport News, Virginia; and Dr. Dean C. Allard, Head, Operational Archives Branch, Washington, D. C.; and Phyllis Akins, Research Librarian, Emma S. Clark Memorial Library, Setauket, New York, are gratefully acknowledged.

I am also indebted to Douglas K. Stott, former radar operator on HMS *Vimy,* now residing in Anguilla, West

Indies; to Rear Admiral Allen Smith, Jr. (Ret.) USN, of Pensacola, Florida; and to Rear Admiral Donald Gay (Ret.) USN, of Menlo Park, California, for information they contributed.

For urging me to get this book written, sincere thanks to Albert Mead and Marion Homire; for helping me to tell this story, my thanks to D. Bruce Lockerbie; for her skill in typing the manuscript, thanks to Mary Rost. For his support and enthusiasm, thanks to Robert T. Heller of Doubleday & Company.

The willing help given by my sister, Mary Bell Whitbeck, Richard Shaw, Joe Greenwell, and George Marano, comrades on both the *SS West Lashaway* and its raft, has been immeasurable.

To the surviving officers and crewmen of *U-66:* Dr. Friedrich Markworth, Klaus Herbig, Werner Fröhlich, Georg Olschewski, Edmund Wilshusen, Paul Breyer, Vinzenz Nosch, Hans Voigt, Helmut Illing, Leonhard Bürian, Richard Kressman, Georg Grölz, Richard Valentin, and Hans Hoffmann, for their many expressions of friendship, thank you.

With joy I acknowledge Karl Degener-Böning, radio operator of *U-66,* and his wife, Hilde, for their gracious efforts to bridge the gap between former enemies by offering the hospitality of their home in Bielefeld, West Germany, as a place to build a bond of friendship.

Finally, my gratitude and love to my wife, Ruth, for her patient encouragement.

Robert W. Bell
Stony Brook, New York

Sunday, August 30, 1942
ONE

A QUIET SUNDAY AFTERNOON

An American freighter plows through the swelling western Atlantic Ocean, 250 miles off the South American coast. It is the 4,600-ton *West Lashaway,* a ship of the Barber Line bound for Fall River, Massachusetts, with a port of call at Trinidad. *West Lashaway* is on its regular route between West Africa and the United States. Its crew of forty-seven, including nine navy men, under Captain Benjamin Bogden, has been at sea since mid-June, making intermittent stops all along the coast of colonial West Africa. Fifteen days ago, this vessel left Takoradi, Gold Coast (now Ghana), laden with tin, copper, palm oil, liquid rubber or latex, and cocoa beans. In addition to this routine cargo, the ship also carries a secret cache of gold known only to the captain and a few select number of his officers.

Now everyone eagerly awaits the first landfall, at Port of Spain, Trinidad, just two days away. Until then, these men busy themselves with prescribed duties or lounge in their quarters, sometimes in their leisure entertaining the five children among the few passengers also on board.

For two of these children—Robert Bell, age eleven, and his companion, Richard Shaw, thirteen—their voyage so far has been a boy's fantasy come true. For more than two weeks they have enjoyed the run of the ship, exploring from the bridge to the engine room, making the acquaintance of the crew, keeping a pact between them not to share the rights of their masculine privileges with the girls—Robert's thirteen-year-old sister, Mary, and Richard's younger sisters, Georgia, ten, and Carol, seven.

Robert's widowed mother, Ethel Bell, age forty-nine, is a veteran missionary to the Ivory Coast. Richard's parents, Harvey and Vera Shaw, are also experienced missionaries. However, because of the outbreak of World War II in Europe and the Pacific, followed by Germany's occupation of European colonies in Africa, missionaries from hostile nations, such as Mrs. Bell and the Shaws, are no longer safe and must be evacuated to their homes in the United States of America.

Although these missionaries expect their crossing to be uneventful, they are aware that German U-boats have been attacking both merchant and military shipping in the Atlantic. Just yesterday, August 29, 1942, the *West Lashaway*'s radio operator, known to the crew as "Sparks," received a suspicious message, so troubling that he asked the first assistant engineer, Joe Greenwell, to double-check its decoding. The message had directed the *West Lashaway* from its course toward Trinidad with orders to proceed to St. Thomas.

"Sounds funny to me," said Greenwell and took it to the United States Navy intelligence officer on board.

"Sure this is for us, Mr. Greenwell?" the navy man had asked.

"Seems to be, sir," Greenwell replied. "Leastways, they knew our radio call letters—W-R-E-A. What's it mean, sir?"

The navy intelligence officer had paused, squinting once more at the message. "Looks like Jerry's up to tricks again, trying to lure us off course and right into a pack of U-boats. They've been pretty active all around the Windwards and Leewards."

"So the message is phony?"

"As a three-dollar bill, Mr. Greenwell! This isn't from our Merchant Marine; it's straight from OKM, the German Naval High Command. Show it to Captain Bogden and tell him to ignore it."

But Captain Benjamin Bogden had done more than ignore the fradulent message; as a precaution that very afternoon, he had required each person to prepare for any possible emergency by placing all valuables in a ditty bag to be kept readily at hand in one's own quarters. Futhermore, the captain had ordered a new round of lifeboat drills, just in case the boats—or the four additional rafts also on board—might be needed.

Both families, the Shaws and the Bells, have had previous experience as transatlantic voyagers; in fact, the Bells' last such venture, in 1938, had been aboard the luxurious Cunard White Star ocean liner *Laconia*—a far different vessel from this workingman's freighter, the *West Lashaway.* Yet they have no complaints. Given the present wartime conditions, the passengers are nonetheless enjoying privileges ordinarily reserved for peacetime cruises. Their cabins are small but comfortable; they eat heartily with the ship's captain in his handsomely appointed dining room. For recreation, the children are delighted by the menagerie of animals and birds brought by the crew from Africa to be sold in America. A baboon and a bevy of exotic African crowned cranes are kept in cages, but a pair of chimpanzees and several spider monkeys roam the ship at will. These animals and birds provide amusement for the children, but they must be careful not to treat them as pets. Just the other day, Robert Bell was attacked by the female chimp and bitten on his left calf. A messboy, carrying a tray of steaks too close to the birdcage, was pecked at by a crane and dropped the crew's dinner.

Meanwhile, the parents and the only other adult passenger, a British customs official named Pearson, are enjoying the leisure of the voyage. In these tropical latitudes in late August, deck chairs offer an ideal opportunity to read or to relax and take the sun, almost without any thought that nearby are those constant reminders of wartime readiness — a four-inch, 50-mm gun mounted on the poop deck and a detachment of United States Navy personnel to use the weapon, if necessary.

On this Sunday a morning worship service, conducted by the Reverend Mr. Shaw and attended by several members of the crew, precedes Captain Bogden's sumptuous noonday dinner. After a memorable slice of pumpkin pie, Robert Bell and Richard Shaw ask to be excused from the captain's table.

"Permission granted." The captain smiles. "More coffee, ladies? Mr. Shaw? Mr. Pearson?"

The Shaw's family cabin sleeps only four; thus Richard has been assigned to a bunk with the navy gun crew below deck, making him feel like a man among men. Of course, Robert, who shares a cabin with his mother and sister, is still a boy! Together Richard Shaw and Robert Bell hurry below deck to visit with Richard's companions, the friendly navy gunners. This afternoon, as usual, they find the men spending their off-duty hours relaxing with letter writing or card games. The navy armed guard welcome their young visitors to an afternoon of ease.

The three girls, Mary Bell, Georgia and Carol Shaw, are also excused to find their afternoon's entertainment — playing with the animals and waiting for the boys to come back from their exclusive visits with the crew. Their mothers, Vera Shaw and Ethel Bell, are lingering over their coffee, while Captain Bogden and Harvey Shaw discuss details of the voyage.

"The radio room tells me that Jerry's U-boats have been pretty busy recently in these parts," says the captain.

"So I understand from yesterday's little incident," replies Shaw. "But if they've let us come this far, I don't suppose they're much interested in a cargo of cocoa beans."

"Let's hope so," Captain Bogden answers as the men rise and leave the dining room.

Still sipping their coffee, the women's conversation has turned to a topic altogether remote from their comfortable circumstances on this tranquil summer day. They are discussing the suffering and martyrdom of early Christians.

"It seems as though God doesn't call on as many people to endure suffering today as in the past," Ethel Bell muses.

"You're right," Vera Shaw replies. "I guess, though, the important thing isn't whether or not we're called to suffer but whether we're ready and willing to accept whatever God brings into our lives."

The women separate and go to their respective cabins for a Sunday afternoon nap. Ethel Bell removes her dress and hangs it in the wardrobe, then stretches out on her bunk.

At that instant—precisely at 2:31 P.M.—the shrieking alarm calling to general quarters pierces the Sunday stillness.

"Torpedo wake, starboard amidships!" screams the seaman on watch. Then, only seconds later, he calls again, "Second torpedo! O my God!"

In the placid waters of the tropical Atlantic, on an equally placid Sunday afternoon, an enemy submarine has found its prey.

On this same quiet Sunday afternoon, some three thousand miles away from the *West Lashaway,* officers and crew of HMS *Vimy* are enjoying shore leave at Norfolk, Virginia. Lieutenant Commander H. G. de Chair, His Majesty's Royal Navy, and his V-class destroyer had arrived at the United States Navy Yard a few days earlier, after escorting the British battleship HMS *Queen Elizabeth* from Freetown, Sierra Leone, on the west coast of Africa.

Built just at the end of World War I and originally named HMS *Vancouver,* the *Vimy* has been busy since being recommissioned in August 1939, just before the outbreak of World War II. At first, patrols out of Plymouth and Scapa Flow protected the homeland; thereafter the *Vimy* saw increased combat action. During the evacuation of Dunkirk, in particular, the *Vimy* won honors. In the five days of that historic event, May 28 to June 1, 1940, the *Vimy* crossed the English Channel repeatedly from Dover to Dunkirk, bringing back almost three thousand troops from certain disaster on the French beaches. The following year, after being refitted to carry extra supplies of fuel, HMS *Vimy* was assigned to the Convoy Escort Force, based at Freetown. Along with other destroyers such as HMS *Quentin* and HMS *Pathfinder,* now the *Vimy*'s task is to ensure the safe passage of troopships and battle ships attempting to make it across the Atlantic from Canada and the USA. Also important are oil tankers from Venezuelan and Caribbean refineries helping to feed the frantic Allied preparations for a return to Europe.

In a day or two Lieutenant Commander de Chair will be heading the *Vimy* out of Norfolk's great port, down the Hampton Roads, and into the Atlantic once again, making this time for Trinidad and antisubmarine protection for tankers plying those U-boat infested waters. But today, de Chair and Sublieutenant R. B. Venables and the rest can relax for a few hours longer, enjoy a languid Virginia Sunday, write a few letters, admire the tidewater scenery, and perhaps even put the war out of their minds, if only temporarily.

At the United States Naval Air Station near San Juan, Puerto Rico, Lieutenant Allen Smith, Jr., commands VP-31, a squadron of naval aviators with a mission. These men fly PBYs, the navy's latest seaplane, in search of submarines and their shipwrecked victims. VP-31 also provides air support for convoys of ships leaving South America for England or the European theater.

Smith's flight crews are on constant alert, day and night. The enemy's seemingly unstoppable success in destroying American and other Allied shipping up and down the East Coast and throughout the Caribbean gives VP-31 all the business it can handle.

On this sultry Sunday afternoon, Lieutenant Smith sits in his operations center. In late August the hurricane season is about to peak upon Puerto Rico and the rest of the Caribbean, making flying even more risky than it is already. Smith is studying the latest weather maps when his radioman calls to him.

"Looks like Jerry's been at it again, Lieutenant."

"Yeah?" Smith responds wearily. "So what else is new?"

"Another tanker's down. Name is *Sir Huron*. About six thousand tons," the radioman answers. "Just before 0930 hours."

"Where?"

"Longitude ten degrees, fifty north; latitude fifty-four degrees even."

"That puts them almost four hundred and fifty miles due east of Trinidad," Smith calculates. "Have you told Trinidad?"

"Yes, sir. They knew before we did. It happened right in their backyard."

"Yeah, well, it's a big pond out there," Smith says.

"By the way, sir, this is the same sub that took down the *Topa Topa* yesterday."

"What's its identity?" Smith asked.

"*U-66*, sir. We've got six sinkings credited to *U-66* since early July."

"All in the same area?"

"All but one, sir, generally speaking. The first, on July 9, was almost mid-Atlantic."

"Just starting the mission," the commanding officer notes. "On the way over from Lorient, no doubt."

"The rest," the radioman continues, "have all been from the Windwards south and east."

"Early July and the Windwards," Smith muses. "Probably the same U-boat that mined Port Castries last month."

Rising from his desk, Lieutenant Allen Smith, Jr., points an angry finger at his radioman. "Get on the horn and tell Trinidad they'd better get that son of a gun before he blows up the whole U.S. Navy!"

The tropical paradise discovered in 1498 by Christopher Columbus and named for the Holy Trinity has been turned into a garrison by the hatred of warring nations. Trinidad, situated a dozen miles across the Gulf of Paria from the coast of Venezuela, was once dotted by cocoa plantations; now oil derricks and petroleum refineries dominate the landscape. Between the two western jaws of Trinidad's configuration—Serpent's Mouth on the southernmost tip, Dragon's Mouth at the northern end— lies one of the great natural havens for shipping. Port of Spain is Trinidad's principal harbor, but offshore petroleum loading may be done at Point Fortin and at Pointe-à-Pierre. There the oil tankers stock up with black gold bound for foundries and factories, trucks and tanks, throughout the Allied countries. Although located five thousand miles from Europe's war-ravaged civilization, Trinidad could not be any closer to the center of Allied efforts at turning back the Axis monster.

Near Port of Spain, the Trinidad Detachment of Patrol Squadron 31, also known as VP-31, has its headquarters. Lieutenant Donald Gay commands fifteen officers and some seventy-five men, flying about a half dozen PBYs; in turn, Lieutenant Gay reports to Lieutenant Allen

Smith, Jr., at the Puerto Rico headquarters. Like their comrades at San Juan, the Trinidad Detachment performs search-and-destroy missions against German submarines preying on the vital oil link between Trinidad and American or British markets. VP-31 also conducts air-sea rescue work, as well as escorting ships within its flight range.

Donald Gay and his men work almost without sleep. At least two PBYs are airborne at all times, using their newly developed technology called "radar." This primitive, still-experimental device permits pilots to detect ships and surfaced submarines at distances up to twelve miles.

Lieutenant Gay has just come on duty with Lieutenant Tom Evert, relieving officers Walter Winika, Jack Hillman, and Raymond North.

"Anything going on out there?" Gay asks.

"Always," Ray North replies. "This place is like Grand Central Station!"

"You know what I mean—any action? Any subs?"

"Yeah, we got word of a sinking this morning," Jack Hillman answers. "Same place as yesterday."

"What's the location?" inquires the commanding officer, and he moves toward the large wall map of the region.

"We already marked it, Lieutenant," says Walter Winkia. "Ten–fifty north, fifty-four west. Called *Sir Huron,* I believe."

Tom Evert goes to look at the map with Gay.

"Say, that's right next door to the *Topa Topa* yesterday," Evert says. "Do you think it's the same sub?"

"Do chickens lay eggs? You bet your boots it's *U-66* again!"

"Maybe we'd better find *U-66* and send him a greeting."

"What have you got in mind, Tom?"

"Oh, something simple like 'God Bless America!' "

The navy pilots laugh, and Gay and Evert prepare to fly. Just as they leave the hangar for their planes on the tarmac, the Trinidad base radioman calls out to Gay, "Message from San Juan, Lieutenant."

Gay pauses and turns around. "Shoot."

The radioman reads, " 'San Juan VP-31 to Trinidad Detachment. *U-66* active in your zone. Get him or scare him away. Smith.' "

Gay nods to acknowledge the message, then says to Evert, "Let's go get him!"

A perfect Paris afternoon is shimmering toward sunset. On the Boulevard Suchet, northwest of the Arc de Triomphe and overlooking the Bois de Boulogne, stands a luxury apartment building. Empty of its former tenants, this building is now the headquarters of the *Befehlshaber der U-boots,* the German Submarine Commander in Chief. There Vice Admiral — soon to become Grand Admiral — Karl Dönitz keeps his twenty-four-hour watch over the daily exploits of his prized forces, eating and sleeping where he works. They are his dedicated heroes at sea in submarines, which he knows and understands better than anyone else in the world. Dönitz loves these men like his own sons. They are young and reckless, wholly committed to the Fatherland, proud to be submariners, proud to be the envy of every red-blooded German! As for Der Führer and his promised Third Reich to last a thousand years, neither Dönitz nor his men care greatly. Hitler and his lackeys are politicians; Dönitz is a German Navy officer; his men are German submariners!

Almost fifty-one years of age—he will celebrate his next birthday on September 16—Dönitz appears much younger, entirely virile, with strong features and penetrating eyes. Dönitz knows his strengths, and apart from any personal vanity, he knows how to motivate and control other men with a word, a gesture, a glance. He knows too that most of the appeal among his submariners derives from the very fact that they belong not to the obese Hermann Göring's Luftwaffe nor to the Wehrmacht of Gerd von Rundstedt; not even to the German Navy, commanded by Grand Admiral Erich Raeder. Instead, they belong to the Freikorps Dönitz, the volunteers of Karl Dönitz's Submarine Service!

To keep this pride, Dönitz ensures that his men receive the best of everything, from instruction and discipline to shore leave and recreation. The commander in chief personally supervises every aspect of the Submarine Service. He has his subordinates, naturally, including his own son-in-law, Commander Gunther Hessler, chief of operations; but Vice Admiral Karl Dönitz—soon to succeed Erich Raeder as commander in chief of the entire German Navy; for a few mad days in May 1945, even Führer himself!—carries the Submarine Service on his own back.

He had taken over the service in 1939, with only fifty-seven U-boats; however, through his dynamic and persuasive influence, Germany is building almost twelve hundred U-boats. Of course half of these will be lost in combat, and with them the lives of his young men. But such is always the price of heroic valor!

In spite of his apartment's ornate chandeliers, Dönitz keeps his operations center dimly lit, wishing to duplicate the gloom of a U-boat's control room. On each wall of his command post hang maps of the world's oceans and seas, with maps of greater detail showing each strait and bay and estuary from the Bay of Bengal to Long Island Sound and the Bering Strait. Each map is dotted by colored pins to represent the current position of every submarine on patrol. Other pins mark the graves of sunken ships. Dönitz knows each U-boat's every move. For example, just passing the Canary Islands, off the coast of North Africa, is a party of five submarines. They are *U-68, U-156, U-172, U-459,* and *U-504.* Departing Lorient on August 17, these submarines belong to the Polar Bear *(Eisbar)* group headed for action in the Indian Ocean.

Dönitz's charts are updated every four hours by communciations officers who are constantly kept informed by wireless communication with radio ships at sea. These ships in turn relay instructions to each U-boat and keep the crew's morale high with news of the latest German success. They can also transmit any submarine commander's information or request directly to headquarters in Paris or relay it to the several submarine bases on the French coast—at Lorient, Brest, St. Nazaire, and La Rochelle.

Because the bulk of Germany's U-boat action has occurred in the North Atlantic and Caribbean theaters, it is this map at which Karl Dönitz most often stares, as if absorbing vicariously the thrill of each submariner's experience. This map, like all others, has been cut up into blocks labeled with double letters. For instance, the waters off the coast of Labrador and eastward across to Scandinavia are designated AH, AJ, AK, AL, AM

(Ireland and the Irish Sea), AN (England and Scotland and the North Sea), and AO (Denmark and the Baltic Sea south of Sweden). The Caribbean region occupies three rows of Dönitz's blocks, beginning with DA on the Texas coast through DD for Bermuda; DL from the western Gulf of Mexico to DO beyond Hispaniola; then EB from Yucatan to EE beyond Trinidad and Tobago.

No one speaks to the *Befehlshaber* while he gazes at his maps, even though he may do so for an hour or more at a time. His underlings wait for Dönitz to summon them. Finally he speaks:

"What is the name of the new commander of *U-66*, the man who replaced Zapp?"

Hessler signals to an aide, who quickly obtains the correct name.

"Kapitänleutnant Friedrich Markworth, Herr Admiral."

"Of course! How stupid of me!" Dönitz exclaims. "He was with me as a cadet in 1935, on the cruiser *Emden*. I had him promoted to midshipman. A very promising young officer. And, I see, making a good start as a U-boat commander."

"Yes, Admiral," says Hessler, pointing to the blocks labeled ED and EE. "I see that he's made a good account of himself on his first patrol."

"A good account!" roars Dönitz with paternal pride. "This Fritz Markworth has five kills already, the first time out! How many did Zapp have?"

The aide loses no time in checking the records. "A total of seventeen in five patrols, Herr Admiral."

"Five patrols! And we gave Zapp the Knight's Cross!"

A communications officer approaches and salutes Dönitz. "With respect, Admiral, make that seven sinkings for *U-66*. We have just received confirmation of two more today."

Dönitz hears this news with a gleeful gig. The communications officer steps to the map and adds two more black pins in block EE, east of Trinidad.

"This morning the *Sir Huron,* a Panamanian registry," he reads from his notes. "This evening, European time, an American freighter, the *West Lashaway.* "

"Send *U-66* my personal congratulations," Dönitz orders and walks away from his maps. "Yes, indeed, Hessler! A young commander to be reckoned with, this Markworth!"

At their Toronto, Ontario, home, the Reverend Alfred Roffe and his wife, Mary, have returned with their older daughter, Nell, from morning worship services at the Christian and Missionary Alliance Tabernacle on Christie Street. As founder and matron of the Missionary Rest Home — a guest house for transient missionaries on furlough, located on the shore of Lake Ontario — Alfred and Mary Roffe are also the parents of five children, four of whom are foreign missionaries themselves. Their younger daughter, Ethel, is on her way home from Africa, bringing with her their grandchildren Mary and Robert.

Over a traditional Sunday dinner, made somewhat skimpy by wartime rationing, Alfred Roffe pauses to give thanks for their food.

"And we also pray, O Lord, they special care and blessing upon our daughter Ethel and our grandchildren Mary and Robert as they journey home. Bring them to us in safety, we beseech thee," he prays. "In the name of Jesus Christ, we ask this. Amen."

Mary Roffe raises her bowed head and, smiling at her husband and daughter, says, "Just think, next Sunday Ethel and the children may be sitting at this table with us."

"The Lord willing," her husband adds.

TWO
DAS BOOT

Like the human aspiration to fly, mankind's attempt to penetrate the ocean depths has a long history. Ancient writers — Herodotus, Aristotle, Pliny the Elder — describe such efforts. According to tradition, Alexander the Great had a glass barrel built for him in which he was lowered to the floor of an Aegean cove. The imagination of Leonardo da Vinci led him to speculate on the possibilities of constructing a container in which a human being might safely explore the world beneath the sea. The first actual submersion of a navigable vessel occurred around 1620, when a Dutch inventor, Cornelius van Drebel, demonstrated his submarine in the Thames River, taking King James I with him on one occasion.

The American War of Independence witnessed the first use of a submarine in conflict. In 1776, a submarine called the "Turtle," built by David Bushnell and operated by Sergeant Ezra Lee, a volunteer, crept into New York Harbor, hoping to fasten an explosive device to the hull of a British man-of-war, HMS *Eagle*. The attack failed, but its tactics established a precedent for all future naval warfare.

Throughout the nineteenth century, experiments and refinements improved the submarine. Robert Fulton, better known as the inventor of the steamboat, also created a submersible vessel with explosives, which he nicknamed after a fish, calling them torpedoes. During the American Civil War, submarine attacks, especially by the Confederate Navy, threatened all enemy shipping. The invention of electrical power in storage batteries gave the next impetus to submarine development. By 1900, John P. Holland had built a submarine fifty-three feet long and ten feet in diameter, fit for total submersion and equipped for warring purposes, complete with periscope and torpedoes.

By the beginning of World War I, Germany had taken over the lead in submarine technology with her *Unterseeboot,* or U-boat. But Germany had disregarded an international understanding, a rule of the sea, that merchant vessels should be safe from attack unless some means existed whereby crew and passengers might be rescued. Instead, in February 1915, just six months after World War I began, Germany declared that her submarines would sink any ship, regardless of the danger to those on board, found within a zone extending from the western mouth of the English Channel in a circle around Ireland and Great Britain. President Woodrow Wilson issued a counterdeclaration, warning Germany not to attack any still-neutral American ship, or else the consequences would be war with the United States. Germany chose, however, to ignore Wilson's threat, determined — as

Thomas A. Bailey writes—to "launch their torpedoes first and write diplomatic notes later."

So the ravaging of commercial as well as military shipping began. In the single month of April 1915, German U-boats sank an astonishing 430 ships belonging to Allied or neutral nations. In three months ninety ships went down in the proscribed German war zone. But on May 7, 1915, the German policy misfired. The infamous sinking of the *Lusitania,* a Cunard luxury liner with 1,198 persons lost—including 128 Americans—created a worldwide terror, discrediting Germany's warriors as barbarous Huns. Yet Germany persisted. Ten months later, in March 1916, a passenger steamer crossing the English Channel was sunk. Now Wilson retaliated against Germany with an ultimatum: Any further sinking of merchant or passenger ships would result in the breaking of diplomatic relations between the United States and Germany.

For almost a year Germany rescinded its attacks; but on January 31, 1917, a new declaration of all-out hostilities against all foreign ships brought Germany face-to-face with America as an enemy. In March 1917, the torpedoing of four American merchantmen left Wilson with no choice but to declare war on Germany.

The Armistice of 1918 required Germany to surrender all her U-boats. In the Treaty of Versailles that followed, one of the conditions imposed upon a defeated Germany forbade Germany ever again to manufacture or obtain submarines. This edict, however, Adolf Hitler arrogantly repudiated in 1935, demanding the right to match Great Britain's number of submarines. Bowing before this pressure, other nations attempted to reestablish a code for humane warfare on the sea. The London protocol, signed on November 6, 1936, by forty-two nations, including Germany, expressly declared that "a merchant vessel must not be destroyed until the crew and passengers have first been placed in safety." If submarines could not meet this provision, the agreement stated, then submarines must "desist from attack and from seizure." Like many other rules for making war a civilized act, these proved to be empty words.

Beginning in 1939, with only fifty-seven U-boats, Germany rebuilt a submarine fleet of more than 1,100 boats, prowling the seas often like a wolf pack, attacking indiscriminately any ship they encountered. Under the command of Admiral Dönitz, his 39,000 volunteers were almost unstoppable until the summer of 1943, when the Allies' new long-range bombers, called Liberators, began to thwart Germany's submarine fleet. But although nearly 800 U-boats were destroyed in combat and 32,000 men died — an appalling loss of life — the Freikorps Dönitz took with them more than 23,000 Allied ships.

Germany's submariners were exclusively volunteers; at least, until late in the war, when conscripts were needed. Confident, eager for action, cocky in the presence of danger, these young men were proud to belong to the elite in spite of the known risk of almost certain death. A typical submariner — perhaps twenty years old — had been indoctrinated by what the Befehlshaber Dönitz himself called "the spirit and pure idealism of patriotism." In such a spirit, he feared nothing. He was ready to taste the excitement of combat; however, he also had to accept the excruciating boredom of inactivity. Mostly he endured wrenching psychological stress, for which his six months of training in submarine school could hardly have prepared him. Nor was he adequately prepared for the insufferable pain within his ears caused by the pressure underwater. Many a submariner returned to Lorient or St. Naziare from his first patrol to discover that he had an irreparable loss of hearing.

A typical submarine mission or patrol lasted from four weeks to as long as four months, during which time sixty men lived on a boat like moles in a tunnel, without fresh water to drink, without bathing. Their craft measured only 250 feet, about three quarters the length of a football field. Inside its double hull, the boat was less than 15 feet wide, with only a narrow passage leading from the control center to both ends. This passage, furthermore, seemed even less accessible because of the array of pipes, valves, wheels, gauges, dials, and other intricate machinery protruding from the walls. Every possible inch of space had been filled by some device essential to the operation of the U-boat.

Its interior had been divided into six main compartments from bow to stern: forward torpedo room; officers' quarters, galley, and communications center; control room; diesel engine room; electric motor and maneuvering room; and aft torpedo room.

Under the U-boat's tapering nose lay the forward torpedo room with its four firing tubes. At the opposite end of the boat, the aft torpedo room contained two more tubes. Each tube was always stocked with an electric torpedo, almost 23 feet long, 20 inches in diameter, waiting to be fired. German torpedoes were powered by batteries stored in the middle of each casing, propelled by an electric motor and steered on their predetermined course by a gyroscope, both at the rear. Up front, the deadly warhead was timed to explode on impact.

Each boat in the *U-66* class carried twenty-two torpedoes upon setting out from home port. Six lay in their firing tubes; four more were ready and waiting in the forward torpedo room, hanging from chains, two more similarly stored in the aft room. Ten additional torpedoes were stored under the top deck and could be lowered into the torpedo rooms as needed. Normally, when these weapons had all been fired, a boat's patrol ended; but every commander was careful not to waste a torpedo on a less-than-certain victim.

But torpedoes were not the only occupants of these rooms fore and aft. Suspended from the ceiling, eight metal bunks in each room provided primitive sleeping accommodations to crewmen. Each shared his bunk with at least one other crew member, working while his opposite slept, then switching places. Crewmen's bunks were outfitted with a coarse woolen blanket and blue-and-white gingham sheets and pillowcases. The choice of colored and checked linens for the crew had little to do with interior decor and aesthetics; instead, it had everything to do with disguising grime and filth. A crewman's bed sheets would be clean upon embarking from Lorient or St. Nazaire or La Rochelle, but there would be no laundry service for the duration of the patrol. Futhermore, with at least two men alternating their sleeping in a bunk, the increased wear soon became apparent. The blue-and-white-checked sheets, however, showed less evidence of dirty linen than would have been true of white bed sheets and pillowcases. Of course, the captain and his officers enjoyed the luxury of clean sheets on a regular basis — always white.

Just behind the forward torpedo room came the officers' quarters, galley, and communications center.

Unlike the crew, whose bunks hung like hammocks and could be flipped back against the hull, officers' bunks were permanent fixtures, set in wood paneling and individually assigned; no officer shared his bunk with another. Petty officers and chiefs had tiny cubbyholes in which to store personal items. Senior officers enjoyed larger closets and their own cabinet of dishes, cups, and saucers. Next to this cabinet hung an autographed photo of Admiral Dönitz.

Next came the galley, a room not unfamiliar to urban apartment dwellers whose kitchens are often little more than closets. Few apartment chefs are responsible, however, for feeding sixty men their 180 daily meals. Nonetheless, the food served was of better than average quality by military standards. A single electric stove with three hot plates and two ovens made the serving of hot meals possible. The galley also contained a refrigerator, a sink, and water supplies, both fresh and salt water. Counter space was almost negligible. Each crewman had his own mess kit, while the officers dined with greater civility, using china, flatwear, and tablecloths.

Food storage, of course, created a problem. More than three tons of food must be taken along to feed so many men for an indeterminate period. Thus at the beginning of a mission, every nook and cranny held provisions. Sacks of potatoes filled the gaps between machinery; canned food occupied every compartment, while from the pipes and lines strung overhead hung fresh hams and sausages, as in any good German butcher shop. Each boat had two toilets, but one of these was fully stocked with food, leaving only one toilet for sixty men. Even the bunks were used for storing food, including the 150 lemons each submariner received and rationed throughout his voyage to ward off scurvy. Yet this food supply supposed a mission of only ten weeks or so; when circumstances of war kept a submarine from returning to its base for another month or more, the men ate half-rations for the final weeks of the patrol.

Next to the galley was the commmunications center, two rooms for the radioman and his sound-detection assistants. The radio room had a powerful wireless unit capable of reaching the relay ships stationed in the mid-Atlantic; from these ships U-boats could receive or send messages direct from the *Befehlshaber's* command post in Paris. After receiving such a message, the radioman, perched on his metal stool, would type out the message on the Enka typewriter, then summon an assistant to deliver the message to the commander or his deputy. Next to the typewriter stood a tiny portable gramophone on which recordings were sometimes played, broadcast over the boat's loudspeaker system. Next door a sound engineer lisened to hydrophones capable of discerning the sound of any ship that might be in the area.

Only the commander knew the privilege of privacy. His quarters, adjacent to the galley and communications center, amounted to little more than a corner curtained off from the busy communications area; but, at least, he could close the curtain if he wished. Inside he claimed a sturdy bunk, ample storage space, including a full-length clothes closet for his dress uniforms, and a wash-stand whose wooden top, when closed, became the commander's desk. Because of the intense physical and psychological tension of a submarine patrol, a commanding officer needed a private place for reflection and rest. But no submarine commander could afford to cut himself off from his men.

The center of the boat, literally and strategically, was the control room. From here the boat received its direction and depth. Technical apparatus astonishing to a novice made possible a cruising speed above water or a sudden dive to more than six hundred feet below the surface or a stable attacking run at just periscope depth. Here the *Obersteuermann,* or chief helmsman, responded to the commander's orders. Here too the official charts maintained a record of the U-boat's journey. Above the control room, with access gained by ladder, stood the commanding officer at his position in the conning tower. The captain's principal instrument was the periscope, through which he could study both the ocean's surface for ships and the sky for planes. Immediately at hand waited an early-stage computer to inform the commander regarding his torpedoes and a preset firing device. Upon the captain's judgment, confirmed by the computer, he gave the command *"Los* [Fire]!" and the devastation began.

Finally, the power sources for a submarine such as *U-66* were found in the diesel engine room and in the electric motor and maneuvering room, aft of the control room. When running on the surface, a U-boat received its power from two diesel engines, each capable of 2,170 horsepower. Oil bunkers supplied fuel sufficient to cover more than sixteen hundred nautical miles. While on the surface a submarine would recharge its batteries for underwater travel. These batteries powered two electric dynamotors, which could propel a submerged boat some sixty nautical miles.

The Submarine Service called for men without nerves. Five dozen men were expected to exist in fetid foulness, in dank, humid stench, imprisoned in a submerged canister, hoping against hope for one gasp of fresh air — all of them unclean, many of them sick from time to time, some wounded in battle and dying without adequate medical attention, several afflicted with venereal disease, a few on every mission slipping temporarily off the ledge of sanity. Malnutrition, anemia, outbreaks of boils and acne, skin color pallid as a corpse: these were the physical signs of a submariner's distress. Under these claustrophobic and enervating conditions, a man had to adjust to the fact that he might not see the sun and sky again for three or four months. He learned to accept his place in the can of worms, to exist through days of tedious waiting, to work without rest through hours of combat, to keep his self-control when his ears seemed about to burst because of underwater pressure, to preserve utter silence as the enemy's sonar instruments probed for the sub's whereabouts. Only one thing made this wretchedness seem worthwhile: his absolute conviction that the German Navy and its submariners were fighting to protect the freedom of the Fatherland.

The officers and crew serving under the submarine commander were divided into three watches. Ordinarily, on patrol, a man could count on working only one third of each day on his watch. Those with specificially technical skills — machinists, firemen, radiomen, the cook, the pharmacist's mate — could count on spending their duty time at their own responsibilities. But every submarine commander maintained a constant round of instruction, teaching every man the jobs of two or three or four other men. It was not enough to have qualified radio operators for each watch, or a qualified pharmacist's mate, or an adequate complement of machinists, firemen, and engineers. Suppose the cook became ill? Who would man the galley? Suppose several seamen were lost in combat? Who would perform their tasks? Many men must know how to serve in any emergency that might arise. So submariners were taught to be versatile, able to fill in for an ailing or fallen comrade with as little loss of efficiency and expertise as possible. Thus, as a patrol lengthened and the U-boat's mission became more dangerous—as casualties rose or men became incapacitated by illness—the normal eight-hour watch could be halved. Now a man would find himself on duty for four hours, off for the next four, on again, until the crisis ended. Under the best conditions, sleep on a U-boat came hard. Dozing in snatches seemed to be the common lot of every submariner.

For recreation during his hours off duty, the U-boat officer or crewman might read, keep his diary, write letters to be mailed at the patrol's end, or engage in one of the perpetual card games that best seemed to occupy men's minds. Seated on lower bunks across the narrow passageway, with a board perched on their knees, groups of four men carried on their *Kartenspiel,* while kibitzers in overhanging hammocks looked on and offered unsolicited advice or comment. From time to time, a commanding officer would instruct his communications officer to play a recording of inspirational, patriotic music on the wind-up gramophone. At the sound of Franz Joseph Haydn's stirring chords, the men would abandon their card games, tumble out of their pipestem bunks, and join in singing the words by Hoffmann von Fallersleben, *"Deutschland über alles."* If the music were Richard Wagner's "Prelude to Act III of *Die Meistersinger von*

Nürnberg" or Richard Strauss's *Also Sprach Zarathustra,* the men could continue to play, knowing that what followed would be a report replayed from Admiral Dönitz's headquarters on the progress of the war. Cheers were obligatory, but no need to interrupt a game or break a fitful sleep.

Formal religious observances were almost nonexistent, except as kept in the privacy of each man's own bunk. When a crew member died in action, a prayer from the Lutheran or Roman Catholic upbringing most men shared might be uttered before the body was committed to the sea. The only other rites were those commemorating any crewman's first crossing of the equator. On the fateful day that a submarine moved from the northern hemisphere to the southern, all those men designated as novitiates were compelled to participate in a comical — and sometimes painful — ceremony. They would crawl the length of the submarine, from the engine room to the control room, all the time being roundly swatted by their mates. Then followed certain forms of mild torture — tickling, torment by ice cubes on their genitals, eating flour balls coated with diesel oil, and so on. At the center of the boat these neophytes were greeted by "Admiral Triton" — an officer and veteran of many such equatorial crossings — before whom they bowed in obeisance, kissing Triton's unclean foot three times. After this ordeal, each initiate received a new "baptismal" name — usually the name of a sea creature — and a glass of rum. The ritual was over. In a pagan parody of Christian redemption, each submariner was cleansed of his sins in the northern hemisphere. He was now a new man.

Sometimes an indulgent commander would allow crew members to take their leisure time on deck, lounging in the so-called winter garden just behind the conning tower. Artillery specialists also spent time on the deck, caring for the 10.5 centimeter cannon up front and the two machine guns and 3.7 centimeter cannon aft of the tower. These weapons were sometimes used offensively but were essential for defense against the increasing threat of Allied air power. Therefore they must be tested frequently to be certain they remained in working condition.

But when the submarine went into action — either attacking or being attacked — nobody slept or played cards, listened to music, or engaged in hijinks. Every man, whatever his regular watch, was roused into action by the boat's Klaxon, ready to perform his assigned task. The call to battle stations was more than just the cry of horns and hounds to a hunt; it was, in every sense, a call for the U-boat's survival.

As far as possible, submarines cruised above water, submerging only for practice dives and for the undetected final approach on a ship about to be attacked. During each watch above water a five-man team occupied the tower above the waterline. A watch officer in the tower assigned the other four men each to stand staring at his ninety-degree sector and report to him at intervals. This duty might be tedious, cold or hot, wet or dry, but it was always a relief to men who would otherwise have been cooped up in the dank and humid dungeon below.

In the late summer of 1942, radar had not yet been adapted for submarine use. Each U-boat depended exclusively on the vision of the men posted as lookouts in the conning tower. Usually their first clue that a victim might be hunted down was a wisp of smoke on the horizon — a ship's smokestacks puffing its exhaust, inadvertently signaling its own doom. Once a sighting had been confirmed by the watch officer's own eyes, the word was shouted down a tube to the control room below.

"Unidentified tanker, possibly five thousand tons, at two miles distance."

Immediately this news would be relayed to the submarine commander, whereupon the customary orders would be given to begin tracking the ship. For their own protection from reprisal, especially by air attack, most U-boat commanders preferred to stalk a potential candidate for sinking, waiting all day, if necessary, until early evening or total darkness before attacking. During these hours of pursuit, the U-boat skipper's preoccupation was always with keeping his own vessel far enough removed to avoid being spotted. Generally he tried to follow the sun's angle in relation to the ship, thus requiring the ship's lookouts to stare directly into the sunlight. Patiently the submarine would wait—unless suddenly the ship began changing its course, tacking at full speed. Then the submarine commander would know he had been seen and would attack without further delay.

The commanding officer might choose to pursue his quarry on the surface, where he could make eighteen to twenty knots; or he might settle for a submerged chase at only eight knots. If so, the commander would give the word to dive below the surface. Quickly the five men on watch and any artillery men also on deck must rush toward the hatch and slide down the pole to safety, the last man inside closing and securing the hatch behind him. Then the submarine tilts forward, flooding its nine chambers with seawater to pull the nose downward. In an emergency dive to avoid bombing, a U-boat could slope to a forty-eight-degree angle and fall more than 650 feet. Usually, however, an attacking submarine stayed just deep enough to allow its fifty-foot-tall periscopes to break the water's surface, scanning both the ocean and sky.

Meanwhile the torpedoes were being loaded and readied for firing.

THREE
"TWO HITS.
STRONG WHITE
EXPLOSION."

Kapitänleutnant Friedrich Markworth, commanding officer of *U-66*, stepped back from the periscope and clapped his hands.

"Direct hits!" Markworth shouted into the speaking tube connected to the control room below the conning tower. "Two of them! She won't last five minutes!"

Oberleutnant Georg Olschewski, chief engineer on the submarine, climbed the ladder to peer into the periscope lens for himself.

"She's keeled over already, Captain. Imagine, less than two minutes! That may be a new record!"

"Do we have her identity?" Markworth inquired.

"I'll find out," said Olschewski, and he slid down the ladder.

"Ask Degener-Böning," Obersteuermann Werner Fröhlich, chief helmsman and third watch officer, ordered a crewman.

The submariner slid from the control room forward

to the radio room, where Oberfunkmaat Karl Degener-Böning sat hunched over his wireless dials and signals, his ears covered by a headset. It was hardly a room, more like a cubicle curtained off from the rest of the submarine to give the radio operator some quiet in which to concentrate. Degener-Böning scowled at the crewman and waved him into silence before the man could speak. Then the radioman removed the headset, stood up, and stretched.

"Nothing," he said in reply to the crewman's unspoken question. "I have no information whatever. The ship's radio never put out a message. It must have been knocked out by the first strike. Tell Captain Markworth that I know nothing at all about the ship."

The crewman returned to the control room with this message.

"Take us to the top, Olschewski," the commander told his engineer. "Let's see for ourselves."

The German submarine known as *U-66* was typical of the boats in action throughout World War II. Built in the Deschimag shipyards at Bremen in 1940, this 750-ton craft had been commissioned on New Year's Day, 1941. The original commanding officer, Kapitän Richard Zapp, and his officers and crew had assembled in Bremen a month before to become acquainted with their boat. Five months after commissioning and training exercises in the Baltic, *U-66* went into service as part of the Second Flotilla, based at Lorient on France's northern curve of the Bay of Biscay. Her first three patrols, in the South Atlantic for the most part, reported little activity. For her fourth mission, however, *U-66* was sent to harass shipping along the East Coast of the United States of

America. This was the beginning of the German Navy's special operation known as *Paukenschlag,* or "Roll of Drums."

Throughout the fall of 1941, even before both Japan and Germany had entered into war against the United States, Admiral Karl Dönitz had been trying to persuade Adolf Hitler to launch attacks against America's vulnerable East Coast, particularly the northeastern ports of embarkation for shipping to Great Britain. For reasons of his own, Hitler had rejected Dönitz's argument; even as late as December 6, the day before Japan's attack on Pearl Harbor, Hitler was still hoping to keep the Americans out of the war. But on December 11, Germany joined Japan in making war on the United States; the American coastline became a German target. Almost immediately, Dönitz sent word to his Submarine Service to head westward toward the sitting ducks in American harbors.

On Christmas Day, 1941, under Zapp's command, *U-66* left Lorient for North America, its fourth patrol. Forty-eight days later, on February 10, 1942, *U-66* returned to base in triumph. Six ships, amounting to 60,000 tons, had been sunk. American defenses seemed nonexistent; naval procedures were careless, to say the least; no alerting of any national awareness, no precaution against danger. For instance, coastal blackouts had not yet been ordered, and so city lights illuminated ships at sea like silhouettes on a firing range. In fact, Zapp joked in the bistros of Lorient that, while he took down the *SS Allen Jackson,* a tanker sunk off New York Harbor, he could watch heedless Americans dining and dancing in skyscraper restaurants.

By the time *U-66* was ready for its next patrol, Admiral Dönitz had shifted his "Roll of Drums" campaign southward to the Carolina and Florida coastlines and into the Caribbean. On this, his fifth and final patrol as commander of *U-66,* Zapp was at sea from March 21 until May 27, 1942. During this time he sank seven more ships. For these and other accomplishments, Kommandant Richard Zapp received the Knight's Cross of the Iron Cross and was promoted to commanding officer of the Third U-boat Flotilla, based at La Rochelle, France.

Zapp's replacement, Kapitänleutnant Friedrich Markworth, took command of *U-66* on June 21, 1942. Markworth, then thirty-two years old—bearded and handsome, with piercing, deep-set eyes—had been born in Wolfenbüttel and schooled at Wilhelmshaven. At age nineteen Markworth had joined the navy. As a cadet, one of his commanding officers had been Karl Dönitz. With Dönitz, in 1935, Markworth sailed on board the cruiser *Emden* around Africa and into the Indian Ocean. Rising steadily through the ranks, Markworth achieved promotion to *leutnant* on April 1, 1937, just three years after having entered the navy. Two years later there was another promotion to *oberleutnant* and the appointment as artillery technical officer on the heavy cruiser *Blücher.* By this time, September 1939, Germany had declared war, and the *Blücher* was singled out to lead the "Weser Exercise," the code name given for the Nazi occupation of Denmark and Norway. This invasion, scheduled for April 9, 1940, was to be under the command of Admiral Oscar Kummetz, with the *Blüncher* as his command post; on board were also many other high-ranking German naval officers. Led by the *Blücher,* the German invasion fleet sailed into the Oslo Fjord. At the narrowest point of the fjord, the Dröbak Narrows, Norwegian defenders began firing on the *Blücher,* using artillery and shore-based torpedoes. Two dozen direct hits, including two torpedoes, ignominiously sank the *Blücher* with its distinguished brass on board. As artillery officer, Markworth received some of the blame for this disaster, resulting in his being given a land assignment for some months following.

During this interim, Oberleutnant Markworth saw a brighter future for himself in the Submarine Service, where his former mentor, Dönitz, was now commander. In the early months of 1941, Markworth trained at several submarine officers' schools; on March 1, 1941, he was appointed first officer of the watch on *U-103,* part of the Second Flotilla out of Lorient, commanded by Kapitän Victor Schütze. *U-103* saw action off the coast of Sierra Leone, West Africa. On September 1, 1941, Markworth was again promoted, to *kapitänleutnant;* two months later he was sent for extensive studies at two more submarine academies, and by May 1942, declared a candidate for command of his own boat. His opportunity came on June 21, 1942, when he succeeded Zapp as commanding officer of *U-66,* lead boat of the Second Flotilla. His first patrol, *U-66's* sixth mission, left Lorient on June 26. By the close of August 30, the day on which this story begins, Markworth had sunk seven ships and damaged several others. An amateur photographer, Kapitänleutnant Friedrich Markworth sometimes amused himself by taking home movies of the havoc he had created, standing in the tower of his boat and panning the scene of destruction and death with his camera.

With a little luck, Markworth could look forward to a brilliant career in the German Navy. Of course, luck could be fickle and calamitous as well as benevolent. Consider the case of his comrade-in-arms Kapitänleutnant Werner Loewe, commanding *U-505,* sister to *U-66.* Like Markworth, Loewe had begun impressively with four sinkings on his first patrol off the coast of West Africa: 26,000 British Registered Tons, or BRTs. Then *U-505* had come to join *U-66* in the Caribbean area: three more ships, 15,000 BRT. But just a month ago, in late July, Loewe the Lion had become ill, so sick, in fact, that his boat had been ordered out of combat and sent back to Lorient. Too bad for Loewe. But good luck seemed to favor Markworth. Along with his fellow officers on *U-66* — men like Oberleutnant Georg Olschewski, age thirty-three, chief engineer; Obersteuermann Werner Fröhlich, age twenty-eight, chief helmsman and officer of the third watch; and young Klaus Herbig, only twenty years old and already second watch officer — Markworth had reached a pinnacle of success many men his age dreamed about but few ever knew firsthand. He was a submarine commander in the Freikorps Dönitz, watching enemy ships crumble into sawdust before his firepower!

But radioman Karl Degener-Böning and most of his fellow crew members never saw the sinking ships, never heard the cries of shipwrecked victims pleading to be rescued before the ocean claimed them. Born in Niederbarkhausen on March 28, 1919, Degener-Böning shared every young man's dream to join the navy and see the world. In 1938, at age nineteen, he had entered the German Navy. But by the time his basic training as a radio operator ended, Germany was once again at war. Degener-Böning's visions of peacetime voyages to exotic ports had been crushed by Hitler's lust for a Third Reich that would last a thousand years. However, instead of waiting to be assigned to some surface vessel, Degener-Böning sought greater adventure as a volunteer in Deutschland's most glamorous fighting force, the Submarine Service.

After training for six months, Degener-Böning had been assigned to *U-66* at its commissioning on January 1, 1941. As one of the original crew members, he participated in every moment of *U-66's* nine missions during its three-year lifespan. Caught up in his own work or in supervising the work of his subordinates — Harry Schöneck, Gottlieb Melmuka, and Helmuth Angerstein — Oberfunkmaat Karl Degener-Böning had little time to theorize about the folly of war. One day was so much like another on board that submarine that, except for a quirk of history four decades later, Karl Degener-Böning would have no reason to recall what he was doing on the afternoon of Sunday, August 30, 1942. He was merely doing his job.

"We'd been at sea almost ten weeks already," says Degener-Böning, now retired from his postwar work as a radio and television engineer for the West German broadcasting system. "Our theater of operations for that sixth patrol was to be the Caribbean. In addition to our routine business of interrupting shipping" — Degener-Böning winces at this euphemism for "sinking ships" — "we also had a special assignment this time. We were to lay mines at Port Castries, Santa Lucia, in the Windward Islands."

From the home base at Lorient to the Windwards, just west of Barbados, took *U-66* three weeks. All this time the supply of mines remained on the floor of the sub's bow compartment, making the crew extraordinarily uneasy.

"We never knew when one of those temperamental devices might choose to go off," says Karl Degener-

Böning. "All we knew was that we were a floating bomb ready to explode."

En route to the Caribbean, *U-66* had sighted and sunk Markworth's first kill, the Yugoslav steamer *Triglav,* on July 9. *U-66* had come upon its prey virtually in mid-ocean, too far beyond the range of American Flying Boats or British Liberators to offer the *Triglav* air protection. Against a single U-boat eager for an attack in open waters, the *Triglav* never had a chance. Now Markworth was ready for more. But first, to get rid of those damnable mines!

On July 20, as *U-66* approached its destination — the idyllic harbor of Port Castries — two torpedo tubes were emptied of their customary weapons and the mines inserted. Now came the tricky maneuvering of the boat. Chief Engineer Georg Olschewski recalls, "At the approach of evening we began carrying out our mine-laying operation. It was a very difficult job for me to keep the boat constantly sumerged in such relatively shallow water. I knew that if we broke through the water surface, we would be destroyed by the shore batteries."

At periscope depth *U-66* crept into Port Castries Harbor to plant its deadly seeds, placing each mine thirty to forty yards apart across the mouth of the harbor.

"We barely made it out of Port Castries," Degener-Böning remembers. "As we were backing out, still at periscope depth, the nets protecting the harbor from subs like us began to close."

But *U-66* managed to slip through the trapping nets and make its way south to the Gulf of Venezuela, then to the waters off Aruba, before returning to the tip of the Windward Islands. Now Markworth was ready to begin attacking Allied ships in earnest.

Six days after the successful mining of Port Castries, Markworth sank the Brazilian ship *Tamandare;* two days later another Brazilian steamer, *Barbacena.* On July 29, and again on August 2, several American and British vessels reaped the harvest of Port Castries, suffering severe damage from the mines *U-66* had hidden in Santa Lucia Harbor. But by this time the reputation *U-66* was acquiring for itself had begun to attract attention from the United States Navy's Patrol Squadron 31, based in Trinidad. One clear night in early August, two PBYs sent out by Lieutenant Donald Gay, commanding officer of the Trinidad Detachment, picked out the moonlit silhouette of a German submarine. Swooping out of the shadows, the U.S. Navy team attacked. Georg Olschewski remembers well:

"The night was perfectly clear, and we were busy scanning the Venezuelan coastline, when all of a sudden there they were! American Navy planes dropping bombs on us! It was the first time we had ever been attacked from the air, and it brought into reality all the drill at diving we had practiced."

For the next few days *U-66* withdrew far from the area off Trinidad, heading southeast along the curve of South America toward Georgetown, British Guiana. "We had to move our reserve supply of torpedoes," says Olschewski, "from the storage area in the upper decks of the boat to the tubes themselves. During this time, we were highly vulnerable, unable to dive, and so hardly able to defend ourselves if attacked. But no attack came."

Instead, *U-66* went back on attack. On August 6, the day that its torpedoes were once again in place, *U-66* destroyed a small freighter with armored sides named *Rosewie.* Markworth seemed able to sink ships almost at will. He and his boat prowled the eastern Caribbean and western Atlantic beyond Trinidad and the Lesser Antilles like a hungry shark, frenzied by the smell of blood. On August 29 yet another ship, the American steamer *Topa Topa*, fell to *U-66*.

The next day, just at dawn, Markworth's spotters found a Panamanian motorized ship named *Sir Huron*. By 9:26 A.M. it had been sunk.

"Often we knew nothing about a ship," says Karl Degener-Böning, "its name or its flag, until after the attack was under way. Then, if the ship had been hit, I'd try to listen in on the SOS call to get the ship's name. I heard the *Sir Huron* call for help, but the next attack was over so quickly, I never heard its name at all."

That next attack is recorded in *U-66's* official log using Middle European Time, a five-hour difference; in Atlantic time, it reads:

	Day: 30 August 1942
7:00 A.M.	Rainy, varying visibility. Just went 184 sea miles above water, 1.8 miles under water . . .
10:00 A.M.	Smoke in view. Proceeding at top speed.
12:00 P.M.	Smoke in sight.
1:08 P.M.	Dived.
1:15 P.M.	At battle stations.

At the position of 10° 30′ north and 55° 34′ west, just after Sunday dinner had been served on board the *West Lashaway,* Markworth gave the command, and the *West Lashaway* was doomed. The remaining pertinent log entries read:

2:31 P.M.	Two individual torpedoes, tubes I and III. Two hits. Strong white explosion. Ship apparently loaded with phosphates.
2:36 P.M.	Surfaced.
2:45 P.M.	Steamer sunk. Now going at 180° on new course.
4:20 P.M.	Wireless message to BDU [Admiral Dönitz' Headquarters in Paris]: Just sunk steamer 4,500 BRT.

Lieutenant Donald Gay, commander of the United States Navy Patrol Squadron 31, Trinidad Detachment, flew his PBY over the sun-blanched western Atlantic. To his right lay the coast of South America, 250 miles away; to the left, his partner, Lieutenant Tom Evert, USN, patrol plane commander of another PBY. Their mission on this Sunday afternoon: to search for enemy submarines and destroy them. Their special object: to hunt down the deadly *U-66*.

"I remember that day," says Donald Gay, now retired as a rear admiral, USN. "We were one of the early squadrons to be equipped with radar. It was very primitive, still experimental, but using it, we could 'see' surfaced submarines and ships at distances up to twelve miles."

Gay and Evert knew where to look for *U-66*. From reports of yesterday and today's sinkings—the *Topa Topa* on Saturday, the *Sir Huron* earlier Sunday morning—they had evidence that the submarine was preying upon ships in the latitudes ten degrees above the equator, just west of the fiftieth meridian. Flying in a half-vee formation, then breaking off from each other for a roll right or left to scan a zone of water, then reforming within hailing distance of each other, the two pilots and friends kept to their course.

Suddenly Donald Gay saw a blip on his radar screen. At the same instant Tom Evert also reacted to what his radar scope showed him. Together the two PBYs rushed toward their target — each other's plane!

"Tom Evert and I had mistakenly honed in on one another," reports Donald Gay. "Each of us thought the blip we saw was the German sub. At about a hundred feet above the water, we finally realized our mistaken and just missed colliding. In fact, as we sped past each other, our wings overlapped."

Gay and Evert recovered control of their planes, gave each the thumbs-up sign, and returned to Trinidad. Once inside headquarters, Gay asked, "Any more word about *U-66?*"

"No sir. Seems pretty quiet out there since this morning. Maybe Jerry's doing a little sunbathing this afternoon."

"That'll be the day!" retorted the commanding officer. "Admiral Dönitz doesn't sunbathe and neither do his U-boats. They're all out there someplace, just biding their time, and we'd better get them before they get any more of us!"

Donald Gay looked around the ward room and said, "Who's up?"

"We are, Skipper," said Lieutenant Jack Hillman, and, after motioning to Lieutenant Raymond North, they strode out on the tarmac to the waiting planes to resume the hunt.

At the first sound of the alarm, Robert Bell and Richard Shaw bolted from the crew's quarters and up a short ladder to their cabins. They hadn't heard the watchman's cry; yet without a word between them or from the crew, each somehow knew that this was more than just another regular drill. Before Robert Bell had reached his cabin, the first shuddering blow of a torpedo struck the *West Lashaway* on its starboard side.

The Bells' cabin was portside, opposite the torpedo's wound in the ship's hull. When Robert came to his cabin, the door had been blown open. Inside he found his mother hurrying to put on her dress, his sister fumbling with the cork life jacket.

"Hurry, children!" Ethel Bell said. "Calmly now, but hurry."

Robert helped Mary fasten her jacket and was starting to put on his own when the second strike came, amidships again and with devastating force. Where the first hit had been only damaging, this second thrust was mortal, exploding the fuel bunkers, boilers, and cargo bays in a spume of fire and steam, oil and latex. Not more than ten seconds had separated the two direct hits. Immediately the *West Lashaway* began listing to starboard.

Across the ship, in the Bell's cabin, the children and their mother froze in panic. Their bunks had collapsed, the light fixture had fallen from the ceiling, the floor seemed to be sliding out from under them. In that moment of stark terror, Ethel Bell called out, "O God, help us!" Then, grabbing their hands in hers, she led her children out of the cabin and up a crazy laddder to the chaos on deck. In their rush they left behind their ditty bags and valuables.

On the deck the sight was not encouraging. Evidence

of disaster spilled out everywhere. Beyond the shattered starboard rail, the waterline rose swiftly. The starboard lifeboats, to which the Bell family had been assigned, had been dissolved by the second torpedo's blast. Ethel Bell and her children were directed across the treacherously sloping deck to the portside boats, tilting steeply as the crippled ship began to slide over on its side. The Bells clambered into a boat, but no sooner had they entered than the officer in charge shouted at them, "Get out! For God's sake, get out!" The ship was now listing so severely that these boats had been forced immovably against their davits; there was no way for them to be lowered. Mrs. Bell and Mary jumped from the boat into the water, but Robert's feet were caught under him. While he struggled to free himself, the entire ship fell away beneath the surface.

"I remember being in the lifeboat," says Bob Bell's sister, Mary, "when we were told to get out. I put my left foot over the side of the boat and was very surprised to see the ocean only three inches away! I realized then that I was going to go down. It seemed so hopeless, I didn't even bother to struggle. I really thought I was only a minute away from death. I remember thinking, 'I'm going to see Jesus and my daddy!' Then, all of a sudden, I was going up — and fast."

As for her eleven-year-old brother, he too was engulfed in a boiling maelstrom, sucked into its vortex along with every other being and the ship's debris. Bodies were first swallowed up, then thrown out into the air as if by a geyser's spume. Furniture, bulkheads, barrels of cargo, chunks of metal — all tossed about while the *West Lashaway* groaned and fought and spun, then disappeared, leaving only a cloud of steam hovering over a massive slick and the acrid stench of explosives to mark its grave.

From first alert to the ship's sinking had been less than two minutes.

When he sank with the ship, Robert Bell knew that he was certainly going to drown. How long he remained in the turbulent suction of the ship's foundering he cannot tell. Suddenly he became aware that he was no longer sinking. Then there was light—and air! But Robert could not see. His eyes seemed almost glued shut by the globs of palm oil and other spillage through which he had emerged. The residue of lost cargo coated his hair and face like a mask. Sputtering, coughing, and gagging— his head barely above the swell—Robert realized first that he could hear the sound of voices, hushed tones, no longer screaming or shouting. Then gradually, through his still-blurred eyes, he began to distinguish objects in the water—bits of planking, articles of clothing, other forms and shapes too terrible to identify.

Robert called out, "Mother! Mary!"

His sister answered, close at hand. Then his mother spoke, some sixty yards away. "Children, over here. O thank you, Lord!"

Together Mary and Robert swam to where their mother was holding on to a plank. Their reunion can be imagined. Conditions were far from promising, but they could have been worse, much worse. Moments before, they had been enjoying their voyage home. Now they clung to life, and their immediate security was a shattered strip of lumber.

As Robert held on to the floating wood, his eyes gradually lost their blurred vision and he saw the two other pairs of hands gripping the plank. On the ring finger of his mother's left hand, he caught sight of her wedding band. The golden circle registered in the boy's consciousness as a sign that all was not yet lost.

"Well, Mother," he gulped between the swell of waves, "at least you still have your wedding ring!"

How absurd! To note at such a desperate time something so trivial as a golden ring! "My remark was impulsive," Bob Bell admits today, "like something someone says in shock, unthinking, with no relation to reality. Yet it's the only thing I said during those first terrible hours that has remained in my mind. To me — somehow — that ring meant security, stability, the past and future compressed into the presence of my mother and memory of my dead father. That ring meant home and safety were as close as my mother's hand holding on to that same splintered timber."

But hope and help were also at hand. Around the perimeter of the oil slick the Bells could discern four wooden rafts. In addition to its lifeboats, the *West Lashaway,* like every other ship, had carried four rafts mounted on steeply angled skids so as to slide easily into the water. Ordinarily, a loosened line would have released each raft. But when the second torpedo ripped into the *West Lashaway,* its rafts required nothing more to set them free; they were blown overboard like chips of wood. These eight-by-ten-foot floating crates, borne up by six watertight drums, weighed almost half a ton each; yet so great was the torpedo's explosion, these boxes had been catapulted from their moorings like rockets.

Other survivors had crawled up out of the water and onto these rafts. Even now the Bells could see people being hauled aboard these bobbing bits of flotsam. The three of them began calling, "Over here! Three more over here!"

While they called and waited for rescue, a strange humming sound filled their clogged ears. Then, as if from a scene in a monster movie, an unthinkable shape from the depths broke the water's plane. Less than fifty yards from where the Bells hung on to their plank, breaching like a whale, the German U-boat appeared. Its gray-streaked tower proudly bore its insignia, the head of a snarling lion with fangs threatening. Then the great hulk of the submarine stood above the surface like an evil spirit in a nightmare. Paralyzed with terror, Robert Bell could hear the metallic grating as the hatch opened and four uniformed officers appeared inside the tower. One of them, bearded and laughing as he spoke, gave orders to the other three. He seemed to be looking directly at the Bells. Could it be the submarine's commanding officer?

Looking at the enemy whose act of war had discarded him like waste, Robert felt the fear that shock and action had forestalled during the ship's sinking. Now, for sure, he would die. His fear found confirmation in the next instant, when the Germans let go with a round of rapid fire from an automatic weapon. Instinctively, Robert ducked below the slime of oil and latex. The firing continued for several more rounds, while Robert waited for the bullets to strike him. But nothing happened, and the boy soon resurfaced. Apparently the Germans were firing aimlessly, not shooting at anyone or anything; they were merely testing the working condition of their weapons in case they should be needed. A few minutes later, the men crawled back down the hatch, leaving their victims without a word — neither threats nor offers of assistance. Like other soldiers and sailors, they simply took no notice of the human consequences of war. The humming of the submarine's diesel engines began reverberating at a higher pitch. Slowly the hull evaporated, the deck with its cannons and, finally, the tower disappeared from view, leaving no trace that *U-66* had ever been there.

Once again the sea was calm.

Klaus Herbig, the youngest officer, closed the hatch of *U-66* and slid to the control-room floor as the boat submerged.

"Did you get the ship's name, Herbig?" asked the submarine commander.

"No, Captain," Herbig replied.

"You are sure?"

"Yes, sir!"

"Too bad. Herbig, tell Degener-Böning so that he can keep his records properly."

Friedrich Markworth paced in the little area dominated by the tower instruments.

"Now, what do you suppose that ship was doing in these parts? She's too small for a tanker; she's just a little *Dampfer,* a steamer that strayed into dangerous waters!"

Markworth laughed again. "And what do you suppose our little friend was carrying in her belly?"

Georg Olschewski spoke up. "Whatever it was, sir, it's no good to anybody now."

"Yes, but what an explosion!" added Frölich. "It was like a pickle factory going off. Did you see that slime all over the water? Poor wretches trying to survive that mess would be better off dead."

"Best not to think about them, Obersteuermann Fröhlich," his U-boat commander cautioned. "We are at war; they are at risk on the high seas. It is all fate. What's more, you'll never see any of them again."

The submarine commander turned and began walking toward the ladder, then stopped abruptly.

"And Herbig, don't forget to ask Degener-Böning if the ship got off any final radio message. I'd like to know whether or not we should expect company later this evening."

Once more, the handsome Markworth laughed. It had been a long day with much excitement. Two sinkings within ten hours of each other! Surely the *Befehlshaber* in his Paris headquarters would soon be informed. How proud he would be of his former cadet Fritz Markworth! Perhaps, with just a little luck, there might be an honor in store. After all, his predecessor, Zapp, had won the Knight's Cross. Markworth fingered the collar of his shirt, feeling for the medal that would someday be there. Enough for one day. Tomorrow there would be more Allied ships to sink.

Kapitänleutnant Friedrich Markworth eased himself onto his bunk and slept soundly.

FOUR
UNANSWERABLE QUESTIONS

When the Bells realized that the submarine had gone, they resumed calling to the rafts drifting or being paddled nearby. Ten minutes—or was it ten hours?—passed before a raft finally reached them. One by one the three victims clinging to their spar rode the swell to grab a hand from the raft. One by one, Robert Bell, his mother, and sister, Mary, were pulled from the water and clambered over the sides of the raft, safe for the moment.

At a glance the rafts looked no different from those afloat off most swimming beaches: a wooden frame of sturdy one-by-six-inch planking, arranged as slats for greater seaworthiness, if not greater comfort for those sitting on the cracks. Unlike such recreational rafts, however, these were sunken in the middle—a well four feet wide running the length of the raft, constantly awash through its wooden slats. This construction hung on six airtight metal drums suspended by ropes within the framework, making the rafts more than four feet thick and elevating them to ride three feet above a calm waterline.

Each raft was completely reversible, so that whichever way the raft tumbled into the water, either side up, the same conditions prevailed. Beneath the floorboard decking of the well lay a treasure of emergency supplies locked in watertight boxes, accessible from either top or bottom, no matter which way the raft surfaced.

The rafts had been roughhewn, unpolished, their grain sharp and grating. Hauled aboard one of these, over its unfinished sides, the Bells never felt the first of many scratches and slivers that would plague them, turning from abrasions into saltwater ulcers and suppurating sores. At this moment all that mattered to mother, daughter, and son was that they were out of the water.

They fell together into the well of the raft, huddling, holding on to each other, while Ethel Bell stroked each of her children, murmuring reassurance and prayers of thanksgiving. At their feet lay a crumpled mass of flesh, two or three bodies heaped on each other, too exhausted to care. On the planking lining the raft slumped several more survivors. Above them stood two Spanish-speaking crewmen attempting to paddle the bulky crate to where another cluster of their shipmates called to them, *"Áqui!* Over here!"

For an hour and more, the four rafts moved through the widening swamp of oil slick and debris marking the grave of the *West Lashaway* looking for any last survivors. From where he lay in the well, Robert could see the face of each person being dragged on board his raft. He knew the names of only a few but recognized most of the others.

While he wondered who might be next to appear, he heard a familiar voice from the sea:

"Take my sister first. She's got no life jacket."

His friend Richard Shaw! Robert sat upright, bumping against the leg of a seaman.

"Damn it, kid! Take it easy!"

His mother reached out and pushed him back into position. Onto the raft crawled seven-year-old Carol Shaw, crying with the pain of a broken arm. She wore no dress, only underwear. The dress had been torn from her body by the suction of the ship's sinking. Later Carol would realize that she also bore a gash in her scalp.

"Here, little girl," said a navy man, "wear this." He took of his pea jacket and placed it around the shoulders of the shivering child.

Then Richard appeared and, finally, his father.

"Vera!" Harvey Shaw called out immediately. "Has anybody seen my wife? Vera? Georgia? My wife and daughter?"

No answer, and he sank down on the planking in despair.

The sailors, relieved at their own rescue, soon regained their tongues.

"Jeez, that was close!"

"How do I get this crap outa my eyes? I'm almost blind."

"Did you see them sons o' bitches on that sub? Lookin' right at us and laughin' in our faces!"

"I swear, I hate Nazis!"

"I'd love to have a friggin' depth charge to put up their—"

"Hold it, there's a woman aboard."

"Where?"

"Down there. Mrs. Bell and her kids."

"Sorry, lady."

Silence.

Now other voices took their place, calling from the other rafts.

"How many y' got?"

"Half dozen. You?"

"Too many. Couple our tanks is busted. Takin' water. We gotta unload some."

"Anybody seen the captain?"

"Right here with me."

"Who's that?"

"Bosun. Captain's hurt, but he's conscious. Says we oughta bunch up."

"OK. Everybody come together."

Slowly the four floating boxes were steered to a junction. Even as they moved, another group was forming, a convoy of sharks surrounded each raft, constant companions for the rest of the journey. Once within reach of each other, the crewmen linked up the rafts like a cluster of canal barges. From the third raft Captain Benjamin Bogden took charge. Although injured, he was nonetheless clearly in command.

"First, men," he spoke to all his crew, "well done. You've done the best you could. Nobody could ask for more." Looking over the survivors, he asked, "Where's Sparks?"

"I don't think he made it, Captain," said a husky voice.

"Last I seen him," added another, "he was sittin' right at his radio, but I ain't seen him since."

"That's too bad," said Bogden. "I'd like to know if the poor devil had time to get off an SOS for us. Well, let's take stock. Number your survivors on each raft. I've got six, counting myself."

"Nine, Captain. But one of our drums is full, and we're listing."

"We've got seventeen, Captain, and we're punctured in two drums."

"Ten, Captain, but we're also taking on water."

Robert heard the numbers and added in his head. Of the fifty-six persons aboard the *West Lashaway* a little over an hour ago, fourteen had been lost. Forty-two survivors were unevenly distributed among four rafts, three of which were damaged.

"All right," said Captain Bogden, "we've got to make some changes. My raft is undamaged. Right, Bosun?"

The boatswain, James Owen, acknowledged affirmatively. "Aye, aye, sir."

"Then we'll take on capacity here and divide up the rest among the three damaged rafts. Women and children first. Mrs. Bell? Mrs. Shaw?"

"Mrs. Shaw didn't make it, Captain," said a seaman. "Her little girl neither."

At this final declaration, Harvey Shaw burst into sobs, clinging to his remaining children.

"I'm sorry, Mr. Shaw," said Bogden. "All right, Mrs. Bell, bring your children and the Shaw children over her. Step carefully. Help her, men."

"Aren't you coming with us, Daddy?" Carol Shaw pleaded. "I want you to come with me."

Harvey Shaw recovered himself and, hugging his daughter, said, "I'll be right here in the raft next to you, Carol. Go with Richard. Go ahead, Son."

"Now, that makes eleven of us," said the captain. "What do you think, Bosun? Can we take six or eight more?"

"Pretty crowded, Captain, with that many," replied

Owen. " 'Course, if we let the woman and children go back to the other raft, we'd have more room for grown men."

"The women and children are in my care, Owen, and don't you forget it!"

Slowly and unsteadily, Ethel Bell and her children, then Carol and Richard Shaw inched from one raft to the other until they reached the raft where Captain Bogden lay in the well. As Robert stumbled on board his raft, the captain reached out a hand and drew the boy down onto his ample belly.

"Here you go, young man," said the captain to Robert. "You stay right here with me."

From raft to raft the survivors shifted, following the instructions transmitted from Captain Bogden by his bosun, James Owen. Obediently, each person remained in place or moved to another raft as ordered.

"How many's that, Bosun?"

"Seventeen-eighteen-nineteen, counting you and me, sir," the bosun answered.

"Looks to me like we're full up," said Bogden. "How about the rest of you?"

From each of the other rafts came assurances that, lightened by the transfer of personnel, the rafts could now carry their remaining passengers, seven or eight each.

"OK, then," said Captain Bogden, "let's check out our supplies."

Owen and another man not yet known to Robert began working loose the clasp that locked the supplies below deck. When they had opened the hatch, they brought out the same cargo found on every raft early in World War II. Each had been equipped with two small kegs of drinking water — about fifteen gallons each — and sealed tins of current technology's finest emergency rations: a quantity of biscuits similar to graham crackers; pemmican consisting of dried meat, sugar, raisins, and other fruits; and both milk tablets and chocolate tablets guaranteed not to melt. In addition, the supply chest included a first-aid kit, a canvas drag to be used during rough seas, and a set of flares to ignite and alert possible rescue vessels or planes. Each raft also stowed two pairs of oars, which had already been put to use as paddles.

Beyond these standard supplies, the bosun's foresight had led him to stow a piece of canvas in each of the four rafts. Like the Bells, none of the survivors had been able to hold on to the ditty bag intended for such an emergency; certain of the merchant seamen, however, had retained their own pocket knives. As it turned out, no one had a compass. Strangely, no one had a wrist or pocket watch. For direction and time both, they would have to read the sky.

While the captain finished hearing about each raft's supplies, satisfying himself that all was in order, the bosun said, "Look, there's a doughnut. Grab it."

Drifting by came a two-man life preserver with a net bottom. This cork dinghy, called a doughnut, had its own set of oars and could be used to ferry salvageable articles from the oil slick back to the rafts.

"Captain," said Owen, "there's still a lot of stuff floating over there. How about I go and see what we can use?"

"Good idea, Owen."

When the doughnut had been secured, the bosun adroitly lowered himself over the side and into the dinghy. He seemed to be luxuriating in the sudden amplitude of space—just himself and no one else in the doughnut.

For the next hour the bosun made forays into the spreading mass of ruin looking for any article amid the debris that ingenuity and imagination might find useful. Owen said little if anything to anyone on his periodic returns to the rafts; he merely looked grim, like a man intent on making the best of a disagreeable situation. Yet no one could fault his industry, rowing back and forth from the rafts to the floating wreckage, depositing his booty at one raft or another, then rowing off again — a man very much in command of himself and his destiny — paddling into the mess of oil and remnants from the sunken ship.

The other men were now taking an active interest in the bosun's expeditions, asking him to look for specific items, suggesting that he bring back articles that they thought they could identify, even from a distance. For instance, scattered throughout the pond of palm oil and latex were sacks of cocoa beans freed from their cargo bays by the bulkheads' collapse.

"Hey, Chief, get some of those cocoa-bean bags," said one seaman.

"What for?" asked another. "To make hot chocolate?"

"No, wise guy! To make shirts. Look at Greenwell and Marano over there on the captain's raft. Look at the lieutenant here. They've got nothing but their skivvies. They're gonna need some protection from the sun."

Several men had surfaced with little clothing on because they had been sleeping, sunbathing, or otherwise relaxing when the ship was hit; they had simply had no time to think about dressing for the occasion. Others, like Carol Shaw, had lost whatever clothes they had been wearing by the force of the ship's descent.

"OK," responded Owen, "I'll grab a few."

"Chief, you'll need this knife," said Woodman Potter.

As Owen reached the first floating sack, he took hold and slit the burlap, dumping the beans into the water, then throwing the empty sack into the doughnut. Back at the rafts, he tossed the bags toward the shirtless. More ripping and tearing opened holes for head and arms.

"It's not exact J. C. Penney's finest," said the first model, "but it'll do, I guess."

"How 'bout gettin' some more o' them bags, Chief?" called a seaman.

"What for? You all got shirts. What do you think I am, in the haberdashery business?"

"Naw, Chief, we don't need 'em to wear. We can fold 'em up like cushions and sit on 'em. These slats are pretty hard on the tail bone, y'know?"

So when Owen returned with another load of empty sacks, the men on each raft took them to reupholster their seating.

Meanwhile, from their cages bobbing in the water came the screeches of the crowned cranes. These strange creatures, with their remarkable golden halos, might have brought a fine price from an exotic collector.

"So much for that investment," said one of the crew who had hoped for a profitable sale to an American zoo.

"Wait a minute," replied another. "They still might be useful. Suppose we're out here for a while, we might want to eat them."

The thought of eating one of those regal birds troubled Robert and made him wince. But a more practical reaction overruled any thought of turning the cranes into food.

"No way, man! There's not enough meat on any one of them to make it worth the noise of keeping them along for the ride. Let them be."

Thus rescued from one form of slaughter, the birds were left in their cages to die. As for the baboon and chimps and spider monkeys, they were never sighted after the sinking. Robert wondered if, perhaps, those animals were better off than the birds. And what about himself and the others around him? Were they, like the birds, prisoners afloat in their cages? Wouldn't it have been better to drown — like the monkeys, like Mrs. Shaw and Georgia, like so many others?

"Captain Bogden," Robert asked, "how long are we going to be out here?"

"Not for long, Robert. I imagine word's already reached Trinidad. They'll have spotters out looking for us before sundown. Sometime tomorrow, for sure."

"Oh, Captain, do you really think so?" Ethel Bell asked.

"I'm certain of it, Mrs. Bell."

Little did anyone, including Benjamin Bogden, realize how much his prediction represented hope-against-hope. A senior captain of the Barber Line — a family man whose wife maintained their home in Brooklyn — Bogden's first concern had been his ship, his passengers, his crew, his secret cargo. He had thought last and least of himself, his own injuries, which had been far more serious than he or anyone else knew at that time. For Bogden had sustained acute acid burns, caused by a mixture of gasses from the torpedoes, compounded by the oil through which each survivor had emerged. These acid burns seemed to afflict the obese more severely than the slender, and Bogden was certainly overweight. How grave his injuries were could be determined only by time, but it was clear to those who knew the captain — and especially to young Robert Bell, seated on the captain's

lap—that in spite of apparent good spirits, Captain Bogden was in pain.

From his vantage on the captain's broad lap, Robert
looked around at all the others squeezed on board with
him. How nineteen bodies—all but four of them mature
adults—could fit on one tiny chip of wood in the horizon-
less Atlantic exceeded his imagination! Yet here they
were, on a life raft not much bigger than the bed in his
mother's bedroom in Africa, a platform about the same
size as the carpet on his grandparents' living-room floor
in Toronto. Nobody on the raft sat upright, occupying
all of his or her own complete body space. Everyone sat
hunched, twisted, or tilted, the body's weight resting on
one buttock, the shoulder forced against one's neighbor,
the knees drawn up tightly. Even normal breathing had
to be constrained—no deep inhaling or exhaling to rob
somebody else's fraction of space.

On either side of the captain sat George Marano, a fireman, and Joseph Greenwell, the first assistant engineer.
Marano had made it to the raft wearing only the swim-
suit in which he had been sunbathing when the first
torpedo struck. Similarly, Greenwell wore only under-
pants because he had been working in the heat of the
boiler room. Now both Marano and Greenwell sported
the newly fashioned burlap shirts made from cocoa-bean
bags. Of course, over whatever clothing each person wore
came the standard life jacket—necessary but, in these extraordinarily crowded conditions, also a nuisance.

Immediately to George Marano's right were several of
the Spanish-speaking crew, deckhands assigned to the bosun. Their names, Robert was to learn, were Frank S.
Flavor, Isbelino Pacheco, known as "Chico," and Servior

Seremos, a Filipino who had a gold tooth that flashed whenever he smiled. Next to them, on the corners of the raft facing westward, five men from the ship's galley had wedged themselves together. Robert knew them all; they had been important to him as providers of the excellent food served on the *West Lashaway*. C. J. Rosibrosiris, called "Rodriguez," a Portuguese from Goa, on the coast of India, had been the ship's chief cook. Now he sat on a water keg. What delicacies would he be offering for dinner on this raft? John Vargas had been the pantryman, the baker responsible for that pumpkin pie Robert had enjoyed less than three hours before. Would there be pastries tonight or tomorrow? Woodman Potter, second cook, and Levi Walker, the messman assigned to pots and pans — both blacks — and Robert McDaniel, the messboy serving meals to the crew, came next. What duties would they perform here? In the well below them, Louis G. Vega, an oiler from the engine room, stared blankly, while the youngest crew member, the signalman Earl Croons, known as "Flags," scratched at his acid burns and whimpered in pain.

Then came Richard and Carol Shaw, sitting next to Robert's mother and sister. By this time one of the men had torn his shirttail to make a sling for little Carol's broken arm. Her head wound still oozed; no one had yet treated it.

Last, the thirty-year-old bosun, James Owen from Pittsburgh, Pennsylvania. A man of slight but wiry build, Owen's competitive nature and combative temperament had served him well in his rise to bosun's rating. But a strange sort of energy seemed to possess this man, as if he drew from the lethargy and listlessness of others. He had already demonstrated his resourcefulness and would do so again. He had no intentions of mere survival; he would fight the very elements and thrive.

Until now each survivor's concentration had been fixed upon saving his or her own life. But as they settled into their respective places on the four rafts, a normal systemic reaction to the violence and shock of their terror set in. Peculiarly, as if on schedule, most of the survivors began simultaneously to feel sudden surges of nausea, sudden flashes of feverish heat, sudden intestinal cramps.

Robert was the first to speak of it. "Oh, Mother," he cried, "I feel so sick!"

Ethel Bell reached out to touch her son's forehead. "Me too, Robert. It's all the nerves just settling down. It'll be over soon."

At that very moment he heard the first sounds of retching and saw Woodman Potter attempt to turn his body to face the sea. Instead, his sickness poured over Levi Walker's shoulders and back.

"For God's sake, man!"

"Sorry, man. I couldn't help it."

As if in concert, other men began to moan and struggle against the rising gorge of vomit; yet unable to restrain the convulsions of their nervous and digestive systems, these sufferers had no recourse for their misery and no way to avoid spewing on those sitting next to them. From each of the other rafts could be heard the same distress. But on those rafts, at least, there was room to lean out over the side. For Robert and his eighteen companions, there was no such luxury of space. Two hours and more would pass before the worst of this aftermath of shock, compounded by their intake of sea water and slime, could be controlled. Then began the process of washing up, for which there was no shortage of water.

"I'm going back in the doughnut," said Owen. "that'll make more room for everybody."

"Yeah, especially you, Chief," said Levi Walker. "Want some company?"

The bosun made no reply except to give a sneering glance. He stepped between Mrs. Bell and Carol Shaw, jostling the little girl as he passed. She screamed as his leg disturbed her broken arm.

"Oh, Mr. Owen, please be careful." Ethel Bell rebuked him.

The bosun never even looked back; instead, he dropped over the side and into the cork dinghy alone.

"Richard? Carol? Are you OK?" Robert heard Harvey Shaw call from his seat on an adjacent raft.

"We're all right, Dad," Richard replied. "You OK?"

"Sure, Son. Take good care of Carol."

Harvey Shaw, born in Violet, Nebraska, on August 11, 1904, had just celebrated his thirty-eighth birthday a few days earlier with a party given by Captain Bogden on the *West Lashaway.* He and his wife, Vera, four years younger, had both attended Moody Bible Institute in Chicago, where they prepared for careers as church musicians. But Harvey and Vera Shaw forsook their music convinced that they must give their lives to serve as foreign missionaries. The Shaws were appointed to serve as Baptist missionaries to Africa, working under an agency known as Baptist Mid-Missions, with headquarters in Mishawaka, Indiana. In 1938 the Shaws arrived to work at Bria and Bambari, in French Equatorial Africa. After four years there, the war in Europe spilled over into colonial Africa, driving the Shaws from their mission base to find an evacuation ship that would take them home, temporarily, to America. At Matadi, on the Congo River, they found space on the *West Lashaway.* Now the Shaw family had been shattered—Vera and Georgia drowned, Harvey and his surviving children separated. If there is a God in heaven, why should this have happened?

And what about the shipwrecked widow, Ethel Bell, and her children? What business did they have riding the high seas in wartime? What terrible twist of fate had brought her and her family to such a crisis, such a doom?

FIVE
THE MISSIONARY

Ethel Bell had been a widow for more than six years. Her late husband, George Noble Bell, born in Omagh, County Tyrone, Ireland, had emigrated with his parents to America, arriving at Philadelphia's Navy Yard in 1904. Young George Bell possessed a feisty temper, which, along with his Irish brogue, led him into many playground fights. He was so combative that his parents had to enroll him in one school after another; he finally completed secondary schooling at night, after he had begun to learn the trade of plumber.

But in 1915 George Bell's life took a different course. The merchandising tycoon John Wanamaker had invited to Philadelphia the famous "baseball evangelist" Billy Sunday to conduct one of his sawdust-trail revivals. For eleven weeks in 1915, from January 3 to March 21, Billy Sunday turned Philadelphia upside down. More than two million people listened to him preach in the wooden tabernacle designed and constructed especially for his meetings; over 40,000 converts registered their names, including 1,858 who "hit the trail" at Billy Sunday's urging on the final day alone.

George Bell had never been a religious person — quite the opposite. But curiosity compelled him to visit the Billy Sunday Tabernacle. There he heard and enjoyed the evangelistic music of Homer Rodeheaver, with his gilt trombone and breezy manner; there he was captivated by the extravagances of the preacher himself — his unconventional language with its heavy emphasis on workingman's slang, his stomping and stalking across the platform, his stripping down to an undershirt in order to do battle with Satan. Bell was amused by all this, but he was also affected by Billy Sunday's direct and personal call for repentance and commitment to God. Almost against his own nature, Bell felt himself drawn to join those walking in the sawdust-strewn aisle to the platform and shaking the evangelist's hand — "Don't grab it, brother! Just a touch is good enough!" George Bell determined to give his life to Jesus Christ; so on a February night in 1915 he walked the aisle of the Billy Sunday Tabernacle, publicly confirming his decision.

In George Bell's case, his conversion was sincere and lasting. He became a devout reader and student of the Bible and joined the Presbyterian Church of the Covenant in Bala-Cynwyd. When the United States of America entered World War I, Bell joined the First Gas Regiment of the American Expeditionary Forces. During the fighting he had sufficient frontline experience to test his faith. He made a promise to God that, if his life were spared, he would commit himself to the Christian ministry in some manner of service. He was subsequently wounded, and in an American hospital in France, George

Bell renewed his vow to serve God. Upon his return to America and discharge from the military in February 1919, he applied for theological education at various Presbyterian institutions; but he was twenty-five years old, with only a night-school diploma. The Presbyterians were not interested in his candidacy.

But Bell remained convinced that he had not been deluded in thinking that he had a call to preach. Although he continued as a member of the Bala-Cynwyd Church, Bell now began to look outside his own Presbyterian denomination and found that the Christian and Missionary Alliance — an evangelical denomination of fervor and dedication — sponsored a school that would accept him, the Missionary Training Institute, located at Nyack, New York. He enrolled at what is now Nyack College in January 1922.

Meanwhile, in London, Ontario, Canada, a young woman named Ethel Gladys Roffe was growing up in the home of a Christian and Missionary Alliance pastor and his wife, Alfred and Mary Booth Roffe. Born on June 11, 1893, Ethel at an early age dedicated herself to serve God as a foreign missionary, influenced by the many missionaries entertained in her home. But just as she prepared to leave home and enroll in the Missionary Training Institute at Nyack, she was stricken by acute pulmonary tuberculosis. Her condition worsened so that she had to be taken to a sanatorium in the Muskoka Lake District of Ontario. There she remained bedridden for almost two years. By April 1921 all medical means of saving her life had been exhausted. Ethel Roffe seemed doomed to die of her tuberculosis.

But her brothers Elroy, Edward, and Paul — each of whom also eventually became a foreign missionary —

believed otherwise. Taking her from that sanatorium, they carried their sister to a healing service in Toronto. Nothing happened. Ethel returned home from that experience disappointed and doubting. The next morning her father said to her, "Ethel, keep looking up. There's plenty of Light up there!" Around midday, this woman nearly twenty-eight years old, dying of tuberculosis, taxed her limited strength to its fullest by rising from her bed, then kneeling beside it. "Lord," she prayed, "give me faith to believe!"

Without any visible sign to rely on, Ethel Roffe began thinking and acting, from that moment on, like someone intending to live. As she was later fond of saying, "I simply gave up my doubts and began living as if I were better." Two weeks later, at the world-famous Gage Institute in Toronto, the same doctor who had sent her to the sanatorium in Gravenhurst pronounced Ethel Roffe free from all symptoms of tuberculosis. Her left lung had been deeply affected, along with part of her right; now neither lung showed any sign of disease.

So far as Ethel Roffe was concerned, there was no question: "God had performed a miracle and healed me," she said. Presumably dying in April, she enrolled at Nyack the following September 1921—a little later than she had planned on beginning her preparation but all the more committed to telling the world about the God in whom she believed.

A few months later, George Bell also arrived at Nyack and soon met Ethel Roffe, who was to graduate in the spring of 1923, a full year ahead of him. Ethel may have been attracted to George—certainly he was to her—but nothing, not even romance, would deter or delay her from her primary calling, to serve God as a foreign mission-

ary. So in the summer of 1923, while George headed to
Alberta to serve as student-pastor on a circuit of country churches, Ethel was accepting an appointment by the
Christian and Missionary Alliance to become a missionary in French West Africa. In October 1924, at the language school in France, George and Ethel became
reacquainted; but not until she was assured that their lives
together would in no way interfere with their individual
commitment to God would she accept his proposal of
marriage. Even when she did, they did not rush into marriage. A year of language study was followed by another
year of apprenticeship in Kankan, French West Africa.
On December 13, 1926, Ethel Roffe became Mrs. George
Bell. Their wedding took place in Carusa, Guinea, and
they honeymooned with a cruise up the Niger River.

The newlyweds then moved to their first station, at San,
in what is now the nation of Mali, where George built
a mission station and their lodging. Their work was conventional pioneering evangelism, preaching and teaching the gospel of Jesus Christ, attempting to win converts
and then instruct them as disciples of Christ. This work
was hard, often lonely, but it was the life to which each
of them separately and now together had been wholly
committed. They had each other, and soon they also had
the joy of a child, their daughter, Mary Ruth, born at San
on September 20, 1928.

The following summer, the Bells returned to America
for a furlough. The Christian and Missionary Alliance
maintains a colony of homes for its missionaries on the
Nyack campus, overlooking the Hudson River. So it was
that in Nyack, on March 5, 1930, Ethel Bell gave birth
to twin sons, David and Paul.

Now with three young children, the Bells were back

in French West Africa by January 1931. But almost as soon as they returned, calamity struck. The infant twins contracted malaria, and in spite of all available medical efforts, on February 20 both her babies died in Ethel Bell's arms. To George and Ethel, their loss took on special significance. Here they were, representatives of Jesus Christ in a pagan culture in which the fear of death is the most powerful factor in human existence; yet, as Christians, believing in the Resurrection and the Life Everlasting, they must show that difference, particularly at a time of personal sorrow. Apparently their witness rang true, for after the death of their sons, the Bells saw more than a thousand converts gradually added to the list of believers in San and its environs.

At the time of her twins' death, Ethel Bell was again expecting a child. Six months later, on July 20, 1931, she gave birth to Robert William Bell. He was her special joy; so when, at age three, Robert suffered an attack of diphtheria, the Bells wasted no time in seeking medical advice. Even as they did, a sudden paralysis afflicted the child. His legs became immobilized. Frantically, George and Ethel Bell sought passage to return to America as quickly as possible for Robert's treatment and care. In December 1934 they once again arrived in America. By this time the diphtheria had subsided, but the paralysis remained. The little boy made a pathetic sight, dragging himself across the floor of his parents' apartment at the mission compound in Nyack or in his grandparents' house in Toronto. Moreover, the diphtheria had left him with a heart murmur.

With a sick child, the Bells' overseas missionary endeavors had to be suspended. While Ethel remained in Nyack, caring for their daughter and praying for their son's recovery, George was busy with an itinerary of "deputation meetings," as missionary jargon refers to them — informational meetings in various churches on behalf of mission work in Africa and elsewhere. The Bells fully intended to return to French West Africa themselves, just as soon as their son's health permitted. In the meantime George Bell would speak for others, increasing general interest.

Gradually Robert began to show signs of restored health. His paralysis diminished, then disappeared altogether, leaving no limp or other weakness of limbs. True, he contracted the typical childhood maladies — tonsillitis and two bouts of measles before he was five — and he continued to be ravaged by severe headaches. But Robert could ran and play almost like any other preschooler, for which his mother and father rejoiced. Furthermore, the Bells could once again plan to resume their work in Africa.

On April 1, 1936, having completed a deputation tour of churches all over New England, George was returning to Nyack from Providence, Rhode Island, riding as a passenger in a bus operated by the Old Colony Coach Lines. At 1:15 A.M., while he reclined asleep in his seat just inside the door, his bus collided with a truck owned by the New England Transporation Company, parked on the shoulder of the highway. The right front of the bus was crushed, and George Bell died while being taken to a hospital in Westerly, Rhode Island.

Mary Bell, age seven and a half, went off to school in Nyack that morning, not knowing that her father had already been killed in the bus collision. Now married to the Reverend Elmer Whitbeck and living in Lincoln,

Nebraska, Mary Bell Whitbeck recalls what happened that afternoon.

"I was so excited by the fact that Daddy would be returning home from New England!" she says. "My best friend in school was Joyce Rankin; when school ended, Joyce and I ran all the way home from school. I burst into the house calling, 'Daddy, Daddy,' but there was no answer. I went from room to room and finally came to the back bedroom; there I found Mother sitting alone with the shades drawn. She told me, 'Daddy isn't coming home. He's gone to heaven.' I ran from the house to find Joyce and tell her my grief."

To Mary, her father had been both provider and defender. She remembers him as the hunter, carrying his rifle with him wherever he went, ready to shoot game for food or kill predators such as the hyenas, which constantly threatened his chickens. On long trips by car, he kept the rifle handy on the front seat, just in case! Now he was gone, and the little girl mourned her lost father.

"I wasn't quite five years old," her brother Bob Bell recalls today, "when my father was killed, and so my memory of him is limited. But from what I do remember, and from what I've been told by those who knew him well, I've acquired some lasting impressions of my father.

"He had a lively sense of humor, and he loved sports of all kinds, especially hiking, camping, and hunting; he would often go with the Africans on their hunts to provide the village with food.

"He was a loving father," Bob Bell continues, "fair but firm and consistent in his discipline. I remember well my being spanked for some disobedience, but afterwards being held on his lap while he made sure that I understood the reason for my punishment and the fact that he loved me nonetheless."

Early in his residence at San, George Bell had constructed a hut apart from the family dwelling, a place set aside exclusively for his spiritual devotions and study. "My father would rise every morning at four o'clock," says Bob Bell, "leave our house, and go to his prayer room. He'd stay there for a couple of hours, praying and reading the Bible, before rejoining my mother and sister and me for breakfast. His habit of beginning each day with prayer made a great impression on me."

Most people would have been devasted by this grief upon grief—their faith shattered, or at least left reeling: her twins taken in one brutal moment of anguish; now her husband was dead, leaving her with a still sickly child, as well as his sister, to care for. But Ethel Bell was never like most people. She lived by what she believed. Call it oversimplification, she nonetheless accepted as true the words of St. Paul to the Christians in Rome: "And we know that all things work together for good to them that love God, to them who are the called according to his purpose" (Romans 8:28). Recalling years later those difficult days in the spring of 1936, Ethel Bell says, "When I learned what had happened to George, it seemed as if the Lord took my hand and whispered into my ear the words from Isaiah 41:10, 'Fear thou not; for I am with thee: be not dismayed; for I am thy God: I will strengthen thee; yea, I will help thee; yea, I will uphold thee with the right hand of my righteousness.' God's presence was just as real as if He were standing there."

Thus, relying on her faith and sustained by it, even through days and weeks of loneliness and sorrow, Ethel Bell determined to continue the work to which she and her husband, individually and together, had committed themselves. She would return to Africa. It was to be two years before she could convince her misson board that she was ready; then there were also the supporting churches to convince that a widow in her mid-forties with two young children could work effectively as a missionary in pagan Africa.

At last, she cleared the final hurdle, and in August 1938 Ethel Bell boarded the Cunard liner *Laconia,* bound once again for Africa. The mission executives had determined that this time Mrs. Bell would work at a new station in Bouaké, Ivory Coast. Her children, Mary and Robert, ages ten and seven respectively, would be sent to a school for missionaries' children at Mamou in Guinea, part of French West Africa.

But a year later, in September 1939, Adolf Hitler began his checkerboard leaps across Europe; by June 1940, France had surrendered to the Nazi tyranny. Throughout the remainder of 1940 and into 1941, the German juggernaut had its way, in spite of French resistance. In French Equatorial Africa the governor of Chad openly supported General Charles de Gaulle and the Free French; but in French West Africa, where the Bells were, the government took its orders from the German puppet, the Vichy regime of Marshal Pétain. After December 7, 1941, when the United States was attacked at Pearl Harbor and joined the Allies against both Germany and Japan, it was no longer safe to hold an American passport in Nazi-controlled French West Africa.

Reluctantly, once more Ethel Bell began preparing for whatever transportation would take her family back home. But it was no easy matter to obtain exit papers from a hostile government, and space for civilian passengers aboard the few freighters still plying the route between West Africa and North America could hardly be found. Not until August 10, after months of official delays by consular bureaucracy, after languishing in shipping offices, did the Bells learn of three places for passengers on a ship leaving from Takoradi on the Gold Coast. On August 15 they boarded the *West Lashaway,* bound for home.

Now that ship lay at the bottom of the sea.

Instead of the role of American missionary among African village women, Ethel Bell now found herself as mother and surrogate mother to four frightened children, the sole woman among three dozen men scattered among the four connected rafts. She had known much about the world of animism and pagan religion in colonial Africa, but she had little firsthand experience with the cynicism and hardness of North American paganism, its scoffing at religion, its contemptuous rejection of spiritual values and concerns. Her life had been closeted within the safety of a godly home, a training school for missionaries, and a marriage committed to Christian service. What defense could she find against threatening attitudes and actions on the part of irreligious and desperate men? What hope could she offer her children and those entrusted to her care?

She had overcome mortal illness herself; she had endured the sorrow of her twins' deaths, the shock of her husband's death; she had persevered when war endangered herself and her remaining children. But what now of this test? Would Ethel Bell's faith in God be sufficient? Only time and experience could tell. Perhaps this raft would be her most important mission field.

For there they were — nineteen bodies, nineteen

souls—like sardines in a bobbing can, derelicts from a disaster at sea, linked together by common hopes, common doubts, common fears. Next to them, the three other rafts jostled and careened, sometimes meeting a swelling wave in tandem, sometimes crunching against the sides of a neighbor raft. This tiny armada, a mere speck on the ocean's vast surface, had no choice but to follow its drift. But to where? What currents would lead them to land? When would they be found? Not even Captain Bogden's optimism could answer these questions satisfactorily.

Already the subtropical sun was sliding toward the western curve, its glare blinding on the water.

"I don't suppose anybody feels much like eating just now," said the captain. "I think we'll hold off on the rations till morning."

"Get comfortable, everybody," the bosun called from his place alone in the doughnut. "It's gonna be quite a night."

"Yea, sure thing," replied Joe Greenwell, noting the bosun's relative ease in the dinghy. "How 'bout trading places, Owen?"

"Sorry, some other time!"

Their wait for rescue had begun.

SIX
PRAYERS

On Sunday evening, August 30, the congregation of the
Christian and Missionary Alliance Tabernacle assembled
in its small meetinghouse on St. Andrew's Lane in Glen
Cove, Long Island, New York. As usual, the family of
Carl and Matilde Koop was present — father and mother
with the infant daughter Linda and her nine-year-old sister Ruth, whose family nickname was "Toots."

Ruth enjoyed going to church on most occasions. A
precocious piano student, she could already play well
enough to accompany the singing at Sunday school. In
fact, she could probably have replaced her piano teacher,
Miss Edna Dalton, who played for the regular worship
services. But on this hot and muggy Sunday evening, little
Ruth Koop had had more than enough of church for one
day. She would have much preferred to spend the entire
day at a Long Island beach. Instead, she had been in
church all day! Sunday school and morning worship. An
afternoon children's meeting. Now the evening service.

The summer was almost over. Next weekend would be Labor Day. Then back to school just a few days later.

The child's wandering thoughts were interrupted by the voice of the pastor, the Reverend Richard Fortran, announcing a song. Ruth liked Pastor Fortran, perhaps because she knew that he was her father's friend. Both men enjoyed playing the violin; both had a passion for fishing. Together Richard Fortran and Carl Koop made music or spent time in recreation; their two families were frequently in each other's home when they were not together in church.

Now Pastor Fortran was speaking about the war. Grown-ups seemed to talk about the war all the time, although it seemed a long way from the mind of a nine-year-old girl.

"We need to remember especially tonight our men in the armed services, fighting in various parts of the world for our liberty. Let's sing a prayer."

The pastor looked over at Edna Dalton, the pianist, and nodded. Immediately she struck up the melody of a simple chorus being sung in churches all over America:

> *God bless our boys, wherever they may be!*
> *God bless our boys, on land or on the sea,*
> *Or in the air, we follow with our prayer,*
> *God bless our boys! God bless our boys!*

Ruth Koop knew of several families in the church and neighbors on the block in whose front windows hung the little white banner with its blue star indicating that someone from that home was in military service. She had also seen gold stars in some windows, and she knew what that meant. So she sang the chorus, thinking about her cousins

95

Ernie and Henry, both serving in the United States Army.

While she sang, Ruth Koop could hear her father's and mother's voices singing the words in their still thick German accents. There was so much anti-German feeling nowadays—on the radio, at school, sometimes even in church. It made her uncomfortable to think that her country was at war with her parents' country, that some of her own uncles and cousins in Germany might be fighting against the Allies. "God bless our boys"—but what about *their* boys?

"These are stormy times we're passing through," said Pastor Fortran. "How good it is to know that we have a Captain, a Pilot, to guide us through the voyage of life. Let's sing 'Jesus, Saviour, Pilot Me.'"

Again the pianist played an introduction, and the congregation rose to sing.

> *Jesus, Saviour, pilot me*
> *Over life's tempestuous sea.*
> *Unknown waves before me roll,*
> *Hiding rock and treacherous shoal.*
> *Chart and compass came from Thee:*
> *Jesus, Saviour, pilot me.*

Ruth looked at her mother, holding her baby, Linda, while the congregation sang a second stanza.

> *As a mother stills her child,*
> *Thou canst hush the ocean wild.*
> *Boisterous waves obey Thy will*
> *When Thou say'st to them, 'Be still!'*
> *Wondrous Sovereign of the sea,*
> *Jesus, Saviour, pilot me.*

The hymn finished, the Reverend Richard Fortran prayed, "O God, we ask you to watch over your children. We are all in need of your guiding hand. But we pray particularly for those tonight who, because of the calamity of war, may be suffering. Those in bombed-out cities of England and Europe, those living under enemy-occupied oppression, those who are in the victims of shipwreck. Be with them, and help them to know your presence. Amen."

It wasn't easy, being a German alien resident, living and working in the United States of America in 1942. True, there were no concentration camps such as those into which Japanese-Americans were being herded; yet every word spoken with a German accent, every hint of Germanic culture—from *wienerschnitzel* to *lederhosen*—caused suspicion. Especially on Long Island, especially in that summer of 1942.

Although German immigrants to America had been highly visible in New York City and on Long Island for generations, anti-German sentiment during World War I had never quite died down. After America's entry into the war in 1917, rumors of sedition and attempted sabotage plagued almost every German-American, whether native-born American, naturalized citizen, or alien. Congress passed laws in 1917 and 1918 under which almost two thousand people were prosecuted for supposed disloyalty to the United States. Words of German origin became anglicized: *sauerkraut* was now "Liberty cabbage," *hamburgers* were known as "Liberty steaks." The study of the German language became suspect and was widely curtailed.

But after the First World War, and until the rise of Adolf

Hitler in 1933, German-Americans enjoyed some measure of reprieve from hostility. August Janssen's famous Broadway restaurant, the Hof Braü Haus, continued to be a meeting place for politicians and other celebrities, as it had since the 1890s. Manhattan's Eighty-sixth Street, the center of the German-dominated Yorkville district, might have been the main *strasse* of any Bavarian city. Maestros Bruno Walter and Otto Klemperer were once again acclaimed conductors of the New York Philharmonic and played their Bach, Beethoven, Brahms, Wagner, and Strauss to cheering audiences at Carnegie Hall.

But on Long Island the German-American Bund—Hitler's scheme for winning converts to the Nazi Party among German nationals living overseas—was holding its youth camp in the woods near Yaphank and Upton, now the site of the Brookhaven National Laboratory. There children were being taught the goose-step march, the *Sieg Heil* salute, and allegiance to the fatal philosophy of Der Führer, whose photograph adorned the camp grounds.

To Carl Koop none of this political fervor made any sense. He was glad to be in America, working toward citizenship through naturalization. A professional musician playing the violin and piano on German ocean liners, Koop had met young Matilde Markant on a 1923 voyage to New York as she emigrated from Germany to settle in America. Koop had jumped ship in New York to court her and, after their marriage, returned to Germany in order to enter the United States legally. By the beginning of World War II, Matilde Koop had received her American citizenship, but her husband's process had been stalled by the coming on of the war.

Carl Koop continued to make his living as a professional musician-choirmaster directing a half-dozen German singing societies in the Borough of Queens and throughout Long Island. But by 1942 to be German-born and not an American citizen—to lead singers in German songs—was considered unpatriotic. The time and place were not appropriate. The war being fought in Europe and the far reaches of the Atlantic since 1939 had come home to Long Islanders. Early in 1942 a submarine called *U-66* had struck ships leaving New York Harbor. Other submarines had sunk ships off Montauk Point, Long Island's easternmost tip, and in the waters bordering the beaches of Fire Island.

More recently, in June of 1942, a massive plot had been uncovered. On the foggy night of June 12 the U-boat *Innsbruck* surfaced near the village of Amagansett, just east of fasionable East Hampton on Long Island's South Fork. Four men, all of them Germans who had lived for some time in the United States, then repatriated to Germany just before the war began, were put ashore by a rubber raft. These men, along with another four who subsequently landed near St. Augustine, Florida, had been selected and trained by *Abwehr II*, a section of German intelligence specializing in subversion, for a mission of massive sabotage to last two years. According to the plan, these two teams of saboteurs were to destroy factories and foundries critical to the American war effort, as well as attack other targets: the Niagara hydroelectric power plant, New York City's water system, and specific railroad bridges and stations.

But the German plot had been foiled almost from its outset; first, seemingly, by accident, then by betrayal. Local residents of Amagansett's beach community had reported hearing a dull throbbing sound on the afternoon of June 12; thick fog, however, enshrouded the beach and water offshore. Nonetheless, the Amagansett Coast Guard Station had been alerted. The sound might be that of a submarine's diesel engines idling. Thus, the four saboteurs had no sooner landed their rubber raft, early on the morning of June 13, than they were accosted by a single coast guardsman on foot patrol. Young James C. Cullen, walking his after-midnight duty, had heard their voices speaking in German before the enemy agents became visible to him or he to them. A strange encounter followed, during which one of the saboteurs first threatened to kill the unarmed youth, then offered him money if Cullen could assure them that he would never recognize any of them again. Wisely, James Cullen agreed, accepted a wad of money—the sum of $260 out of the $200,000 the sabotage team had brought with them!—and retreated to his command post. There he told his amazing story. A detachment of coast guardsmen, now armed, hurried back to where Cullen directed them.

Meanwhile, George Dasch, leader of the German raiding party, and his compatriots had made their way into the sand dunes. After burying boxes of munitions and other supplies off-loaded from the submarine, they walked to the Long Island Railroad depot at Amagansett and boarded the first train to New York City. Having made plans for their respective missions, the saboteurs dispersed to visit family and friends still living in America. But George Dasch—a naturalized American citizen who had served in the U.S. Army Air Corps in the early 1920s—had decided on a different course. Along with Ernest Burger, another member of his foursome, Dasch had determined to inform the American authorities and thus defuse the sabotage plot. He had nothing but contempt for Hitler and the Nazi Party, and he hoped by turning informer to be cited as an American hero.

Upon arriving in New York City, Dasch telephoned the Federal Bureau of Investigation, but his call was regarded as a twisted joke. When he called the Washington headquarters of the FBI a few days later, the reaction was considerably different! By that time the report from the Amagansett Coast Guard Station had been circulated, and the FBI knew that their caller was telling the truth. Dasch and Burger were taken into custody immediately; a little more than a week later, they were joined by their six colleagues. Two months later, following a secret military trial, all eight saboteurs were condemned to death. As their reward, Dasch and Burger had their death sentences commuted by President Roosevelt and reduced to thirty years of imprisonment. (In 1948 both Dasch and Burger were deported to Germany, where they were scarcely greeted as heroes.) Only after the other six saboteurs had been electrocuted was the story released to the press. Naturally, the German sabotage plot on Long Island made national headlines. Once again propaganda stirred up a frenzy of suspicion and hatred against innocent and loyal German-Americans.

Thereafter, wherever Carl Koop conducted his German choirs, even in rehearsals of his 150-voice children's choir in Astoria, Queens, it was considered necessary to national security that a federal marshal be present to observe.

"It was tough to be a German-American in those days," recalls Ruth Koop Bell, now the wife of Bob Bell. "Neighbors we'd known for years on Lafayette Avenue in Sea

Cliff made remarks about my father and mother and their German-accented English speech. We had a bomb threat to our property, I remember, and the police had to come. My father was restricted from visiting his relatives in New Jersey because it was out-of-state. I think there was a lot of unnecessary harassment."

As the sun turned to a great red ball and dropped below the waterline, a pale cold moon, dull as a pewter tray, replaced the sun. Across the moon's face, great clouds moved rapidly, and as the moon rose behind the rafts, its dim light created an eerie counterpoint of shadow and substance. The tiny boxes somehow seemed larger; yet the sea was just as close at hand, the confines of each raft just as limiting.

The survivors began to feel again the dampness of their clothing and the chill of darkness coming on. To add to their discomfort, the greasy residue of oil still coated their bodies, turning to film on their skin, making their hair stink, blurring their vision. Those who had been scraped or cut or gouged during the sinking or their subsequent rescue could now feel the sting of oil in their wounds. But any temptation to hold a bleeding foot over the sides and soak away its hurt in salt water quickly disappeared whenever one of the several sharks tracking the rafts cruised alongside.

The captain had been right: nobody hadd any appetite for food. Well on into Sunday evening the sounds and stench of physical illness hovered over the four rafts like smog. At last, however, the retching subsided, and an exhausted silence seemed to settle over the rafts.

"Move just a little, Robert," said the captain, and he struggled to raise himself and sit on the food box in the middle of the well. Thus elevated, he could see and be seen by most of those on the other three rafts. He cupped his hands to command attention and, with a nod to Ethel Bell, addressed the survivors once again.

"Mrs. Bell, men," said Benjamin Bogden, "I don't need to tell you that we need everyone's total cooperation and support. None of us has ever been in such a tight place before, I'm sure. I hope it'll be the last time for all of us. But until help comes — and, I repeat, I expect that help tomorrow morning — until that time, we've got to help each other."

There were sounds of general agreement from each of the rafts.

"Sure, it's going to be uncomfortable," the captain went on, "but no more so for you than for the person next to you. So, I ask you, *think!* Think about what's best for the whole group."

The captain paused and sighed deeply to overcome his own pain. "If everyone thinks on behalf of the group, then everyone will be taken care of. And, I remind you, that naval regulations still apply, and orders given will be obeyed! Now, rest easy, and get some sleep, if you can."

The effort to lift himself and project his voice had wearied the captain, and he slumped off the food box and back into his corner of the well. Robert wondered where he should sit, but with a smile Captain Bogden reached out and drew the boy down again.

No one said a word, but Robert could see in the moonlight the silhouettes of several heads nodding in affirmation of the captain's speech. What the captain had said was true — selfishness could lead only to chaos. As Robert looked at the faces surrounding him, he realized for the first time, and with an eleven-year-old boy's illumination, the meaning of the cliché, "all in the same boat," which indeed they were — quite literally. Total strangers to him, casual acquaintances, as well as his own family, now found themselves cast upon each other for support and survival. To the degree that each individual survivor subordinated his own interests to the good of the whole company, they would make it. Without this spirit, they were lost.

He heard his mother softly speak his name. "Robert, slide over as close as you can. Richard, lean over this way. Captain Bogden, you don't mind, do you?"

The captain stirred and looked quizzically at the woman.

"The children and I are going to have our evening prayers. It's something we never miss at home, just before bedtime, and there's no reason to give it up just because of these circumstances. In fact—"

"I know, Mrs. Bell," the captain interrupted, "there's probably better reason than ever to say our prayers, all of us."

Robert could hardly change his position; so, instead, he turned his head to come as close as possible to his mother's knees. With her arms tightly around her own daughter, Mary, on one side of her, and motherless Carol Shaw on the other side, Ethel Bell began speaking the words of Psalm 23. Her children, well acquainted with the words from much required memorization and recitation, both at home and at school, followed along. Richard Shaw gradually lost his shyness and joined in, helping Carol to say what little she knew.

> . . . *Yea, though I walk through the valley of the shadow of death, I will fear no evil: for thou art with*

> *me; thy rod and thy staff they comfort me. Thou*
> *preparest a table before me in the presence of mine*
> *enemies: thou anointest my head with oil; my cup*
> *runneth over. Surely goodness and mercy shall fol-*
> *low me all the days of my life: and I will dwell in*
> *the house of the Lord forever.*

This psalm finished, the mother shifted to another favorite passage, Psalm 46.

"Perhaps you don't know this one quite as well, children," she said to them, "but it's one we can learn to say
together." She began saying the words slowly, almost stilt-
edly, like a primary school teacher attempting to imbed
a lesson in her pupils' minds.

> *God is our refuge and strength, a very present help*
> *in trouble. Therefore will not we fear, though the*
> *earth be removed, and though the mountains be*
> *carried into the midst of the sea; though the waters*
> *thereof roar and be troubled, though the mountains*
> *shake with the swelling thereof. . . . The LORD of*
> *hosts is with us; the God of Jacob is our refuge.*

Phrase by phrase, the woman repeated the psalm again,
the children speaking the lines after her.

"Now, let's play a game and see who can memorize
Psalm 46 first," she said with animation. "Richard, can
you begin?"

"I'm not ready yet, Mrs. Bell. Make somebody else go
first."

"All right. How about you, Robert?"

"Let Mary go first, Mother. She knows it already
anyway."

"I do not! You're just saying that, Robert!"

"Children, let's not quarrel. We'll all say it once more together. Then perhaps tomorrow evening—"

"But the captain says we won't be here tomorrow evening," Robert interrupted.

"I know, dear, and I pray he's right. But perhaps God intends for us to be on the raft a little longer. So we'll just wait and see. Now, all together one more time."

Holding tightly to the two girls, her head bobbing like a conductor's baton, Ethel Bell led the children through their halting recitation.

"God is our refuse . . ."

"Refuge, Robert, not refuse, like trash. Start again, children."

"God is our refuge and strength, a very present help in trouble. . . ."

"Just *in trouble,* Mary. Not *in time of trouble.* We don't need to add any words to the psalmist's. Let's try it again."

"God is our refuge and strength, a very present help in trouble. Therefore will not we fear, though the earth be removed, and though the mountains be carried into the midst of the sea; though the waters thereof roar and be troubled . . ."

"That's just like what happened to us, Mother," said Robert. "Our ship was like a mountain, and it got carried into the sea."

"Yes, Robert, but, thank God, the LORD of Hosts is with us; the God of Jacob is our refuge."

For an instant, she was quiet, unable to speak.

"Now, children, let's sing a hymn. Richard, Carol, do you know 'Jesus, Saviour, Pilot Me'?"

The Shaw children nodded, and Ethel Bell began in a voice uncertain and still rasped by seawater:

Jesus. Saviour, pilot me
Over life's tempestuous sea.
Unknown waves before me roll,
Hiding rock and treacherous shoal.
Chart and compass came from Thee:
Jesus, Saviour, pilot me.

As she sang, the children joined the woman, singing just barely above a whisper.

What a peculiar song to sing, thought Robert. Too young to know the meaning of the word *irony,* he nonetheless could sense its effect. Wasn't it a little late to sing "Jesus, Saviour, Pilot Me"? Where was the Pilot when they needed Him?

"I'll teach you the other stanzas another time," his mother was saying. "Now, let's say the Lord's Prayer together. We all know that."

They began reciting the familiar words — "Our Father, which art in heaven" — a widow and four children huddled in the deepening darkness of a night at sea. Five voices, speaking huskily into the void, uttering their petition: "Thy will be done in earth, as it is in heaven. . . ."

Then there were six voices: "For thine is the kingdom, and the power, and the glory for ever. Amen."

"Thank you, Captain Bogden," said Ethel Bell. "Children, now let's do our best to sleep — or, at least, sit as still as we can."

Hell is a long night on a crowded raft.

Yet, in retrospect, that first night may have been the best, so far as sleep was concerned. The day's events had extracted a heavy toll in fatigue. Once the initial shock to the physical system had worked itself out, all that remained was the body's yielding to weariness. Furthermore, the desperate realities of their situation left the survivors with little else to do other than drowse, hoping perhaps to sleep.

Lying on the bulk of Captain Bogden's frame, in the well of the raft, Robert felt each current of ocean water as it surged through the slats. He was all but immersed, like a child soaking in the family bathtub. But here he had no way of stepping out of the water and feeling the warmth of an enveloping towel. All night he seemed to be moving through several levels of consciousness toward the blankness of sleep, without ever quite reaching that comfort. Whether near or far from being fully awake, the boy nonetheless seemed removed from his immediate circumstances — almost as though he were a spectator at the drama being played out on some distant movie screen. He could sense the presence of his mother and sister, but what were they doing here in the motion picture that kept on replaying itself in his mind, like the battlefront newsreels he had recently been allowed to view in Accra? And who were these strangers whose breathing seemed to suffocate him, whose mumbling voices pressed upon his ear, whose faces — even in the darkness — seemed so masked by anxiety?

"I can't tell you how we got through that first night," Bob Bell says more than forty years later, "or any of the other nights that followed, for that matter. All I know is that, every time I twitched or fidgeted the slightest bit, my mother cautioned me with a word or a touch. I knew that she was right there, and I knew that she was awake every moment, watching out for us."

The two girls had each placed her head in Ethel Bell's lap, and the woman sat bowed over them, like a hen sheltering her brood from the surprisingly chill wind that arose as soon as darkness fell. Richard Shaw leaned against his sister, trying to be as careful as possible not to bump her fractured arm in its sling. Even so, Carol Shaw could not be entirely free from pain, and off and on all night, whenever her arm was disturbed, she cried out. One of the crew, anonymous in the darkness, reacted to the child's crying.

"Stuff a rag in that kid's mouth, lady!"

But the captain was quick to rebuke the voice from the dark. "That's enough of that, mister!"

Thereafter an eerie silence blanketed the rafts, as if an informal moratorium on talking had been declared. Only the sound of the four boxes colliding or scraping, as they pitched one way or the other, interrupted the stillness. No more mumbling or crying out: just heavy silence, the kind that seems to precede a great explosion of thunder or rage. Nobody wished to speak or be spoken to; nobody had anything to say or any desire to listen to the complaints of anyone else.

After only an hour or so of presumed sleep, those men sitting around the edge of the captain's raft had locked themselves into a permanent hunch of shoulders, with their chins resting on the life jackets or supported by hands and arms braced against their thighs. The mere crush of bodies — like a Manhattan-bound subway train during morning rush hour — maintained the rigidity of each man's position. No individual shift of body weight would have been possible without an adjustment of the entire mass of bodies in a prearranged sequence. There simply was no place to go.

So the long night passed, second by second, ache by excruciating ache, in a slow-motion horror of helplessness.

Monday, August 31
SEVEN
PEMMICAN

A gray stillness preceded the first rays of dawn. On each raft the survivors shuddered with the cold. Not even the life jackets seemed able to ward off the chill. How could your teeth chatter in the tropics? How could your skin freeze in gooseflesh in such latitudes?

As one after another of the survivors stirred, suddenly a navy man on one of the less-crowded rafts jumped to his feet:

"Look, there's a ship!"

"Where?" asked Elliott Gurney, an able-bodied seaman.

"About one o'clock, just above the horizon. Here, give me one of the oars. Gurney, give me that torn shirt."

Quickly the shirt was tied to the oar, and the navy man began waving wildly.

"Hey, Mac, you gotta be kiddin'!" said a realist. "Nobody that far away is gonna see you wavin' that flag. Save your energy."

Reluctantly, the navy man acquiesced and sat down.

"Nice try," Gurney told him.

"Well, we have to do something! We can't just sit here."

The ship the navy man had seen was a British tanker, formerly known as *Pulpit Point,* now called *Winimac.* Her smokestacks puffing grandly, her cargo bays full of precious Venezuelan petroleum, the *Winimac* made her way toward distant England without benefit of convoy protection, fully aware that she was an easy target for any lurking submarine. So far, *Winimac* had managed to elude any enemy threat. If she could just get beyond the U-boats' apparent favorite hunting grounds, east of the Windwards, perhaps *Winimac's* luck would hold all the way to Liverpool.

"My God, look at the size of that monster!"

The first words to be spoken on the captain's raft summoned Robert out of his lethargy. Joe Greenwell and George Marano, on either side of Robert and the captain, were studying the scene just a few feet from where they sat. Cutting through the water came a dorsal fin belonging to one of the sharks of the school that had become attached to the rafts.

"It's twice as long as the raft!"

Robert twisted to look between the men, sending a groan through the captain.

"Easy, son. It'll still be there if you move slower." He spoke kindly.

"Sorry, Captain Bogden," the boy apologized. "I'll try to be more careful."

Nonetheless, Robert's curiosity compelled him to look. There next to his raft, just inches below the surface, lay the most frightening reminder of their condition—a shark some twenty feet long! Its bulk swelled beyond any terror Robert had ever imagined.

"Here, Joe," said George Marano, "gimme that oar."

Greenwell reached for an oar and handed it to Marano with a cautioning word.

"Careful, Captain Ahab!"

Standing gingerly, Marano began thrusting at the shark as if with a blunted harpoon. After a half-dozen jabs, Marano ceased his oar spearing, and the huge beast glided away in disdain.

"I sure wouldn't want to meet that big bugger in a swimming pool!" said Marano.

"Best to leave him alone," Greenwell responded, "or else he might come back and bring his big brother with him."

"Who d'ya mean? Moby Dick?"

"Well, that's a whale, but I guess sharks might attack a raft, I dunno. . . ."

"My goodness, men," spoke the captain, "what a delightful topic for the first conversation of the morning. And I haven't even had my eye-opener cup of coffee yet."

"You know something, Captain," Rodriguez the cook spoke up, "I came to just now dreaming about the breakfast I had planned for this morning on the *West Lash.*"

"Well, don't talk about it unless you can serve it!" said the bosun from his doughnut alongside the raft.

"I think we ought to get on with the food we have on hand. What do you say, Mrs. Bell?"

"I wholly agree, Captain Bogden," she replied.

"Bosun, come up here, please. I'm going to need your help on the other three rafts. Trade places with the bosun, somebody."

Three or four men moved suddenly to claim the enviable position alone in the dinghy.

"Not so fast, men." the captain rebuked them. "Take it slow. We can't have people jumping up and down like that. We'll swamp. Potter, you and Walker both go into the doughnut. Make room for the bosun."

Back onto the raft crawled Owen, looking a trifle miffed at having to yield his place. The captain noted his expression.

"Did you have a comfortable night's rest, Bosun?"

"Not with those sharks nosing around all night, sir."

"Too bad," said Bogden with no trace of sarcasm. "Go to the other rafts and supervise the distribution of rations. I want one man responsible on each raft, and I want the daily rations strictly adhered to. You know what your mothers used to say, men? No nibbling between meals!"

The men laughed at the captain's humor, the first sound of laughter Robert had heard since Sunday lunch the day before. The thought of that meal and the present talk of food made him suddenly aware of how hungry he was.

"Mr. Greenwell and I'll take charge of food here, Bosun," the captain went on. "You handle the other rafts."

"Children," Ethel Bell said, "before the captain passes out our food, we need to wash up."

Slowly she bent over and reached into the well of the raft, where a constant basin of ocean water sloshed through. Cupping her hands, she brought them back dripping to her face and scrubbed, then rubbed her teeth and gums with her forefinger, as if she were performing ablutions in some luxurious lavatory.

"Be careful not to get any of that salt into your mouth, lady," the bosun called from another raft. "If you do, you'll tack on a raging thirst to the rest of your troubles."

"Thank you, Mr. Owen, you're right," Mrs. Bell acknowledged. "Children, don't swallow any of the water as you brush your teeth."

But for all their earnestness and obedience, the children did taste the salt water, and their washing did nothing to remove the grime of their baptism in fire and oil.

On each raft the floor hatches had been opened and the food boxes and water casks removed. Owen stood where the men on the other three rafts could see him and relayed the captain's orders.

"We don't know how long we'll be out here, so we're holding to strict rationing of this food. Like Captain Bogden says, no snacks; just regular mealtimes, twice a day."

The food had been packed in small tins for individual portions. The captain had decided that rations for each day would consist of two tins of pemmican, each to be shared with someone else, one half at each time, early and then later in the day. To this would be added a small piece of chocolate, a biscuit, one malted milk tablet, and two ounces of water per person with each meal.

On the first morning the food boxes seemed amply supplied. Robert wondered why it was necessary to limit himself to only one half of his pemmican. Why not eat it all? If the captain was right, if they were going to be rescued soon, why not enjoy themselves while they waited? The food being passed around the raft by Joe Greenwell, the captain's right-hand man, reached Robert last. As he gripped his share, the boy's resentment welled up and spilled over.

"How come we can't eat the whole tin now, Captain? We've got lots of food."

"Yes, my boy," Bogden replied, "and when we need it, the food will be there. And when we don't need it any longer, I'll see to it that you get a nice big steak, instead of tinned rations! For now, you share with your sister."

Robert found the metal key attached to the tin of food, snapped it off, inserted the key in the metal tab, and wound it around the vacuum-sealed can. A tiny gush of air released with it the oily, sweet smell of its contents. Around him the men were already sampling the mixture with their fingertips.

"Well, Rodriguez," said one, "this stuff sure makes me appreciate your cooking!"

The evening before, Ethel Bell had maintained her family's customary bedtime devotions. Now, as soon as the children and she received their first distribution of rations, she kept up another custom in the Bell household, grace before meals. As she and the children with her held their bits and pieces of foodstuff in their hands, Ethel Bell bowed her head and prayed, "Our heavenly Father, we thank Thee for the food that Thou has provided. We pray for strength to endure our difficult circumstances. We pray for courage this day. Our trust is in Thee, O God. In Jesus' name. Amen."

When he raised his eyes and looked around, Robert was not surprised to see that most of the men were already busy chomping at the hardtack biscuit or chewing through the sticky pemmican. Some men, however, had waited until his mother's quiet prayer had ended, respecting the woman's religious convictions before beginning to eat their portions.

"Now, children, it's time for breakfast," she said cheerily.

"What's this stuff, Mrs. Bell?" asked Carol Shaw, pointing to the pemmican. "I don't like it."

"It's a mixture of fruit and nuts with a little dried meat,

Carol. It's called pemmican," Ethel replied. "We have to eat all our rations to keep strong until we're picked up."

"I don't like it," the little girl insisted. "Richard, do I have to eat the pelican?"

"It's not *pelican,* silly! It's *pemmican,*" her brother told her, "and Mrs. Bell is right. You do have to eat it." With that the older boy dug his fingers into his rations.

Robert's turn came soon, and he sympathized with Carol. He regretted having demanded a full tin for himself and was glad to eat only half a tin.

"I'll never forget the oily flavor of that pemmican," says Bob Bell today. "Maybe it wasn't the food. Perhaps it was the all-pervasive oil that still coated our mouths and hands. But to this day I can't stomach coconut, which was one of the fruit ingredients in the pemmican. And I don't care much for chocolate either."

To help wash down the food, each person received an inch of water served in a porcelain mug. This container was greasy; yet who could waste water in washing it? Certainly it could not be rinsed in the sea water so readily at hand. As for the drinking water, it had been stored months before and had acquired a rank flavor. As a beverage, this water left a good deal to be desired. But it was all they had.

To eat the small supply of food each person held in hand, to refill and pass the cup of water once around the raft, might have taken as little as ten minutes. But for this first meal and every meal that followed, the time consumed equaled any state occasion in a palace. Chewing became a dawdling pleasure. Eating meant masticating every morsel until its juices had been thoroughly savored, then holding the pulp in the mouth as long as possible before the inevitable swallow. Then began the search for any last fragment of food lodged in some crevice between the teeth. This preoccupation itself could last another long duration.

"To this day," says Bob Bell, "I eat my meals very slowly. I can't understand how people can gulp and wolf their way through a three-course dinner. I learned to treasure every bite; every glass of water is a precious gift.

"I'm also dismayed," Bell goes on, "whenever I see good food being thrown into the garbage. So many people today—not just on rafts but in our cities and even on our own block—may not have enough to eat. We waste food by buying and cooking too much, then discarding what we don't want. It's a crime against the human race."

While Captain Bogden and his companions ate, the same procedure was being followed on the three adjacent rafts, with James Owen supervising. Even though each of these rafts carried only half as many persons as the overcrowded captain's raft, their rations remained the same. Nobody complained. Fair for one, fair for all seemed to prevail.

When the morning's rations had been eaten, the food box was tied down in the raft's well instead of being returned to the hold under the decking. What was lost in leg room seemed to be made up by additional seating. Furthermore, the two water kegs now also served as stools, providing seats for John Vargas—who commenced beating out Spanish rhythms on the side of the keg as if it were a conga drum—and the bosun, now returned from the other rafts.

By this time the morning sun had risen behind the rafts and begun its climb toward full noonday brilliance. At first its rays were welcome, dispelling the cold that had troubled the survivors throughout the night. But soon the sun's near-equatorial heat would give real cause for each survivor to wish for the night's chill air once more.

Again Captain Bogden hauled himself to sit upright on the food box. He addressed his own company. "Hope you ladies and gentlemen all enjoyed your breakfast." Then raising his voice, he spoke to the survivors on all the crafts. "It's time to organize ourselves into duty watches. We need two men to stand each watch, and they'll be two-hour duties instead of the regular four-hour watches on board ship."

Like a sacred ritual among men at sea, the watch began immediately. Everyone except Ethel Bell and the children was assigned to a partner and expected to stand the watch — literally *stand* in a corner of the raft, looking for any sign of help or impending danger. Joe Greenwell and George Marano took the first duty, with time being estimated by gentleman's agreement. Together they stared at the glistening water, shielding their eyes from the sun's blinding glare with a hand held to the forehead. From time to time they turned to study each quadrant of the infinity that stretched before, behind, and to either side. They saw nothing except the omnipresent sharks.

"Where do you think that sub got to?" one man asked another.

"Who cares, just so it don't come back here!"

"What makes you ask anyhow?" inquired a third.

"I dunno. Them sharks sure remind me of that U-boat."

"Don't worry. Jerry's long gone by now."

In fact, *U-66* was only a few miles away.

After Karl Degner-Böning assured Klaus Herbig that no SOS from the *West Lashaway* had been sent, the submarine had no need to flee the area. With her radio apparently damaged or her radio operator dead after the first torpedo's impact, the *West Lashaway* could attract no other ships or planes to come to her aid, could summon no help, either for rescue or reprisal.

As soon as night fell *U-66* emerged from hiding and spent the hours of darkness fully surfaced and with engines idling. Just at dawn, a member of the watch called out, "Smoke ahead!" The news was hollered down below. Commmander Markworth, summoned from sleep by his standing orders whenever a ship was sighted, rushed from his quarters to the tower.

"Position?" he demanded while squinting through his binoculars.

"Must be around ten degrees, thirty north, and fifty-four west, Captain."

"Distance?"

"Not more than three miles, Captain."

"Estimated size?"

"Larger than either of yesterday's ships. Possibly six thousand, maybe seven thousand tons."

"Attack!"

By 9:15 A.M. the British tanker *Winimac*, caught totally by surprise and struck by only one torpedo, had carried her 8,600 tons to the bottom of the Atlantic. Markworth had sunk his eighth ship, his fourth in three days. It was time to return to base at Lorient.

EIGHT
DAYDREAMS

While Joe Greenwell and George Marano stood the first watch, the bosun ordered Woodman Potter and Levi Walker out of the dinghy. James Owen had decided to resume his scavenging among the debris from the doomed ship.

Robert was surprised to see that the rafts had not drifted farther away from the site of the shipwreck and asked Joe Greenwell about it.

"Oh no, my boy," the engineer answered, "we've drifted a good long way, I'm sure. But, you see, the same current that's moving us is also moving all that junk out there. So it's trailing alongside us. It just seems that we're in the same place because all that mess is still so close to us."

"How fast are we drifting?" the cook, Rodriguez, asked.

"Hard to say," George Marano replied. "Of course, without any propulsion, we fall back a little every time we move a length forward."

"Well, why not crank up some propulsion?" said Joe Greenwell. "We don't have much steam power, but we sure got enough arm power. Let's row."

"Row!"

"Are you kiddin'?"

"Get off it, Mac!"

"Hey, why not?" Greenwell answered his critics. "We got four rafts with two pairs of oars each, right? So we rig some line for oar locks, and we use one of the light-weight rafts as the powerhouse. We can rotate the rowing duty, just like we rotate the watch."

"Can't hurt to give it a try," one of the navy men on an adjacent raft conceded. "Let's set up shop on this raft," he said, indicating one of the three damaged rafts. "We've got a complement of eight men here already. We'll take the first shift, right, guys?"

"Yessir! Aye, aye, sir!"

So began the brave experiment with inadequate oars and flimsy hemp oarlocks, not to mention dubious, if not disbelieving, men to pull upon those oars. Years later Bob Bell would read Stephen Crane's story about another shipwreck and of four men at sea in "The Open Boat." When he read of these men and their futile attempts at rowing, he could empathize with them. Like Crane's victims, these men on the rafts rowed and rowed. "And also they rowed," wrote Crane. But the ocean was tractless, the horizon a blur of mist and glistening sunlight upon the water; direction and distance seemed meaningless. With all the goodwill in the world, the rowing got nowhere and ended without either ceremony or regret.

"I remember the men's attempt at rowing," says Mary Bell Whitbeck. "It took so much effort, and they made almost no headway whatever. It was so discouraging."

Joe Greenwell concurs. "It was pretty easy to tell we weren't getting anywhere, and we were wasting a lot of strength we might need later on. So among us all we decided to give it up. Nobody complained about that decision, let me tell you!"

Meanwhile the bosun had resumed his place in the doughnut, as if by rank and privilege. Once again he set out to forage among the debris. His return trips seemed to be bringing back fewer and fewer treasures, but at one point he called to his crewman Isabelino Pacheco, "Chico, come with me."

"¡Sí, señor!"

Curious to know what was happening, Robert peered throught the cracks in the raft just at the waterline. He could see the blue-gray cork dinghy edging away from the raft with Owen and Chico aboard.

Fifty yards from the rafts, the bosun and his companion plied their way through the scattered debris, picking at remnants from the ship. Robert could hear their voices but could not understand what they were saying. It seemed as though they were weighing the merits of salvaging one item or another. After a while, he heard the men on his raft speaking to the two men in the doughnut dinghy.

"What's that stuff for, Owen?"

The bosun had dragged back to the rafts some boards, a wooden ladder, and a mattress.

"Gonna make a trailer," Owen replied. "We'll lash these boards to the ladder and put the mattress on top. Somebody can stretch out and get a little leg room from time to time."

Several men on the captain's raft leaned over to hoist the bosun's cargo aboard. It was tricky business, mov-

ing planks, a ladder, and the soggy mattress onto an already crowded raft. To make room, a couple of men
moved temporarily to the adjacent rafts. Almost immediately their added weight caused the damaged raft to sink
lower into the water. Clearly, those rafts with punctured
floats could not be counted on for long.

Together the men bound the boards at right angles to
the rungs of the ladder and attached a line to the captain's
raft. Then they threw the mattress onto the makeshift raft.
It floated, but just barely.

"Why don't you give it a try, Captain?" Owen invited.
"You'll be more comfortable."

Robert moved so that Captain Bogden could raise his
bulk over the side and onto the mattress. At first he smiled
with relief, but in only a few minutes it became plain that
Owen's invention suffered from too much weight.

"Maybe it'll hold a lighter man, Bosun. I'm coming
back in," said the once-more soaked captain.

Together several men reached for the line connecting
Captain Bogden's waterbed and drew him back to the raft.
Now Bogden's internal injuries seemed more searing as
he attempted to roll his overweight torso from the water-
logged mattress back onto the raft. Few, if any, of the men
had known heretofore what Robert Bell knew: that Captain Bogden was an injured man attempting to conceal
his injuries. But in the process of his moving back to the
raft, his moans and wincing face could not be hidden.

"You look like you're hurt bad, Captain," said Woodman Potter.

"It's all right, Potter. Just some burns, I guess. We
mustn't make too much of them, you know."

"Captain, you gotta take care of yourself," Potter re-
joined. "You can't be no sofa for the kid, not if you got

burns on your body." Turning to Robert, the second cook told him, "Boy, you gonna have to sit somewhere else."

"Robert," his mother called him, "come over here."

The boy crawled over the food box and the men sitting on it, then squeezed himself into the family group in the corner opposite where the captain now lay alone. Bogden's face was a grimace of restrained anguish.

"How he held back from crying out in his pain is a wonder to me," Bell now recalls. "His pain must have been excruciating; yet never once did he allow himself the normal man's expression of suffering. He was a superb example of personal courage on behalf of us all."

Meanwhile, Joe Greenwell and the bosun were having words.

"That's enough of those bright ideas, Owen. What you wanna do, kill the old man?"

"Get off my back, Mr. Greenwell," Owen retorted. "The captain can take care of himself. He knows what he can do and what he can't."

"Yea, maybe so. But as for you, Bosun, remember your place!"

"Yes, *sir!*" the bosun sneered back at the officer. Then he said, "How about putting Mrs. Bell and the kids—or at least some of them—on the mattress? They're lighter than the captain. They'll float."

Incensed, Greenwell doubled his fists on Owen. "I'm telling you, Bosun, lay off that lady and those kids. They don't go nowhere, you hear me?"

To ease the tension, George Marano spoke up.

"Hey, since we didn't get far rowing, let's use the oars for something else. How about making a mast and using the canvas as a sail? How about wind power?"

"Great idea, George!"

"Sure beats rowing!"

Other men chimed in their assent.

"Yeah, I'll buy that," Owen responded. Then turning to his crew of deckhands, he instructed them in erecting a double-masted sail.

"Hey, Flavor, Seremos, Chico, step lively. Lash these two pairs of oars so each one's the same length. Then we'll fasten the canvas between the two masts. When it's secured, we'll stand the masts upright at the back of the well."

The three deckhands rose from their seats on one side of the raft. Greenwell and Marano eased away from their places to make room at the captain's end of the raft, taking Robert with them. Together with the bosun, the four men worked to bind first one, then a second pair of oars to form two poles some eight feet long. The task was far from easy. The bucking raft made standing treacherous; the press of bodies and the length of oars left little space in which to work. But these were experienced mariners — Flavor, a utility deckhand; Pacheco, an ordinary seaman; Seremos, an able-bodied seaman. Under James Owen's scrutiny, they knew their skills would be tested, and so they took pride in their work. When the oars had been tied fast, the bosun produced from the hold beneath the flooring his prize, the piece of canvas with which, in forethought, he had outfitted each raft.

"Here, men, let's see what kind of yachtsmen you are!" Owen said.

Woodman Potter passed along his knife, with which Frank Flavor cut slits in the canvas for the fastening ropes. At last the canvas was attached; then the masts were raised and bound into the corners of the well nearest to Captain Bogden and Ethel Bell. Immediately the sheet caught the wind and stretched taut.

The survivors on all the rafts cheered.

"Good work, Bosun," the captain commended. "I think that will do very nicely. We should get quite a bit of benefit from that sail."

"Where do you think it'll blow us, Captain?" Robert McDaniel asked.

Bogden squinted at the sky to judge direction. The sun was over his left shoulder, just passing the crest of the improvised sail.

"Well, if we went down where I think we did, less than two days out of Port of Spain, and if I take my bearings correctly, we're right in the middle of the Windward currents. That means we'll probably drift northerly as much as we go westwardly.

"But," he continued with regained energy, "I don't see us drifting far at all. We're not going to be out here that long. Unless I'm mistaken, we'll be spotted this afternoon."

General agreement flooded the raft like a breaker swamping a surfboard.

"Oh, Mr. Greenwell," the captain beckoned, and Joe Greenwell leaned in for a private conversation.

"OK, sure thing, Captain," Greenwell responded. Standing up and worming his way toward the corner closest to the other rafts, Greenwell called out to them, "Captain Bogden wants another piece of canvas from one of you." In a moment, a rolled sheet was being passed across to Greenwell. Taking the roll and summoning George Marano to join him, Greenwell began attaching the second canvas to the uprights just below the billowing sail.

"What's the idea, Mr. Greenwell?" the bosun asked. "You won't get any more wind at that level."

"Captain's orders. Ask him."

Ignoring Owen, the captain turned and spoke quietly to Ethel Bell. "Mrs. Bell, for you and the girls. In case — you know—you need a little privacy. A courtesy curtain."

"Thank you very much, Captain," the woman replied. "That's very thoughtful of you."

"What does he mean, Mother?" Mary Bell asked.

Mrs. Bell whispered in her daughter's ear. The teenaged girl blushed and put her hand to her mouth.

Until that moment Robert had given no thought whatever to the need for a toilet. He could not have explained why, but since yesterday afternoon's attack of nausea and vomiting, his bodily functions seemed suspended because his intake of nourishment had been entirely absorbed, leaving no waste in his system. So it was for the remainder of this ordeal. Yet the "courtesy curtain," as Captain Bogden called it, represented order, decency, and civility, even in such desperate straits.

"Tomorrow morning at the latest," the captain resumed his optimism. "We'll be off these rigs by then, you mark my words."

"You bet, Captain!"

"That's the spirit!"

Robert smiled at the encouragement from so many men around him. These were experienced merchant seamen. They knew the sea and its ways; they knew how ships keep track of each other, how shipping companies watch for the first signs of need and respond to them instantly. If these men could feel so confident, so assured, why should he be afraid?

Then there was the United States Navy! After all, there

was a war on, wasn't there? The navy had to know by then that the Nazi submarine wolf pack had been smelling blood. *It won't be long before we're rescued,* Robert told himself. *In the meantime, what an adventure! What a story to tell the kids when we get back home to Nyack!*

"SOS. SOS. SOS. HMS *Winimac* damaged and sinking. Positon, ten degrees thirty-six minutes north, fifty-four degrees thirty-four west. U-boat surfaced but unidentified. Repeat. SOS. HMS *Winimac* damaged and sinking. Over."

"Roger, HMS *Winimac.* VP-31, Trinidad Detachment, reads you loud and clear. Position, ten degrees thirty-six minutes north, fifty-four degrees thirty-four west. Rescue patrol alerted. Try to identify the U-boat. Repeat. Try to identify the U-boat. Over."

"Roger, VP-31. Thanks, Yank. We can use all the help you can send. Jolly good, here's a report on Jerry. Just got a look at his numbers. It's *U-66.* Over."

"Damn that German! What's he doing, fighting the whole bloody war himself? Roger, HMS *Winimac.* Keep on the horn as long as you can. Help is on the way. Over."

The radio operator at Patrol Squadron headquarters on Trinidad hurried from his desk to inform Commanding Officer Donald Gay. He handed the written SOS to the officer and said, "Guess who, Lieutenant?"

Gay took the note without a word. Then looking around the ward room at his weary comrades, he motioned toward the planes and said, "Sorry, fellas, but we just got a mission." Together the group of navy pilots and their crews jogged in double time to their aircraft.

"Where we headed, Lieutenant?"

"About two hundred and fifty degrees due east. I'll give

directions when we get upstairs. The Brits have a tanker in trouble. By the way, a special prize to the pilot who lands the big fish. We're looking for a certain U-boat with a big double six. Let's go, and happy landing!"

"And how did you spend your summer vacation, Robert?" some schoolteacher would ask him. Would she be surprised!

"My mother's a missionary in Africa," he'd answer, "and our home is at Bouaké, Ivory Coast, about a hundred and fifty miles inland from Abidjan, the capital city. We used to live almost four hundred miles farther inland, at San in Mali, but that's when my father was still alive. My sister Mary and I went to a school for missionaries' children at Mamou, maybe five hundred miles away from Mother, in Guinea. That's part of French West Africa, and it's controlled by the Vichy French. Those are the guys who sold out to the Nazis, not General de Gaulle's Free French. . . ."

John Vargas was drumming out a Latin rhythm and singing a Spanish song, barely audible. Most of the other men sat motionless in the early afternoon stupor. The captain, exhausted after his exertion, lay gasping in the corner. Robert returned to his reverie.

" . . . As I was saying"—Robert pretended to be addressing his teacher and classmates at Liberty School in Nyack—"after Pearl Harbor, it wasn't safe to be an American in that part of French West Africa controlled by the Nazis. So Mother began making plans for us to leave. Only it wasn't as simple as just calling up a shipping company and paying the fare. There weren't many ships carrying ordinary passengers; everything was tied in with the war effort. Every morning Mother would go to the government offices and try to convince the Vichy French officials—who were really acting on whatever orders their Nazi bosses gave them—to give us papers to leave.

"Late one afternoon, a month after we'd arrived in Ouagadougou, Mother got word that we had clearance to leave Upper Volta for Gold Coast, a British territory. Mother is a naturalized American citizen and Mary and I are Americans; so as citizens of an Allied country, we could gain entry to the British colony of Gold Coast.

"The British provided us with transportation by lorry and train, and we traveled the 375 miles to Accra, the capital city, on the coast of the Gulf of Guinea. It's a beautiful city, and our hotel was right on the ocean. Accra has no harbor, and there were always ships anchored offshore, where dories would go out and bring their cargo back. I remember seeing one ship that never seemed to move; finally, somebody told me that it had been torpedoed by a German sub and had sunk as much as it could in the shallow water.

"Mary and I had a great time in Accra. We were still supposed to be leaving for home soon, so there were no classes. All we did was play on the beach or stroll around the streets of Accra. We had delicious food—lots of fresh fish—and sometimes at night Mother would let us watch the current newsreels from the war in Europe and Asia. Of course, sometimes she didn't, and we'd spend those evenings in our hotel room memorizing Bible verses. Mother always was a great one for memorizing Scripture. . . ."

"Do you want to play, Robert?" his mother interrupted his musings. "Mary and I are quizzing each other."

"What about? What for?"

"Oh, about anything. State capitals, authors, Bible

verses, anything we think might stump the other person. We're just doing it to pass the time. Would you like to play, Richard? Carol?"

"I don't know how to play," the little girl whined. "I just want my mommy. Why can't I be with my mommy?"

"Hush, Carol," her brother spoke forcefully. "Mom's not here anymore, but Dad's right over there on the other raft, and Mrs. Bell is trying to be kind to you. Now you hush up and try to understand!"

Ethel Bell hugged the tiny waif seated next to her. Across from her, on an attached raft, sat the forlorn figure of Harvey Shaw. From the moment he had been pulled from the water and informed that his wife and daughter Georgia were missing, Shaw had sunk into gloomy resignation. His only words since sending Richard and Carol to the captain's raft had been spoken after yesterday's nausea. Ethel Bell's own spirits were far from hilarious, but she knew she must keep herself and the children entrusted to her from early despair. Perhaps if they could speak across the rafts to their father! She would try.

"Mr. Shaw," she called, but her voice seemed dry and weak. She turned to Joe Greenwell, now relieved from watch. "Mr. Greenwell, could you get Mr. Shaw's attention on that raft over there. I think it would help if he could talk with his children, especially Carol."

"Sure, Mrs. Bell." The robust engineer cupped his hands and called the name several times. Then he stood to gain a better view. "He don't seem to take no notice, Mrs. Bell. He's just sitting there, looking at the floor. Maybe it's best just to leave him alone. He's got a lot on his mind, poor fellow!"

Ethel Bell nodded and returned to her game with the

children. "Now, who's next? Who has a question that no-body can answer?"

"I do, lady," spoke a voice from the other end of the raft. The youth known as "Flags," the signalman Earl Croons, had been listening. "I got a question. When do we get off this stinkin' raft?" Then he broke out into hys-terical laughter, trying to thrash about with his legs. The men at that end of the raft grabbed him and attempted to subdue him quietly, but his laughter now turned to loud cries of pain.

"O God, it hurts! It hurts! O God, I wanna die!"

Then he was still, and the raft returned to normal.

Whatever interest Robert might have had in playing his mother's game had been dissipated by the discourage-ment of Carol, her father's silence, and Croons's outburst. For his part, the boy preferred his daydream.

" . . . I had my eleventh birthday there in Accra, July 20, 1942. We had a real nice party. Mother found some-body at the hotel to bake me a birthday cake with can-dles, and we had my favorite meal, roast beef and gravy, mashed potatoes and peas, just like Grandma Roffe's, es-pecially when we visit her summer house at Gravenhurst, Ontario. I suppose I could have stayed in Accra forever, we were having such a good time. But it was hard on Mother, I know. She kept worrying about when we were going to get out of Africa and back home to Nyack and to Grandpa and Grandma Roffe in Toronto.

"Finally, on August 10, word came that a ship would be arriving sometime soon at Takoradi, one hundred miles or so from Accra. There were only three passenger bookings available, and there were two families of three persons each. How they decided I don't know, but the grown-ups decided that the Bells would go on this ship.

I hear the other family went home by airplane! We loaded all our baggage — everything we owned — into a bus and rode to Sekondi, near Takoradi, where we stayed four days, waiting for our ship to arrive. It came on August 14. Almost as soon as we got into our cabin, Mother shut the door and called Mary and me together to pray, thanking God for giving us places on this ship. She prayed for our safety on the *West Lashaway*. The next day, August 15, we sailed. Then, fifteen days later . . ."

As Robert thought about telling his classmates of his mother's prayer, he wondered if they would laugh at its absurdity.

"Mary! Robert! Look! Look over there! Richard! Carol!" Ethel Bell pointed toward the western horizon. "See, children, a rainbow!"

From south to north, in radiant hues, stretched the bands of color, disappearing at either end into the gray distance. Some of the men, hearing the woman direct the children's attention toward the sky, turned their heads.

"Hey, a rainbow! That's good luck!" said Levi Walker.

"Yeah, maybe we'll find a pot o' gold!" replied Robert McDaniel.

"Yeah, and maybe we won't!" growled James Owen.

Ethel Bell said nothing. She simply smiled and squeezed her daughter's shoulder.

"We saw that same rainbow every day," says Bob Bell. "It never failed to bring us hope."

NINE
WAITING AND WONDERING

By midafternoon the near-equatorial sun beat down upon the survivors in furnace heat. With nothing shielding them from the sun's full force, the men gasped and cursed.

From their heads to their feet, each of the nineteen adults and children on the captain's raft knew intimately the meaning of discomfort. Every part of the body ached or stung with numbness or pain, Globules of grease coated their heads, draining over their faces and necks or streaming from lank strands of hair, irritating their eyes and lining their lips with its foul taste. This filth clung to their clothing, to their bare arms and legs, so that they looked like swimmers preparing to cross the English Channel. Some bore deep gashes; some, like Carol Shaw, had broken limbs; some, like Captain Bogden and Flags Croons, had internal injuries no amateur medic could diagnose. Already, after only a few hours with their feet in the open well of the raft, the effects of prolonged immersion in salt water were beginning to show. Itchy, puckered skin would soon yield to weakened flesh, in which would then break out suppurating ulcers.

Now that routines had been established—food distributed, watches assigned, seating arranged—there was little to do but wait. The burden of time fell crushingly on the hunched shoulders of each survivor. Bent almost double, most of the men could not see beyond the waterline. For hour upon hour few words passed among them. The burden of tedium, unknown to most of these hardworking seamen, now oppressed them.

"Hey, I got an idea how we might pass the time," said Joe Greenwell.

"Yeah, what's that, Joe? Count the sharks?"

"Let the man speak!"

"I'm thinkin'," Greenwell went on, "here I am with you people, and I don't even know that much about most of you, and you don't know much about me."

"What's to know?"

"Lots," Greenwell continued, "like where you came from, how you happened to be on the *West Lashaway,* how you made it here instead of endin' up in Davey Jones' Locker, like some of our people."

"OK, man, shoot," said Woodman Potter. "Tell us 'bout yourself, since it's your idea."

"Sure, why not?" And Joe Greenwell began.

"I was born near Bardstown, Kentucky, in 1898, so that makes me"—Joe Greenwell tilted back his head to calculate—"forty-four years old, or thereabouts. My father went to Cuba to fight with Teddy Roosevelt and the Rough Riders and got himself killed there. My mother received a pension for her, my two sisters, and me until we reached the age of sixteen. Two-fifty each, it was—a great big ten dollars per month for the four of us.

"Thank God, my grandfather had left my mother the farm, so we had a place to live. We kept some livestock, horses, cows, sheep, pigs, a few of each, and plenty of turkeys. We also had geese, ducks, and chickens. I ate a lot of eggs growing up. And we had a big vegetable garden. We managed to keep food on the table.

"Our schoolhouse was about three miles from home, right in a patch of woods. Course it was one room with a big wood stove in the middle. Families who sent their kids to school got together and cut and hauled wood, and the kids did the stoking of that stove. We carried our lunch from home, drew our water from a spring some one hundred yards down the hill from the schoolhouse, and we had two outhouses, his and hers. We weren't much on education in those parts of Kentucky. I guess the whole school budget wasn't more than four hundred dollars a year, including the teacher's pay.

"I left school at fourteen, but stayed around the farm to help my mother and sisters for a year or two. Then I went off to Galesburg, Illinois, and got a job there. Nice town, by the way. College town. Knox College was one of the hotbeds of the Abolitionists, and Lincoln and Douglas had one of their debates there, I believe. Anyway, I stayed there for a while; then I went out to Wyoming and got a job as a telegraph operator with a railroad. Lousy job.

"Then I got restless again and decided to go to sea. I was strictly a landlubber—not much salt water in Kentucky and Wyoming!—but I joined the navy in 1915. Well, by that time the Huns had started trouble over in Europe, and we finally got into it in '17. Where do y' suppose I got assigned? To a mine layer in the *Pacific!* The service is the service, don't y' know, but what a way to go! We were based in Honolulu, and there wasn't much action in that part of the the Pacific. . . . "

Hoots of recognition and knowing glances full of double entendre from seamen recalling their own adventures in exotic ports goaded Joe Greenwell on.

"Nice work if you can get it, Joe!"

"Not much action at sea, maybe, but how about the action on shore?"

"Did you get in a little hoola dancing, Joe?"

Greenwell smiled and ignored their gibes.

"And so I served about six years, and then got my discharge in 1921. Came back home to Kentucky for a short stay. Hadn't seen my folks since I left almost ten years before that. But, y' know, once you got seawater in your veins, it's hard staying down on the farm! So I joined my first commercial ship, out of St. John's, Washington. It was the SS *Nebraskan,* a ship of the American Hawaiian Line. . . . "

"Just couldn't keep away from them Hawaiian women, right, Joe?"

"Well, do ya blame him?"

"I was a fireman, shoveling coal. There were nine of us, three on each watch. My watch, I had a guy from Bombay and another from Hong Kong. The three of us left that ship first time we got to the East Coast. From that time on, I guess I worked at every unlicensed job there is on a merchant vessel, really learning at firsthand. I took my time before I sat for my engineer's license. I had correspondence courses, and I even went back to school for a few months. Then I was ready for my first test, to get my third assistant engineer's license. Stayed with that until I'd learned enough to work up to the next grade. Finally, after about ten years, I got the top license for chief engineer."

Applause and approving nods, along with "Nice going, Joe," greeted his accomplishment. These men knew from their own experience how demanding the process of obtaining a top-grade merchant marine license really is. Not unlike the rigor required for a surgeon's diploma or a lawyer's admission to the bar.

"All this time," Joe Greenwell continued, "I'm working for many different steamship companies, usually as an assistant engineer, until this war started. I joined Barber Lines just after Peal Harbor and shipped out of New York as first engineer on the *West Lashaway*. As most of you know, this was my second voyage. And here I am! Now, who's next?"

Slowly, one by one, two or three other men spoke, telling with self-consciousness the narrative of their lives, the string of circumstances that had brought them to their present situation. C. J. Rosibrosiris, the chief cook — whom the crew insisted on calling "Rodriguez" — described his childhood in the Portuguese colony of Goa; Servior Seremos told of growing up in the Philippines, of running away to sea as a boy, then jumping ship in New York and hiding out as an illegal immigrant until he could find a sponsor and another job with the Barber Line. Most of those who spoke seemed aware of the minor coincidences, the strokes of luck, that had landed them, by seeming chance, in their common straits; few, however, made anything of the irony. No one blamed anyone — neither God nor man — other than the German submarine and its crew.

George Marano, a twenty-three-year-old fireman from

White Plaines, New York, had a typical story. After early years of working in the merchant marine on various ships, Marano found himself between jobs. So he went to the Seamen's Institute, down by the docks of Lower Manhattan, where he would be fed and housed until his next opportunity came through. He didn't wait long. By June of 1942 ships' firemen were in short supply, and a call for volunteers was issued. "There were eight of us who signed on," Marano told his audience, "and they gave us a choice of three ships. I turned down the first two because they were tankers — sure bets to be target practice for Admiral Dönitz and his boys. Then I chose the *West Lashaway* because it was only a freighter! And, like Joe says, here we are!"

"Yeah, but how'd we get here?" inquired Greenwell. "I don't mean where we've come from and all that crap; we know that already. I mean, where were you when general quarters sounded?"

"I'll tell you," Marano picked up eagerly. "I was supposed to be down below finishing up my stint at the boilers, but my relief man, Victor, showed up ten minutes early. I don't know why, he just did. Offered to take over for me right then, so I said, 'Sure thing!' and promised to do him a good turn sometime. Well, so it goes!

"I was wearing these swim trunks," Marano continued, pointing to his shorts, "because I'd decided to go up to the poop deck and relax in the sun. Just sort of taking it easy on a Sunday afternoon. So there I was, stretched out like a tourist, when I heard the bells and felt the first torpedo hit. There wasn't much to do but start reaching for the supply of life jackets and pass them out to everyone coming up on deck. After the second hit, I took a vest myself and went over the side. I didn't wait around for the ship's suction to pull me in. I swam for the nearest raft right away."

"What about Victor?" someone asked.

"How the hell do I know?" Marano rasped back. "Poor devil probably never had a chance. It could have been me, but it wasn't, that's all I know."

A silence full of memory and laden with premonition took over momentarily. It was broken by Joe Greenwell's good cheer.

"Yeah, well, George, you got a lot to be thankful for. I guess we all do. Take me, for instance. Another engineer, God rest his soul, was sick, and I was doing his duty as well as my own. So I was down below. The watch officer saw the first torpedo coming and signaled the captain, who called for all possible power. So I climbed up on top of that old turbine and was just beginning to open it up for more speed when the second hit came. That first torpedo, I figured, might have sunk us all by itself, but it would have taken an hour or so before the old *West Lash* went down. But by the second torpedo, we were blown to bits!"

General agreement with the first engineer's assessment stirred around the raft, and Joe Greenwell continued his story.

"Well, that second strike hit us just forward of the boiler space, right up with the cargo of palm oil and latex. I guess that explosion simply blew the bulkhead away because all that gooey mess of oil—plus the seawater!— just poured into the engine room. Everything fell in on me. I was caught in it, and the force simply shot me up and out the engine room's skylight door."

"What happened next, Joe?"

"Something I'll never forget, I tell ya!" Greenwell continued. "I was pulled down like by a whirling corkscrew, maybe a hundred feet — or so it seemed to me at the time. Then I shot back up again, much faster than I'd gone down. I barely had time to realize I was on the surface of the water when the whole thing repeated itself. Down again in that whirlpool of water, oil, latex — far faster and far deeper this time than the first — and then back to the top again, so fast and so hard, I shot clear of the water like a porpoise."

"Way to go, Joe!"

"Yeah, well, thanks, but let me tell you guys, on both trips down to the bottom, my plans for the future were pretty dim, I assure ya!"

"Yeah, but you made it, Joe, that's what counts."

"Sure, thanks to a couple of cocoa-bean bags, I landed right in the middle of those floating bean bags. I just grabbed a couple of those suckers and put 'em under my armpits. Then I held on and prayed! I couldn't see a thing for a long time because of all the slime in my eyes, and I couldn't let go of the bags to wipe the junk out of my eyes."

"Wouldn't have done no good anyhow, Joe," retorted Robert McDaniel, the messboy. "I been wipin' and wipin' ever since I got on this rig, and I still can't get my eyes clear. Feels like paste on my skin and lard in my hair!"

"Yeah, well, you may be glad of it," spoke the bosun, his first remarks in some hours.

"How's that, Chief?"

"Because all the glop is like suntan oil — you know, the stuff your girlfriend puts all over when she goes to the beach to keep from turning lobster-red?"

"This stuff?"

"Sure, why not?" Owen continued. "It's oil mostly, just like Johnson's Baby Lotion. Keeps your skin fresh like a baby's instead of blistering in this rotten heat!"

"But, Chief," another man protested, "you make it sound like we're gonna be lyin' out in the sun for a long time."

"You never know," Owen replied. "Maybe we will, maybe we won't. Whatever way it goes, I know this — you don't need to spend more than one afternoon at Jones Beach to come back home sore and swollen with sunburn. Mrs. Bell here maybe ought to offer one of her prayers of thanks for all this garbage we crawled through. It might turn out to save our lives. What do you think, Mrs. Bell?"

Captain Bogden stirred as the bosun addressed the woman; he eyed Owen carefully, as if to catch the nuances of his remark. But Ethel Bell's reply ignored any recognition of the bosun's veiled sarcasm.

"I think that's a good idea, Mr. Owen," she said. "Before this trip is over, most of us will have many things to thank God for, I'm sure."

The bosun offered no reply. Without explanation, he left the raft and crawled back into the doughnut dinghy alone.

"What do you think, Captain Bogden?" Robert Bell asked.

"About what, son?"

"About what the bosun said. The oil and all that."

The captain winced and straightened himself to speak, by means of reply to Robert, to all on board the four rafts.

"Listen up, everybody. The bosun here has just made a good point. I know we're all uncomfortable with this sticky mess all over our skin and clothes, but it might be a blessing after all. We're all hoping and praying and expecting to be picked up soon, but we've got no way of telling how long we might actually be out here. We're not expected in Port of Spain till tomorrow, and so they won't even be missing us until then.

"In the meantime," Bogden continued, "I suggest you do your best not to scrape any of the oil off your skin. As Owen says, it can serve to prevent some of the worst sunburn you'll ever see, reflected straight off the water surface. So just sit tight, and get yourself a nice suntan!"

"Like me and Woodman here!" joked Levi Walker.

Everyone on the captain's raft joined in the good humor. For a moment the sound of hearty laughter eased the afternoon tension. Then the survivors were quiet again.

Throughout the rest of the afternoon the captain lay speechless, as if exhausted by his most recent effort at communication with the four rafts. Throughout the rest of the afternoon the bosun sat by himself in the dinghy. Throughout the rest of the afternoon several pairs of men exchanged their watch duties, standing back to back in front of the sail at the captain's end of the well, scanning the ocean's expanse and seeing nothing. Throughout the rest of the afternoon Frank Flavor sat silently next to Chico Pacheco, who sat silently next to Servior Seremos, who sat silently next to Robert McDaniel and Woodman Potter and Levi Walker and Louis Vega and Flags Croons and John Vargas and Rodriguez Rosibrosiris. George Marano and Joe Greenwell had also had their say. Throughout the rest of the afternoon Ethel Bell held her daughter, Mary, and Carol Shaw, while Richard Shaw sat silently looking at his father on the next raft. Throughout the rest of the afternoon Robert Bell sat leaning against his sister, waiting and wondering.

What if— he wondered —*my father hadn't died six years before? What if my parents had never become missionaries and we lived in New York or Ontario, like other people? What if Mother hadn't decided to go back to Africa after Father's death? What if our family had been the one chosen to fly from Accra and the other family had taken the ship from Takoradi? What if there'd never been a war?*

Richard Shaw coughed, breaking Robert's musings and changing momentarily his point of view.

What if Mrs. Shaw were the woman holding Carol and Mary?

What if there'd been only one raft afloat?

What if all the rafts had been destroyed like the ship?

What if the sharks had appeared right away?

A chill of fear went through the boy, and he looked up at his mother for reassurance. Strangely, she seemed to be asleep. After remaining stoically awake all night to watch over and comfort her four children — by now she had taken full responsibilty for the Shaw children as her own — she had at last yielded during the oppressive afternoon heat to weariness. Head resting on her life jacket, arms still encircling Mary and Carol, Ethel Bell dozed.

"What day's today?" asked Earl Croons, sitting up in the well.

"What's it to you, Flags?" Robert McDaniel responded.

"I want to know, is all. Is this the thirtieth or thirty-first?"

"The thirty-first. Don't you remember? Yesterday was the thirtieth, the day we sank."

"One date I'll never forget!" said Levi Walker.

"Then I made it! Today's my nineteenth birthday!"

"Hey, Flags!"

"Congratulations, Flags!"

"Many happy returns, Flags!"

"Yeah, but not to the same bar and grill! Next time, Flags, make it the Waldorf-Astoria!"

"Let's sing to celebrate."

Eveyone on the raft chimed in, joined by others on the adjacent rafts:

> *Happy birthday, dear Flags!*
> *Happy birthday to you!*

"How 'bout a treat for the birthday boy?" Woodman Potter suggested. "How 'bout an extra cup of water?"

"Sorry, men," the captain said. "We can't afford to offer anyone special favors. But, Flags, I promise you the biggest birthday cake you ever saw, soon as we get to Port of Spain."

"Thanks, Captain," said the signalman, "but I just think I'll help myself to a drink anyway. See, this here water will do."

Reaching both hands into the water that washed through the well, the young navy man cupped the seawater to his mouth, gulping it down.

"Stop that, you crazy damned fool!"

"Ah, what the hell?" and Croons slumped back into his corner of the well.

This midafternoon lethargy lasted while the sun passed through its most furious intensity, turning the ocean's surface to steam, grilling the shipwrecked survivors with its reflected heat. Slowly, as the run rolled toward the horizon, the rafts came to life again. Soon it would be time to eat the day's second meal.

As if by agreement, no one wanted to rush the procedure. A general stirring, a few exchanges of conversation, a laugh here and there, a gratuitous curse: these were the preliminary signs that rations were about to be dispensed. The bosun crawled out of his private quarters in the dinghy and addressed Captain Bogden.

"What do you think, sir? Is it time to break out the rations?

Bogden twisted his neck to catch a glimpse of the sun's progress, his only timepiece.

"I think we might begin, Owen. Same instructions as before. You take the other rafts. Mr. Greenwell, you take charge here."

"Aye, aye, sir," the bosun replied and made his way cautiously to one of the adjoining rafts. This was no easy matter, moving from raft to raft, because even on a calm sea the rise and fall of each raft bore no exact correlation to the others. They were not synchronized in their response to the ocean's pitch. But the bosun made it and could soon be heard repeating the orders from the morning, almost twelve hours earlier.

"Remember, men, only half a can of pemmican each. You share with the same person you ate with this morning. Two ounces of water. Measure it carefully, and don't spill any! Milk tablets, chocolate, and a cracker, same as before," Owen told them.

"OK, everybody," Bogden said, "you've all heard the bosun on the other rafts. Same goes here. Mr. Greenwell, you can distribute the rations, if you will. Take it slow and make it last."

Since moving from his place with Captain Bogden, Robert Bell had been sitting on his mother's side of the raft, closest to the bosun.

"Mary, come just a little closer to me, dear," Ethel Bell said, "and that'll make more room for Robert and Mr. Owen."

Mary Bell shifted her position just a fraction, but as she did, the bosun swung his body into Robert's, expropriating the added inches of space.

"Like I told you, kid, there's no room for you here. Better go back down into the well." The bosun leaned into the swell as he spoke.

"Oh, but Mr. Owen," Ethel Bell retorted, "I'm sure . . ."

Robert saw the bosun's balance falter ever so slightly and, grabbing the initiative, slipped back into place on the rim of the raft.

"See, Mr. Owen, there's lots of room!"

The bosun cursed and looked away.

From Joe Greenwell, bent over the food box, the cans of pemmican were passed around the raft, the first reaching Mrs. Bell, then the children next to her, and finally the men. When the pemmican containers were opened, some of the men made faces or uttered a rude description of the concoction, but nobody declined to eat his share. Most of the men went right to eating their portions, but a few—notably the Latins—looked expectantly at Ethel Bell. They did not have to wait long.

"Children," she said, "let's give thanks for our evening meal."

Once again she bowed her head, and the children with her, while she prayed, "Our heavenly Father, again we thank Thee for this food provided by Thee. We pray for strength for each of us to endure these difficult circumstances, especially through the hours of the night. Our trust is in Thee, our Father. In Jesus' name. Amen."

When Robert looked up, he saw that several of the men—Flavor, Chico, Seremos—were just completing the sign of the cross.

Then it was time to eat!

TEN
THE FOOD GAME

Admiral Karl Dönitz stood before his maps in his Paris headquarters listening to the latest reports.

" . . . and the Polar Bear group, Admiral, continues to proceed on course without incident."

"Good."

"Now, turning to the western Atlantic and Caribbean zones, we have much activity to report."

The briefing officer read from his packet of dispatches relayed from transmitter ships, telling of attacks by submarines and attacks upon submarines, sinking freighters and tankers, sunk or damaged U-boats.

"Special notice, Admiral, may be made of the next report."

"So?"

"Yes, Admiral. We spoke yesterday of *U-66* and her recent success? Well, another sinking today, 2:15 P.M., Middle European Time. A British tanker here."

The briefing officer stepped to the map of the western Atlantic zone and marked the spot where the *Winimac* had been sunk.

"That makes four successful strikes in just three days, Admiral. Do you wish to send a commendation to *U-66* and Kapitänleutnant Markworth?"

"All in good time. I prefer to keep Fritz Markworth and *U-66* eager and hungry, like young wolves. Too much praise too soon makes a man complacent. Go on with your report, *Oberleutnant.*"

Back on the rafts the ceremony of eating proceeded at its dignified pace. Each person savored the tiniest particle of food, like a gourmand about to pronounce judgment on a new restaurant's fare.

"You know what would make this stuff more edible?" George Marano asked.

"Nothing in the world!" replied Robert McDaniel, who nonetheless kept on eating.

"No, I'm serious," Marano went on. "I know how to make these rations taste better."

"How's that, man?" Levi Walker inquired.

"We use our imagination," said Marano. "We pretend. Instead of eating pemmican or whatever the hell it's called, we make believe we're eating our favorite food — something delicious — something like . . . like lasagna!"

Groans and protests rose from the other men.

"Go 'way, Marano!"

"That's kid stuff, playing games about food!"

"Not wop slop!"

"Hey, watch your mouth! That's my mama's cooking you're talking about! And what's so bad about kids' games? What else is on your agenda?"

The men grumbled some more. Only Rodriguez Rosibrosiris picked up on the idea.

"OK, I'm the chef," said Rodriguez. "I'll start the game. I'm not eating pemmican and malted-milk tablets. I'm eating biryani—"

"Beer what?" someone asked.

"Hey, that's what I'd like right now—a nice cold beer!"

"Now you're talking! How about playing *that* game?"

"Yeah," said Marano, "we can do that too, but let's stick to one game at a time. Go ahead, Rodriguez. Tell us about your food. What's it called again?"

"Biryani. It's a favorite dish in India and wherever Indians have traveled."

"What's it made of?"

"Well, you can make it with either chicken or lamb—"

"Not lamb, man. It's too greasy."

"Not chicken. There's only one way to do chicken, and that's southern-fried!"

"Let Rodriguez talk!" Marano shouted. "He'll never get this dinner cooked if you guys keep interrupting. Nobody says you have to like it. After all, it's *his* meal, right? I didn't hear none of you guys volunteering."

"OK, OK, Marano," Robert McDaniel spoke up. "But if we're going to play this game, one of the best parts of it ought to be the fact that our dream meal is something other people might enjoy."

"Yeah, like inviting folks to dinner," said Levi Walker. "I mean, when my old lady and me has folks over for an evening meal, we don't serve them something they can't even say!"

"Yeah, well, all you eat, Levi, is chitlins and greens!"

"Maybe so," Walked replied, "but at least we know

what we're eating. Not some Hindu food all covered over with tea leaves!"

"Come on, Levi," Marano pleaded. "Let Rodriguez have his turn. Maybe you'll like—what's it called again, Rodriguez?"

"Biryani."

"That's it, *beery-anny.*"

"No, biryani."

"Yeah, well, whatever. Go ahead, Rodriguez. Now, listen up, everybody. Give the cook a fair chance. Do your stuff, Rodriguez. Make us smell and taste your *beer-anny.*"

C. J. Rosibrosiris shook his head in amused dismay at George Marano's inability to pronounce the dish. But he had been challenged as a professional to whet the appetites of his diners. His reputation as a ship's cook, as well as his pride in his national cuisine, must be defended.

"Look, I don't care whether you use chicken or lamb or beef or kangaroo. Just think of some meat you like. You can make biryani any way you want."

"What about pork?" Woodman Potter broke in.

"No pork, man! I mean, Goa, where I come from, maybe more Christian than anywhere else on the subcontinent, but we still have too many Muslims to go around eating pork. So, I'm sorry, no pork in this dish."

"OK, Rodriguez. Just asking. But you guys ought to taste my mother's stuffed pork chops!"

"Shut up, will you, and let Rodriguez speak!"

This time the cook waited until everyone was quiet. Then he began his recipe for his favorite dinner.

"Like, I say, you pretend whatever meat you want. If it's chicken, you need a good-sized broiler or fryer. If it's lamb, something like two or three pounds will do. You start out by cutting the meat into cubes."

"Have you cooked it yet?"

"No, it's still raw. And before you cut it, of course you've got to wash it in cold water. Then you go to your spices. Every good cook has a collection of spices. What you don't have on hand, you have to go out and buy. But you won't find some of these at your local grocery store. I'm talking about coriander powder—"

"What's that, coriander?"

"It's an herb that's been used since ancient times. Got a very strong aroma to it. You probably have tasted it in curries and other sauces. Another spice is cumin seed. It's pretty strong too. So is cardamon—"

"I'd like to send a card to Mom. I think she'd like to hear from me. 'Dear Mom, Having a wonderful time. Wish you were here.'"

Protests greeted the silly humor. Robert Bell looked over at Richard Shaw and saw him bite his lower lip to keep from crying. The cook ignored this latest interruption and continued his recipe.

"You also need some cinnamon, some black pepper—"

"Hey, finally something I know we've got in our kitchen!" Joe Greenwell interjected.

" . . . some tumeric to make it yellow—"

"I knew I wouldn't like the looks of this stuff!"

" . . . about one inch of ginger root, a lemon, enough salt to taste, probably three cloves of garlic—"

"That's why you've got such bad breath, Rodriguez!" the bosun chimed in for the first time.

"Let's not get personal, Owen!" Greenwell warned.

" . . . and four large onions," the cook continued. "Now all this gets mixed together in about a half pint of yogurt."

"Yogurt? What's that?" asked George Marano.

"Another name for sour milk," Woodman Potter replied.

"It is not!" the messboy Robert McDaniel objected. "Woodman, as second cook you should know at least that much!"

"Well, it tastes like sour milk to me!" Potter protested. "Just because you give it some fancy Turk name doesn't mean it tastes any better. Still just sour milk. Anything I hate, it's sour milk!"

"OK, Woodman, you made your point," Marano chided him. "It's probably not half as bad as you make out. This yogurt stuff, Rodriguez, is it anything like ricotta? My mother uses a lot of ricotta, 'specially in her lasagna."

"George, now you're the one butting in," John Vargas, the ship's baker, rebuked him. "You'll get your chance to tell us all about your mother's lasagna. Go on, Rodriguez."

"No, George, yogurt's a lot creamier and smoother than ricotta. And yes, Woodman, yogurt is sort of sour-tasting, but nobody ever got a bellyache from eating yogurt the way you do from drinking sour milk. What's more, yogurt can mix with anything and take on the flavor of what it's mixed with. Say, you mix it with fruit, like strawberries or blueberries, and stir them into the yogurt. Really, it tastes like a king's dessert.

"But to go on," C. J. Rosibrosiris continued, "all these spices get mixed into the yogurt, which is going to become a sauce for the meat—"

"You mean like a cream sauce?"

"No, he means like something called beef stroganoff,"

said Captain Bogden. "My wife back in Brooklyn cooks it sometimes."

"That's right, Captain," Rodriguez confirmed. "Only the Russians usually make beef stroganoff over egg noodles . . ."

"Pasta!" said Marano triumphantly.

" . . . while we use a seasoned rice for our biryani."

"What's a seasoned rice?" asked Joe Greenwell.

"It's rice mixed with lots of seasoning," the cook explained. "You know, if you go to a Chinese restaurant—"

"Who goes for that chink food?"

"Come on, man! A little chow mein would taste pretty good right about now!"

"Chow mein! That's about as Chinese as Hungarian goulash! If you call chow mein 'chink food,' then you're even stupider than I thought!"

"Who's calling who stupid?"

"Settle down, settle down," Marano and Greenwell spoke in one voice. "Let Rodriguez talk," Greenwell urged.

"Yeah, and let's leave off the racial and national business," Marano continued. "Look around you. We got the whole League of Nations right here on this raft. Me, I'm Italian, some of the rest of you are some sort of Spanish; Woodman and Levi here are coloreds; the cook is Portagee and Indian; only God knows what the rest of you are. So let's not knock anybody else's background. OK?"

The tension eased, C. J. Rosibrosiris began again, describing how rice should be mixed with cardamom, cloves, cinnamon, peppercorns, salt, and bay leaves to create an exotic dish fit for the finest dining.

" . . . and you bake it for about thirty minutes. Then

you lower the heat, say to three hundred degrees, and let it bake another half hour."

"Oooh, what an aroma! I can just begin to catch it now!"

"Yeah, it smells better than I would have expected."

"Finally," the cook said, "you sprinkle the remaining fried onions on top of the meat mixture, and you serve it over the seasoned rice."

Rodriguez Rosibrosiris paused; then, extending his empty tin of pemmican to his mates around the raft, said, "Anybody like some of my biryani?"

The imaginary feast began. Like the hungry beggar in *The Arabian Nights*, served from an array of vacant dishes, these survivors gorged themselves on a banquet created by fantasy. For a few moments their raft seemed changed into a large refectory table at which they sat to dine on Indian cuisine. On its white linen cloth rested the two bowls of seasoned rice and meat, as well as other condiments to enhance the main dish—coconut flakes, peanuts, chopped scallions, chutney. To this festive board came not half-naked derelicts drawn from the sea but elegantly attired merchant seamen in their finest uniforms. The thought of food had transformed these men and given them hope.

Then the bosun spoke.

"What are you talking about, Rodriguez! That's not biryani! That's a lousy tin of crap called pemmican, and you know it!"

"Ah, come on, Chief," said Levi Walker, "it don't hurt none. We know we're only fooling. It's a way to pass the time."

"Then it's a damned stupid way, is all I say!"

Suddenly the banquet disappeared. The taste lingering in the men's mouths was no longer spiced lamb or curried chicken; instead, it was the taste of fear. Around the raft sat not guests at some elegant table but fellow survivors whose every twitch seemed irritating, a deliberate intrusion upon one's own limited space. Just an arm's length away waited instant terror in the shape of huge sharks. Ahead of them lay a second night, soon to fall upon them in its subtropical chill. The spell had been broken, and the survivors knew it. How could they have sat there, fantasizing about food? Could anything have been more futile?

Yet the food game, as they called it, was a diversion to which the survivors would return many times during their ordeal. Bob Bell remembers:

"It started out as nothing more than one man's whimsy, a way of taking our minds off how hungry we were and how awful-tasting those rations were. By the way," he adds parenthetically, "I've often wondered if the lab experts responsible for creating those emergency rations ever ate that food themselves! It was almost deliberately unpalatable, like a bad meal in a cheap restaurant.

"Getting back to the food game," Bell continues, "it soon moved from being an occasional source of entertainment—something we did to pass the time—to becoming much more than that. The food game took on a kind of necessity. In our minds it took the place of real eating. It became a means of survival. I wonder if we'd have been able to last without the hope and expectation we received from pretending to eat those imaginary meals. You see, from that hope we took strength."

The early evening meal had formally ended with the bosun's rebuke. Now the men began closing up the food box, lashing it tightly to prevent either seepage of seawater or—the worst disaster of all—the box's being jolted overboard. As if on cue, the sun quickly retired for the day, bringing on the night winds and, with them, the biting cold. The day had been long; the night would seem even longer. Already the chitchat among the men had subsided. They were settling themselves, getting into positions of weight distribution and balance, leaning left or right against a neighbor.

"Flavor and Seremos," the bosun addressed them, "before you get too comfortable, take a turn in the doughnut."

"No way, Chief," Frank Flavor retorted. "I'm not spending no night in that doughnut with them sharks."

"Me neither," Sevior Seremos concurred.

"Are you disobeying my order?" the bosun spoke angrily.

"Nobody gives orders but me, Owen," the captain interrupted. "Go to the doughnut yourself, if you care to. Otherwise, let the men be."

"Aye, aye, sir," Owen grunted. All eyes waited to see him move from his place at the back of the raft, but he stayed put.

Ethel Bell hovered over the children like a mother hen, her arms and fingers trying to reach all four of them at once. On her right, her son and daughter leaned toward her; on her left, Richard and Carol Shaw.

"Are we going to say our Bible verses, Mrs. Bell?" Carol asked. "I've been practicing all afternoon. I can say part of 'The Lord is my shepherd. . . .'"

"Why, that's wonderful, Carol!"

"Bet you can't," her brother teased.

"I can so, Richard!" And she began, confidently at first, then haltingly after a couple of sentences. The woman looked at her lovingly, mouthing the phrases in tempo with the child's recitation. By "He restoreth my soul . . ."

the little girl had exhausted her memory.

"That's very good so far, Carol," Mrs. Bell encouraged her. "I'm sure you'll learn the whole psalm very soon."

"But I don't know what it means," the girl replied. "I've never seen a shepherd. And what's a green *pastor?*"

Richard snorted an older brother's disdain. "There you go again, Carol. You're always getting words mixed up. It's not *pastor,* like the minister of a church. It's *pastures,* like where the animals eat their grass."

"But I'm not an animal. I don't eat grass."

Ethel Bell broke in. "Maybe we ought to talk about the psalm while we learn it. What does David mean when he says, 'The Lord is my shepherd'?"

"We didn't have sheep at Bambari," said Richard, "just goats."

"Neither did we," said Mary. "But I've seen sheep on farms near Nyack."

"And near Gravenhurst, at Grandpa and Grandma Roffe's," Robert added.

"I know that, Robert! You don't have to be so smart!"

"Children, that's enough! God doesn't bless us when we fight with each other. It's a bad testimony to the men."

The children instantly ceased their bickering.

"Now, about Carol's question," Ethel Bell continued, "what do you think David means when he says, 'The Lord is my shepherd,' Richard?"

The boy looked around at the men nearest him, embarrassed at their overhearing this conversation.

"Speak up, kid," said Robert McDaniel. "It's been a long time since I was in Sunday school. I never could understand the Bible either."

Taking courage, Richard Shaw said, "Well, it doesn't mean that God is really a shepherd; you know, somebody who spends all his time with sheep. It means that God is *like* a shepherd."

"What's the difference?" Carol asked.

"I know," replied Mary. "God is *like* a shepherd because God takes care of us just like a shepherd takes care of his sheep."

"You call this taking care of us!" spoke Flags Croons.

"Yes, I do," said Mrs. Bell, addressing the man as well as the children. "I certainly do. Why, it's perfectly obvious that God has cared for us. The very fact that we're on this raft, with food and water, instead of facing those sharks—that's proof enough for me!"

"But, Mrs. Bell," McDaniel protested, "if God's so caring, why does He let things like this happen in the first place? Why aren't we still just cruising along, a few hours out of port, like we're supposed to be?"

"Because there's a war on, stupid!" George Marano took up the argument.

"And whose fault is that?"

"Well, I don't know, but it certainly ain't God's!"

"I don't see where God fits into this, one way or the other. To me, it's all dumb luck. I'm a seaman. I coulda gone to sea in one ship; I chose the *West Lash*. So it goes down. Whose fault is it that I'm on board? Hitler's? Roosevelt's? God's? Naw. It's just dumb luck, that's all."

"No, forgive me, but it's not a matter of luck," Mrs. Bell replied. "Luck has nothing to do with our lives. God is in charge. Don't you believe that, Captain Bogden?"

"Oh yes, Mrs. Bell," the captain answered. "It's like the poet says, 'God's in his heaven, all's right with the world.'"

"Yeah, well, I wish that poet was here right now!" Joe Greenwell spoke up. "I'd throw him to the sharks!"

"And what about the Shaw kids' mother, Mrs. Bell? How'd you like to explain God's goodness to her! And to them?"

Ethel Bell looked fiercely at the man who spoke so cruelly in the presence of Carol and Richard. His lack of tact could hardly have been unintended. She met the challenge head on.

"Forgive me, Carol and Richard, but I'd like to answer that question. In fact, I'd like to answer Mr. McDaniel's question first. I'm sure God would much prefer to have had us arrive safely in Trinidad, then go on to our final port. But God has given human beings a very risky gift. It's called free will. We're free to behave any way we choose. Because we're sinners . . ."

"Who's a sinner? I'm no sinner. I go to church."

"I'm sorry, but we're all sinners, including those of us who go to church," Ethel Bell went on. "Because we're sinners, we lash out at each other, just like these children quarreling or some of you bickering with each other. Quarrels lead to fights. When nations fight, it's called war, but it's just the same as two children scrapping. When children or nations fight, somebody always gets hurt. God doesn't want it that way, but we human beings seem to prefer war rather than peace."

"So then, why doesn't God stop us?"

"Because the one thing God won't do is take away our freedom to choose. He wants us to choose right over wrong, and he makes that possible by believing in His Son, the Lord Jesus Christ."

"Ah, come on, lady, now you're preaching!"

"Call it preaching, if you wish. I'm merely answering the questions some of you asked. So, when we choose to fight and kill each other, God is pained by that."

"OK, but what about . . . you know . . ." The seaman nodded his head toward the Shaw children.

"Mrs. Shaw and, I'm sure, her daughter Georgia are with the Lord right now. Nobody knows why they aren't with us now. All we can say is that they are surely better off in the presence of God in heaven than we are on this raft, wouldn't you agree?"

"Yeah. This raft is hell."

"If I didn't believe that God loves me and these children and every one of you men, I wouldn't want the sun to come up tomorrow," the woman continued. "But I do believe that God is in his heaven, and as long as I trust him, all's right with the world. You see, the Bible puts it another way—'All things work together for good to them that love God.' I believe that."

Ethel Bell sank a little lower, slumping into her life vest as if worn down by her defense. She remained slumped in silence for a moment, then she spoke again:

"And now, if you gentlemen don't mind, I'd like to say our evening prayers with the children. Any of you who care to join us, please do."

She summoned the children's attention and began leading them in the Lord's Prayer.

"Our Father, which art in heaven, hallowed be thy name. Thy kingdom come. Thy will be done in earth—"

In the middle of the prayer they were interrupted by the insane laughter of Earl Croons. Suddenly he stood up, still laughing, and shouted, "Dammit, Mrs. Bell! It hurts too much to pray!" Then the young man lunged to attack, but he was the full length of the raft away; in his path were the food box and the legs and feet of many others. Joe Greenwell stood and swatted Flags across the face.

"Shut up, you fool!"

Flags crumpled in the well and lay there moaning.

The captain spoke curtly to the men nearest the whimpering youth. "Vega, Vargas, keep an eye on him. Don't let him make another move like that. He's badly hurt inside."

"Aye, aye, Captain. We'll sit on him."

Mrs. Bell had never ceased the prayer. When she and the children had concluded, she looked up and said, "Thank you, Mr. Greenwell. Now, I'd like to pray for us all.

"Our heavenly Father, we are all afraid. Some of us seem unable to accept the conditions in which you have placed us. But we know we are in your care. You are the Good Shepherd, and you care for your sheep. Protect us this night from the dangers we see around us and from dangers we know nothing about. And, please, dear Father, bring us in safety to harbor soon. Our trust is in Thee, O Lord. In Jesus' name . . ."

A chorus of response rose up from the raft:

"Amen. Amen. Amen. Amen."

ELEVEN
ANNIVERSARY

Somehow they made it through that second night.

If the terror of the unknown has any equal, it must be the terror of the known. The first night's discomfort — its numbing cold, its cramping congestion of bodies, the later realization that the sharks had arrived to stay — had at least been new and shocking. Now, however, the survivors were no longer blessed by blissful ignorance. They knew and could anticipate the coming on of night, each night more dreaded and more dreadful than the night before. Yet, somehow, they made it through that second night.

As the cold gray curtain of darkness gave way to the first rays of dawn, the earliest survivors to come awake could see that nothing had changed. If anyone had dreamed that his present circumstances were nothing but a nightmare — that upon opening his eyes, he would find himself safe in his own bed or safe aboard the still-seaworthy *West Lashaway* — those eyes opened upon stark disappointment. He was far from being safe, whether at home or on board his ship. His present circumstances were indeed a living nightmare, a dungeon of horrors fitted out with rack and iron maiden, a living death.

Yet this was only Tuesday, only the second day after the sinking. Less than forty-eight hours had passed since the submarine's attack had thrust them out upon the water. It was far too soon for melodramatics! After all, this was the day of the *West Lashaway's* expected arrival at Port of Spain, Trinidad. You couldn't expect anything much in the way of rescue before anyone knew the need for rescue. There had been no SOS; the ship's radio had been knocked out too quickly for that. In wartime, ships kept as silent as possible, looking to avoid the unnecessary communication that might be picked up and give a clue to the enemy. So what's the big deal? A little inconvenience for a few hours, and then . . .

As dawn overtook the last shadows of darkness, the rafts remained still, the survivors silent. Even so soon into their ordeal, the survivors had already developed a pattern of behavior, a code of ethics that would become their law. With sleep so scarce, so precious, the first rule was obvious: Nobody does or says anything to waken somebody else. No rousing morning greetings, no "rise and shine" summons to duty. Just let everybody else ease into the day. After all, nobody had anywhere to go.

Robert Bell awakened from fitful sleep, shuddering with the cold. His first conscious thought was of rescue. He remembered Captain Bogden's assurances of yesterday: "Tomorrow morning, for sure!" Well, today was tomorrow morning!

"Any time now, Captain," Robert spoke eagerly.

"What's that, son?" the man answered weakly.

"Like you said yesterday, Captain. Today's the day we're due to land at Trinidad. They'll miss us and send out looking for us, right?"

"Yes, Robert, let's pray they do."

Young as he was, the eleven-year-old boy caught a tone of pessimism in the captain's voice.

"You believe they'll find us, don't you, Captain?"

"Sure he does, kid," Joe Greenwell interrupted and, sitting behind the slumped Bogden, motioned to Robert to cut short his talk.

The boy caught the gesture and its meaning. He complied instantly, but now he was troubled by doubts no one had dared to think before. A whole new set of "What-if's?" occurred to him for the first time.

What if nobody knows our ship's been sunk?

What if nobody cares?

What if the ocean's too big and the raft's too small for planes to spot it?

What if a ship sees us and mistakes us for a surfaced submarine?

What if another German sub comes along and fires on us?

What if . . . ?

To these worries three more words were added:

How much longer?

How much longer will it be before we will be rescued?

How much longer can we hold out?

Surely, he reasoned, there was still enough food and water to last for several days; perhaps even for a couple of weeks, if they were careful. But what about other kinds of strength besides that sustained by nutrition. What about moral strength? "Intestinal fortitude" it was called in polite terms, but the older boys at school called it just plain *guts*. Well, what about it? Did they have the *guts* to hold out as long as they might need to?

Robert looked around the raft. Joe Greenwell and George Marano — he could count on them to pull through. They wouldn't give in, no matter how tough it got. But he couldn't feel quite so sure about some of the others.

Earl Croons, for instance. Something was seriously wrong with him, the way he talked and cried out every so often. Imagine, leaping across the raft to attack a woman for praying! He must be crazy with some pain. How much longer could he last? Robert McDaniel was also ailing. Even beneath the smeared grease, his face seemed paler than the rest. Louis Vega, the oiler, also looked weak. He had said almost nothing from the moment he stepped onto the raft, and his head drooped constantly, as if before an axman's blade.

John Vargas, the baker, looked strong, sitting upright on the water keg, from time to time beating out a rumba rhythm on the keg. Rodriguez, the cook, was also in good spirits; so too were the American blacks, Levi Walker and Woodman Potter. Servior Seremos smiled a lot, his gold tooth gleaming in the sunlight's brilliance. Most of his conversation was in Spanish with Frank Flavor and Chico Pacheco; even though Robert could not understand what they said, he could detect nothing threatening or discouraging in their tone.

Not so with the bosun. Whenever James Owen spoke, it seemed to Robert as though a thumbnail had been scraped across a chalkboard. There was something caustic in the man's tone, something unpleasant in his demeanor, something abrasive about his conduct that grated on others. Robert sensed the bosun's hostility toward his mother and the children. There had also been sharp words between the bosun and the captain, angry words between Owen and Joe Greenwell. Would there be other incidents — perhaps even a fight? Robert hoped not.

Most troubling to the boy was the captain's condition. Overnight, it seemed, Captain Bogden had changed. Of course, he had been hurt during the explosion and sinking — everyone knew that. He had strained to assert his responsibility and maintain control over the four rafts and survivors. He had even struggled to participate in the mattress experiment. But now, as the sun began to crawl over the horizon and illumine the morning, Robert could see a look on the captain's face that frightened him.

By common consent, everyone had waited for Captain Bogden to decide when it was time to eat each of the two daily meals. But on this morning, even after some preliminary conversations had broken the quiet, the captain seemed to remain inert. Joe Greenwell and George Marano, sitting nearest to Bogden, spoke to him; then Greenwell leaned over to address C. J. Rosibrosiris.

"Take charge, Rodriguez. Captain's orders."

"Chow time," announced Rodriguez.

Immediately a streak of sunlight seemed to burst through the morning gloom. Whenever the food box was opened, things looked better all around. Even the captain stirred and drew himself into a more upright sitting position.

"What's for breakfast?"

"As if you didn't know!"

"Sure, same diet as before."

"Leastways, you ain't troubled by no choices."

"You mean like in a cafeteria?"

"Yeah, man! That's where I like to eat!"

"You said it! Give me a Morrison's any day over them fancy French restaurants!"

"We don't have no Morrison's in New York," said Levi Walker, "but we got us this Bickford's on Lenox Avenue — and, man, they got some food there, like to make a body sit up and say, 'Jim, now that's what I call *food!*' "

George Marano interrupted. "Levi, don't say no more. Let's pass around our rations, then when everybody's got his share, why don't you take us down the cafeteria line? Sort of like we were filling up our trays?"

"Good idea," the survivors concurred.

Once more the rations were handed out — the pemmican, biscuits, and tablets — and the drinking water passed around. When the last person had been served, Marano said, "OK, Levi, we're your guests."

The messman from the *West Lashaway*'s galley rolled his eyes back in thought and began.

"The way I know 'bout cafeterias, man, is I used to work in restaurants before I shipped. Busboy, dishwasher like on the *West Lash,* even a little short-order stuff. Rodriguez here can tell you — I ain't no ordinary pots-and-pans scrubber, no ways.

"Well, like I say, this Bickford's is part of a chain all over New York. Maybe other places, too. The place I'm talking 'bout is right on the corner of 125th Street and Lenox Avenue —"

"That in Harlem, Levi?"

"The crossroads, man! Anyway, this place ain't nothing fancy, just like every other Bickford's I ever seen, but the food —"

"Yeah, let's get to the food!"

"Like I say, the food has got to be tasted to be believed!"

"So, make us taste it, Levi."

"Well, first you got to pick up your tray and *u*-tensils."

"Your *what?*"

"U-tensils. It means knife and fork and spoon. It's a fancy word Levi must have learned in the restaurant business."

"Then you get in line. Now every cafeteria starts out with the sweet stuff first—appetizers and desserts and all that. Your fruit cup, your Boston cream pie, your rice pudding all right there at the head of the line. Know why they do that?"

"Tell us, Levi."

" 'Cause that way they get you while your eyes is still bigger than your stomach. Iffen they wait till you put the main course on your tray, then they worry that maybe you won't take no pie or no cake, and they won't make that sale. They don't care whether you eat it or not, just so you buy it!"

"OK, so we're standing at the head of the line. What do we put on our tray, Levi?"

"Well, I don't know 'bout you, but I'm gonna have me some of this applesauce right here . . ."

Levi Walker reached out into the vacant space before him and scooped up an imaginary dish of applesauce, then placed it gently on his imaginary tray.

" . . . and maybe this slice of blueberry pie."

Robert Bell felt his stomach churn as he heard the words "blueberry pie." Early in the morning though it was, and even though he'd never tasted pie before noon, the boy knew that nothing could have tasted better at the moment than a pie made by Grandma Roffe with fresh Muskoka berries. Right there he resolved that if he ever got off this raft alive, he'd eat what he wanted when he wanted, whatever the time of day.

"Now a little side dish of salad. Could be I might fancy a tossed salad with lots of creamy dressing. Or how 'bout some cottage cheese inside a big half of a pear?"

Other men were now warming to the fantasy, nodding their heads in agreed pleasure, some actually pantomiming with Levi Walker his tray with its accumulating menu.

"Now we come to the hard part. Here's the main course, and there's eight, maybe ten, different choices. You got the big steamboat of roast beef . . ."

"That's it! Fill my plate, Levi!"

" . . . or the Southern fried chicken with lots of deep-fried batter crust . . ."

"That's for me, man!"

" . . . or the pastrami and cabbage . . ."

"None of that kraut crap for me!"

" . . . or the pork chops . . ."

"Yessiree!"

" . . . or the liver and onions . . ."

"Oh no!"

"Well, you can have bacon instead of onions."

"That's better."

"And then there's always the daily specials. Let's see, today we got, maybe, a nice veal chop or maybe a ham steak with a slice of pineapple . . ."

"Hey, Greenwell, that's for you! Just like in Honolulu again!"

" . . . and 'specially for us Harlem folks, there's some pigs' feet and greens!"

"You people actually eat that stuff?"

"It ain't Christian!"

"What you mean, it ain't Christian!" said Woodman

Potter with a laugh. "Man, that's what makes the angels sing so sweet!"

"Levi, let me ask you one thing."

"Sure, George."

"When's the last time you ate in this cafeteria?"

"Oh, back in June, just before we shipped out on this trip."

"This past June? Of 1942?" Marano asked incredulously. "And they had all that meat? All those choices? Where'd they get that stuff? Don't they know there's a war on?"

"Yeah," chimed in Rodriguez, "lot of places I know had to shut down. Couldn't get enough provisions to carry a decent menu. Course, like anything else, if you know the right people, war or no war, you just keep goin' business as usual."

"That's true," said Greenwell, "it all depends on who you know. Folks in Brooklyn I know, they got relatives in City Hall—eat like kings every meal. Rationing? They never heard of it. Some guy comes to the back door every Friday afternoon with bags of groceries, meat, butter, eggs."

"Ain't it the truth!"

"Meanwhile, we're bustin' butt for a plate of beans and franks, or some slop like that!" said Robert McDaniel.

"I never gave you slop!" the cook declared defensively.

"Naw, I don't mean us on the *West Lash*. You fed us good, Rodriguez. That's one reason why I signed on the merchant service. Good food. I mean all the rest like us—the poor S.O.B.s who don't have connections. The hardworkin' sweathogs who take it on the chin, all for the sake of the war effort! Baloney!"

"Hey, let's not get political. Let's go back to Levi's cafeteria," said George Marano.

Levi Walker nodded and grinned, ready to resume his rapturous selection of food. "Now we come to the vegetables, a dozen or more. Corn on the cob in melted butter, pickled beets . . ."

"I like Harvard beets better."

"What are you, a college man?"

" . . . all kinds of potatoes, peas, lots of beans, including my favorite — southern green beans with a nice slab of fatback to give it some flavor. Oh my!"

"What else, Levi?"

"Well, there's okra and squash and zucchini and cauliflower with cheese and brussel sprouts and broccoli . . ."

"Any rice, Levi?"

"Sure, Chico, how much you want?"

Levi Walked had dipped his imaginary serving spoon into a steaming tray of rice and was just preparing to dish it out for Isabelino Pacheco when a screech stopped him.

"Cut it out! For God's sake, cut it out!"

The voice came from a corner of the well, where Earl Croons lay crumpled and almost buried under a tangle of legs.

"I can't stand no more talk about food. It's driving me crazy!"

"Let him up," Joe Greenwell spoke. "Let him have some air. But, Flags, no more rough stuff. Just take it easy."

Greenwell looked over at Levi Walker and shook his head. Walker shrugged his shoulders and looked away. For now, at least, the food game was over.

Robert Bell was disappointed. Since the slice of blueberry pie, the boy had freed his imagination, greedily sampling every food mentioned. He'd pretended to reach in among the lighted shelves of food for the largest portions and set them down on his imaginary tray. All except the pigs' feet, that is! Robert preferred his pork as bacon or chops or a ham and cheese sandwich on rye bread with lots of mustard! A drumstick of fried chicken and a wedge of beef from the outside cut, even some liver and onions! And lots of vegetables—mashed potatoes and gravy with peas and carrots and beets—he didn't care whether they came from Harvard or Yale or the commissary at Nyack College!—and corn on the cob and string beans with some bacon fat and more mashed potatoes. To top it all off, a tall glass of cold milk, maybe with a little chocolate syrup to make it even sweeter.

But now, it had all disappeared.

The pemmican never tasted so awful.

Throughout the playing of the food game, Ethel Bell sat quietly, holding tightly as always to the two girls on either side.

"Mother," Mary whispered to her, "they didn't talk about my favorite food."

"What's that, dear?"

"Cream puffs!"

"Yes, I know, Mary. You certainly do love that dessert."

"Yes, Mother, I think about cream puffs all the time. Light pastry filled with whipped cream! I'm just dying for a cream puff!"

The mother let go of her daughter's shoulder and pointed to a band of billowing white clouds passing overhead. "Look, Mary! God's got his own supply of whipped cream. I'm sure we'll have cream puffs before too long."

Mary followed her mother's pointing finger. As she looked into the bright sky, two large tears formed in her eyes and spilled down her cheek. "I don't want to have to go to heaven to eat cream puffs. I want cream puffs right now!"

With that, the thirteen-year-old girl burst into sobs.

"What's wrong with Mary?" asked Carol Shaw.

"Oh, she's just a baby!" answered Robert Bell.

"Robert, that's enough!" his mother rebuked him. "There's nothing wrong with Mary, Carol. Sometimes it does people good to cry, that's all. Let's just leave her alone. She'll be all right, won't you, Mary?"

Mary Bell wiped her eyes with the back of her oil-stained hand, smudging her face like a chimney sweep's. "I'll never be all right until I get off this raft!" she screamed. "I hate it here!" She threw herself into her mother's lap, once more sobbing.

"Mary," the mother spoke softly to her daughter, "let's pray, just you and me."

The girl nodded, still sobbing, while her mother drew her as closed as possible.

"Oh God, please look upon us in our need. Give us confidence to believe that Thou art with us. Help us to be strong."

"And, please, God, give me my cream puffs," Mary added.

"In Jesus' name. Amen."

The food box had been clamped shut; the men had returned to their customary places. Now there was nothing to do but sit and wait.

"Hey," said Joe Greenwell, "anybody know what day this is?"

"Sure, it's Tuesday."

"I know *that,* man! I mean, do you know what the date is and why it's important?"

"September 1, right?"

"What day did the *West Lash* go down?"

"Sunday, August 30."

"Yeah, that's right . . ."

"Thirty days hath September, April, June, and November, all the rest have thirty-one . . ."

"Which means that, if we went down on August 30, yesterday was August 31. So that makes today September 1."

"Just like I already said!"

"Who's arguing?"

"Come on, you guys, knock it off!"

"So what if it's September 1 or September 31? One day's just like all the rest on this trip!"

"Hey, where's your sense of history?" Greenwell teased. "Isn't there anybody here who knows a little history?"

"You mean something important that happened on this date?"

"That's it."

"September 1, let's see . . ."

"Babe Ruth hit his sixtieth home run on this date?"

"Naw, that's not it."

"Abe Lincoln got shot?"

"What do you know about history? Lincoln got shot on February 12."

"February 12 is his birthday, dummy!"

"Who cares!"

"I know," said Robert McDaniel. "Hitler invaded Poland on September 1. Let's see, must have been two or three years ago, right?"

SS *West Lashaway.* Owned by American West African Lines, Inc., and managed by the Barber Lines, 5,637 tons. Photograph was taken in June 1942 before its last trip to Africa in August 1942. Note the life rafts on racks on side of ship and the "defense" gun on poop deck. *U.S. Coast Guard, courtesy of The Mariners' Museum, Newport News, Virginia*

The raft (eight by ten feet). Storage area beneath the floor. Note door latches. Food, water, first-aid and emergency supplies were pulled out of the storage area and lashed to the floor for easy access. Airtight barrels for flotation were under the seats. Water flowed through the raft but no large fish (sharks) were able to get inside. Construction was the same on each side and reversible. Very seaworthy. Sufficient space to accommodate ten people with reasonable room. We were packed with nineteen people: fifteen adults and four children. *United States Navy*

German submarine *U-66* entering home base harbor, Lorient, France, on the Atlantic coast, after a long voyage, circa 1943-44. This photograph was captured when *U-66* was sunk on May 6, 1944, by Task Group 21.11. *Karl Degener-Böning*

Kapitänleutnant Friedrich Markworth, circa 1943. In late July 1943 Markworth was awarded the Knights Cross to the Iron Cross. A week later, August 3, 1943, the U-boat was heavily attacked by two carrier-based planes from the USS *Card* near the Azores, and Markworth was wounded. At the end of the patrol, Markworth was relieved as commanding officer and succeeded by Oberleutnant S. Gerhard Seehausen. *Dr. Friedrich Markworth*

British destroyer HMS *Vimy.* During the evacuation from Dunkirk, May 28–June 1, 1940, *Vimy* brought over 2,976 troops. In January 1941 she was taken in hand at Portsmouth Dockyard for an extensive refit as a long-range escort. In August 1942 *Vimy* joined HMS *Quentin* and *Pathfinder* escorting damaged battleship HMS *Queen Elizabeth* to Norfolk, Virginia, for repairs, then proceeded to Trinidad, where she departed from Port of Spain, September 17, with a special tanker convoy bound for Gibraltar. The next day, September 18, *Vimy* sighted and rescued us. *Imperial War Museum, London*

Rescue. September 18, 1942. 1020 hours. 12°45′ N — 60°24′ W. Twentieth day on the raft. This picture was taken by a crew member on board HMS *Vimy.* The flag (large canvas) is being waved as a signal to cease firing deck guns.

Hastings—Christ Church, Barbados, October 1942. Left to right: Richard Shaw, Mary Bell, Joyce Baynes, and Robert Bell. Note bandages on feet. Joyce was a niece of Mr. and Mrs. Mahon, at whose home Mary stayed when released from the hospital and where this picture was taken.

Visiting in Dr. Friedrich Markworth's home, September 18, 1981, in Detmold, West Germany. Left to right: Karl Degener-Böning (radio operator, *U-66),* Dr. Markworth, Robert Bell. We are looking at photographs of the raft when the survivors were rescued and pictures of *U-66* under attack in 1943 when Markworth was wounded. Neither man had ever seen these pictures before, part of my collection. *Author photo*

Petty officers, *U-66,* May 1944. Prisioners of war. Standing, left to right: Werner Pasedag, radioman, third class; Bernhard Terinde, machinist; Werner Fröhlich, chief warrant quartermaster, head helmsman; Wolff Loch, pharmacist's mate; Werner Hartmann, machinist's mate, second class. Seated, left to right: Richard Hohn, warrant quartermaster; Karl Degener-Böning, radioman, second class; Franz Nirnberger, fireman, first class; Walter Landvoigt, machinist; Georg Grölz, fireman. *U.S. Naval Archives, Washington, D.C.*

Officers, *U-66,* May 1944. Prisioners of war. Left to right: Ludwig Flintsch, ensign, engineering duties; Georg Olschewski, head engineer; Klaus Herbig, executive officer; Richard Ketelsen, engineering duties. *U.S. Naval Archives, Washington, D.C.*

Thursday, October 1, 1981, the *U-66* reunion in Schmittlotheim, West Germany. This reunion was the first that some of the men attended. They were curious to know about the person who wanted to visit them after they had brought such a horrible experience to him. Standing, left to right: Werner Frölich, Paul Breyer, Robert Bell, Hans Voigt, Richard Kressmann, Georg Grölz, Helmut Illing, Karl Degener-Böning, Richard Valentin, Georg Olschewski. Kneeling, left to right: Vinzenz Nosch, Hans Hoffmann, Edmund Wilshusen, Leonard Bürian. *Author photo*

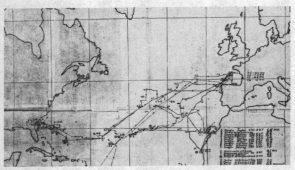

U-66 patrols from June 26, 1942, to September 1, 1943. VIII included the sinking of SS *West Lashaway*.

Thursday, October 1, 1981, Schmittlotheim, West Germany. Left: Edmund Wilshusen. Right: Robert Bell. Edmund, the torpedo-man on the *U-66*, fired the two torpedoes that hit and sunk the SS *West Lashaway*, August 30, 1942. *Author photo*

A life raft mounted on a ship. Note the airtight drums for bouyancy.

Reunion in Chicago, Illinois, August 2, 1987. Left to right: Richard Shaw (SS *West Lashaway*), Joseph Aucoin (USS *Buckley*, DE51), Robert W. Bell (SS *West Lashaway*), Mary Bell Whitbeck (SS *West Lashaway*), Vinzenz Nosch *(U-66)*, Donna Taylor (Carol Shaw, SS *West Lashaway*), Robert Burg (USS *Buckley*, DE51), James O'Keefe (USS *Buckley*, DE51). *Author photo*

"Three years today," Joe Greenwell confirmed. "September 1, 1939."

"And they used to call it 'the phony war'!"

"What I say is, I'd like them know-it-alls to trade places with us! Let 'em find out how phony it is!"

"Yeah."

"So where were you when World War II began?"

"I wasn't paying attention," said George Marano. "Why should I? We weren't in it, and Roosevelt kept telling us we wouldn't be in it. And like a jerk, I believed him!"

"Yeah, most of us could tell you where we were last December 7, Pearl Harbor Day. That's something I'll never forget. But September 1 three years ago? I have no idea."

"Out with some broad probably."

"You wish!"

"Naw, it's not an anniversary I keep tabs on. Now, speaking of anniversaries, I'm gonna remember August 30, for sure!"

"Yeah, red-letter day on my calendar from now on!"

"Anybody figure out what this war's about anyway? I mean, why did Hitler go after Poland three years ago?"

"To clean up Europe. Get rid of the Jews."

"Good, if you ask me. Dirty kikes!"

"Not all of 'em."

"Well, most I know. I think Hitler had the right idea."

"FDR's a Jew, you know. That's why we're in this stupid war!"

"Who told you that? President Roosevelt's an Episcopalian!"

"Pretends he's one anyway. No Jew could get elected President."

"Or Catholic either."

"Good thing, too. Oh, no offense to all you R.C.s, but you can't have your President swearing allegiance to the Pope."

"That's why Al Smith lost."

"Yeah, and gave us Herbert Hoover instead! I'd rather have voted for the Pope!"

"You know," Joe Greenwell interrupted, "for a bunch of sailors, most of whom haven't made it out of high school, you guys sure know a lot of wonderful knowledge about almost everything! And most of what you know is hooey!"

"From now on, let's cut the talk about religion and politics and all those hot topics," George Marano added.

"Mrs. Bell talks about religion."

"No she doesn't. She talks about God and the Bible, and that's not religion. That's *faith*. Besides, she's different. She can talk about anything she wants, right?"

Marano looked around the raft and waited. Each man seemed to agree.

"OK, we stay away from knockin' anybody else's race or religion or politics. There's no percentage. It just riles us up."

"So then, what do we talk about? You've eliminated all the good topics."

"Maybe we talk about nothin'! Maybe we talk about baseball or places we've traveled or . . ."

"Women?"

An embarrassing stillness covered the raft.

"Sorry, Mrs. Bell."

"Or maybe we talk about our future plans, like what we expect to do when the war ends."

"Right now, I'd just be happy to have this part of the trip end!"

"Speaking of which, aren't we supposed to be arriving in Trinidad today?"

"Yeah, where were you this morning? The kid and the captain, they already talked about it."

"I didn't hear them. What'd the captain say?"

"By the way, the captain's been awful quiet all day. He OK?"

"Let him be. He's takin' it easy. He's been under an awful strain, y' know."

"Sure, sure. Just askin', is all."

"Back to Trinidad. They know we're due, right?"

"Supposed to. It was a regular port o' call. Fact is, we had a cargo drop scheduled at Port of Spain, didn't we, Bosun?"

James Owen grunted his reply, his only communication since the morning meal's distribution on the other rafts.

"Well then, when we don't show today, won't somebody take notice?"

"What do you expect them to do? Send a St. Bernard dog and a search party?"

"I dunno. I guess they'll send somebody."

"And do you expect them to find us?"

"Pretty big ocean out here."

"Well, I'd hope . . ."

"Just don't hope too hard."

Robert felt a great stone of doubt come crushing down upon his chest. The very men he believed in most! What had happened to their confidence? How could they sit so blithely and say such discouraging words? Yet, what if their words were true?

"Yep, September 1, 1939," Joe Greenwell was saying again. "What a day! World's never been the same since. I reckon it'll never go back to what it was before Hitler invaded Poland. Quite an anniversary!"

TWELVE
ADJUSTED SCHEDULES

The Union Jack waved above the harbormaster's head-quarters on a pier facing Port of Spain's busy harbor. British soldiers and members of Trinidad's colonial forces patrolled the docks, stopping all vehicles and pedestrians, requiring identification and often a search. In the harbor itself, ships seemed to be in constant motion—tankers and freighters tying up to unload their cargoes, then loading again to return to the open sea. Beyond the Dragon's Mouth to the north and south through the Gulf of Paria to the Serpent's Mouth, vessels of the Royal Navy kept on guard against enemy intruders—whether by sea from the Caribbean hunting grounds or by land from neighboring Venezuela. For Great Britain and all her Allies, the port of Trinidad had to remain a safe haven.

In his office the harbormaster checked with his subordinates on the comings and goings of several ships.

"Did you hear, sir," said one assistant, "that HMS *Winimac* took it on the chin yesterday?"

"That so?" The harbormaster raised his eyebrows in surprise. "Too bad. She was just here in port until Sunday. My, my, it's been a rough past few days for Allied shipping. Lots of Jerry's subs seem to have got into the fishing tank!"

"None inside our defenses, sir!"

"Right," replied the harbormaster, "but no need for us to get cocky. Nothing would please Jerry more than to lay a few mines inside Port of Spain's seawall."

Then, turning to a sheaf of papers on his clipboard, the harbormaster asked, "Now, who else do we expect today?"

"Hard to say, sir. Since the recent flurry of attacks, most ships have been going on radio blackout. We don't really have a lot of current information."

"Well, let's run down the original manifest and see who's arrived and who hasn't." The harbormaster began reading a list of ships whose announced course had called for them to make their landfall at Trinidad on Tuesday, September 1.

"Three of our destroyers seemed headed this way— HMS *Vimy,* HMS *Quentin,* and HMS *Pathfinder.* Any sign of them?"

"Not yet, sir."

"Well, perhaps they're serving tea for Jerry this afternoon!"

"How about this America freighter, *West Lashaway?* Listed as coming from Takoradi, due in today?"

"No word."

"Right. Not sunk, you suppose?"

"Oh no, sir. The Yanks over at VP-31 keep a pretty keen eye. Now that they've got this new toy *radar,* they don't miss much."

"Particularly if it's one of their own, I suppose?"

"Right, sir. We'll see *West Lashaway* any time now."

So it was that on this Tuesday, September 1 — some forty-eight hours after the *West Lashaway* had been sunk — no one was searching for Captain Benjamin Bogden and his fellow survivors because no one knew of their plight. British authorities at Port of Spain had only the Barber Line's anticipated course for the *West Lashaway,* filed in June before the ship had ever left New York, bound for Africa. In time of war, many changes of course might be necessary; a ship might be delayed by fuel shortages or rerouted by the demands that its cargo be delivered elsewhere than originally planned. Only the unexpected could be expected! As for the Americans based at Port of Spain, Lieutenant Donald Gay's Trinidad Detachment of Patrol Squadron 31 had no information either. In fact, at the moment the *West Lashaway* was sinking, Gay and his companion, Lieutenant Tom Evert, were almost colliding overhead. In their excitement and chagrin, these navy pilots never saw the signs of distress at 10° 30′ north and 55° 34′ west. Besides, with the *West Lashaway*'s dead radio and dead operator in a ship sinking in only two minutes, who could have been informed? Of course, the commander in chief of the German Submarine Service, Karl Dönitz, in far-off Paris, France — he knew all but the name of the *West Lashaway;* but for Admiral Dönitz, that single ship was merely one more pushpin in his maps. No one who cared knew anything at all.

But on the clustered rafts, as they bounced off each other, sliding down a cresting wave, everyone was certain of rescue today. How could it be otherwise? Over and over, the men on Captain Bogden's raft assured each other. After all, they reasoned, the shipping company had certainly filed the proper papers with Port of Spain, as with every other port along the *West Lashaway*'s charted course. Hadn't the Baber Line's vessel been expected at each and every port of call so far? Tadoradi, Accra, Lagos and Apapa Quays, out and back, with one-shot stops at Douala and Matadi? Every port, right on time. Two o'clock in the afternoon, arriving as scheduled at Takoradi on July 1. Five days later, on July 6 at six o'clock in the morning, embarking for Accra exactly as posted weeks in advance.

"You know why we kept so close to schedule, don't you?" the bosun asked with a gleam in his eye.

"Naw. Why's that, Owen?"

"Because of good planning on the decks, that's why. I knew where every stick of cargo was, how much it weighed, how long it would take to heave it over and off, and what was coming on to take its place. Me and my men, we kept the *West Lash* on time. Right, Flavor? Isn't that so, Chico? Seremos?"

The three deckhands, part of the bosun's crew, nodded unenthusiastically, as if embarrassed to accept their part in the bosun's self-congratulations.

"What's more," Owen went on, "you can thank me — every last one of you — that you're alive at all!"

"Come off it, Owen!"

"Go, 'way!"

"I mean it!" the bosun replied angrily. "I checked these rafts every day. I had a feeling that, if we ever got smacked, those lifeboats wouldn't hold up, and I was right. I stocked these rafts with extra supplies — like that roll of canvas the captain put up for the lady and girls.

Hadn't been for me, most of you would've been shark bait in the first hour!"

Joe Greenwell spoke up above the hoots of disdain that covered the bosun's ears. "I gotta hand it to you. You know your business. Only, where I come from, it's customary to let somebody else toot the horn for you."

"Maybe so, Mr. Greenwell, maybe you Kentucky colonels can afford all that politeness. But in Pittsburgh, where I come from, we're used to the steel foundry and the blast furnace. We learn early that the only way to stand the heat is to be tougher than the heat. I don't make no apology to anybody. I'm looking out for James Owen, and I'm gonna make it! And when I do, the world's gonna know who's responsible for the rest of you deadbeats and holy joes!"

From the floor of the raft, the weakened voice of Benjamin Bogden suddenly took on booming authority:

"That's enough, Owen. I'll hear no more from you. Is that clear?"

"Yes, sir!"

The bosun retreated to the dinghy behind the raft.

The rest of the men were silent for some time. Then once more they took up the former topic, their certain and impending rescue on this expected day of arrival at Port of Spain.

It is a difficult, if not impossible, task for the victim of some terrible force greater than himself to see his real situation in proper perspective. It is a difficult, if not impossible, chore for any man to contemplate his own insignificance. Here were thirty-seven men on four connected rafts, along with one woman and four children—two girls, two boys—forty-two persons in all, nineteen of them on a single raft. They had been thrown together by misfortune or bad luck or chance or fate or even Providence — call it what you will. Their ship had been sunk, some of their comrades killed, and they had survived. Now, it seemed clear, the world owed them the dignity of rescue, soon and without further delay. Each man, thus convinced of his own importance, presumed that the world-at-large shared this opinion and must even now be summoning all its resources to come to his aid. It must be so!

"Where are those damned search parties they keep telling us about?"

"Don't we have no bases in the Caribbean anymore?"

"Maybe the Nazis have taken over the zone, and we don't even know it!"

"Well, where's the navy?"

"Beats me."

"They gotta know we're out here somewhere!"

"Yeah, but where? That's the whole point."

"Right *here!* See me? I'm standing up on this friggin' raft, and I want some friggin' flyboy to look down from his almighty seat in the sky and throw me a line!"

"Easy, George, easy."

"Is anybody sure that Sparks got off a signal before we went down?" Robert McDaniel asked.

"Nobody's sure of nothin', man."

"What's the difference? Sparks is dead, right?"

"Yeah, but I'd like to know if he got off a call. If he did, then there's some reason to hope for rescue today. But if he . . ."

"Don't say there's no reason to hope!"

"I didn't say there's no reason to *hope.* I said, there's no reason to hope for rescue *today,* 'cause if he didn't get through an SOS call, then who knows we're in trouble?"

"I see what you're saying."

"And if there's nobody out there holdin' his breath, waitin' for the *West Lash* to pull into port, then there's not much point in me holdin' my breath for some jerk to come rescue me. It'll happen when it happens. That's all."

McDaniel held out his upturned palms in a gesture of quandary and submission to the facts.

"Maybe you're right, Mac," said Woodman Potter, "but I still think it's a good idea to look for somebody to come today. I intend to keep looking every day. That way, I won't never be disappointed. I'm just gonna say to myself, 'Woodman, if it's not today, it'll be tomorrow.' And one of those tomorrows, I'll be right!"

"That's the spirit, Woodman!"

By sundown, the survivors knew the worst. The day had come and gone — their day of certain rescue — with no sign of any search party. No glint of a plane against the sun, no roar of engines; no smoke from a ship commissioned to find them. After such hopefulness, some of the men seemed to have succumbed to discouragement. Two or three tried to pass up their rations, but Joe Greenwell insisted that everyone should take his share. They ate their evening meal without anyone's suggesting the food game.

"Come on, you guys," said Joe Greenwell, "nobody swore on a stack of Bibles that it would be today. I mean, we gotta be reasonable!"

"Whaddya mean, reasonable! My rump's aching from these boards, my feet's festering with salt water sores, and you tell me to be reasonable!"

"Of course, you're uncomfortable, McDaniel. We all are. And we'll probably be uncomfortable for another day or two."

"Yeah, I heard that before — like, yesterday maybe?"

"That's what I mean. You guys are too cynical. What are you, a bunch of babies? Mommy doesn't come and pick you up the moment you fall and bump your nose, so you bawl like hell? What kind of seamen are you, anyway?"

"Whatcha getting at, Joe?" asked George Marano. "How come the chewing out?"

" 'Cause I'm tired of grown men pouting. Look at these kids here. You don't hear them bellyaching or see them pulling a long face. And you guys have all been to sea. You know how things work at sea. The moment something goes snafu, we don't drop everything else. There's such a thing as standard operating procedure, right?"

"Yeah, OK. So what?"

"Well, standard operating procedure takes time. There's steps to be followed. It doesn't just all of a sudden sprout like a flower in one of those Walt Disney movies. We gotta be patient."

"Mr. Greenwell's right, men."

A hush fell over the raft. The captain, still slumped in the well, had spoken his first words since early morning.

"Perhaps I owe you all an apology. I led some of you to assume for certain that we'd be picked up today. I still believe it was possible, but I should have left the door open. Obviously, we'll have to wait till tomorrow or maybe the next day. We've got to give Trinidad time to miss us before they can start to hunt for us. Then we've got to give them time to find us — and that won't be easy."

The captain's speech had slowed to a word-for-word crawl, but something suggested that he hadn't completed all he intended to say.

"But the main thing is not to give up hope. We may have to adjust our thinking somewhat, change our timetables a bit. But don't give up hope."

A long wheeze of stifled pain cut off the captain's utterance. Each seaman's face turned toward the captain, a new sense of alarm in every eye.

"What's wrong with Captain Bogden?" Carol Shaw asked Ethel Bell, her little girl's voice penetrating the raft's stillness.

The woman did not answer.

"He isn't going to die, is he?" Mary Bell asked.

Her mother still did not reply in words. Only a slow nod of her head assured the children. Then she said, "We need to pray for Captain Bogden and for Mr. Croons too. Children, let's pray."

Nightfall came like a cloak thrown over a candle. One moment, it seemed, the sun was still visible, low on the horizon; the next moment, darkness had enveloped the rafts.

"It was always worse to be adrift in the dark," says Bob Bell. "Somehow, bad off as we were, we never seemed to be as uncomfortable during daylight as we were at night. The distance from the edge of the raft to the waterline was only a few inches, but at night it seemed like a drop into the abyss. We didn't know where we were going—morning, noon, or night—so seeing shouldn't have made any difference; but at night, not being able to see a thing, we felt abandoned, literally lost at sea."

That night, Tuesday, September 1, Robert Bell prayed for rescue. He had prayed before, as part of his mother's routine devotions, entering into her prayers; but until this time, he had never voiced any petitions of his own. Now he focused his prayers on one single desire. *Dear God, he said in silent prayer, please send the rescue planes tomorrow.*

And if not tomorrow?

His doubts revised his prayer: *Soon, please, God, soon.*

DISCOURAGEMENT

The rescue planes did not come.

If all the power of wishing, concentrated upon the single desire for one PBY to appear overhead, could have produced its successful results, an entire squadron would have appeared. But mere wishing proved futile.

Instead, the sun rose as before, dispelling the night's unbearable cold but all too soon replacing it with suffocating heat.

The morning rations were dutifully dispensed as before, inedible yet necessary, tasteless yet better than nothing.

Only one aspect of this fourth day on the sea seemed different to Robert Bell: the absence of chatter. Each morning previous he had been summoned from his semi-sleep by the sounds of men's voices. But not today. From yesterday's expectations and optimism, the men on Captain Bogden's raft had fallen into silence. Their eyes were uniformly downcast, except for the pair of men still assigned to watch duty. But even they—Woodman Potter and Levi Walker at the moment—seemed hardly looking as though they anticipated seeing anything.

Except the sharks. Everybody was conscious of the sharks. Those beasts were constantly alongside, lending an element of fear to the whole experience, which Robert preferred not to contemplate.

With a shudder, the boy looked away from the sharks' fins and found his mother's face. He saw nothing that had changed. Unlike most of the men, she still seemed strong, her arms extended to enclose her daughter, Mary, and Carol Shaw.

She caught his eye and said, "Did you sleep, Robert?"

"Yes, Mother. I think so. Did you?"

"Not much, Son. There'll be lots of time to sleep once we're picked up."

"What do you do all night, if you're not sleeping, Mother?"

"Oh, I think about your father, and I remember happy times we had together at San and at Grandpa and Grandma Roffe's house."

Robert's grandparents were now both seventy-five years old. Grandpa Roffe had been in the Salvation Army as a young man, and Robert could recall having seen photographs of his grandfather in the uniform of a Salvation Army officer. Later he became associated with Dr. A. B. Simpson, founder of the Christian and Missionary Alliance, and Grandpa then had become the pastor of The Missionary Tabernacle in Toronto. But then Grandpa and Grandma Roffe had established the Missionary Rest Home in a big house near Lake Ontario, at 119 Lakeshore Road in Mimico, a western suburb of Toronto. There missionaries newly arrived from many different lands could come and spend a few days resting up from the rigors of their travel before setting out again on their itineraries of speaking in many churches.

Robert had always felt slightly uncomfortable at the Missionary Rest House, as though he were disturbing godly folk at their devotions. All that hush and piety seemed stifling to the young boy. He much preferred to visit his grandparents at their other house, called "Mapleholme," in Gravenhurst, Ontario, near Six Mile Lake in the Muskoka region north of Toronto. There he felt more at ease, more like a boy able to romp and make a noise, less like a so-called M.K., a missionaries' kid. The last time he'd visited his grandparents at their Muskoka home had been — let's see, he pondered — five years ago, in December of 1937, when Robert was just six and a half years old. His mother and sister and he had spent Christmas at Mapleholme, as they often did whenever the Bells had been on furlough. One Christmas, he remembered — it must have been when he was only three or four — most of his uncles and aunts and cousins had been there, too. In fact, all but one of the Roffes' five children, including three of their four missionary families from Laos, French West Africa, and the French Sudan, had been together for Christmas. Only Uncle Paul Roffe and his wife had been missing, needing to remain in Peru on their mission station. It had been quite a family reunion; important enough, his mother told him, to be written up in the Toronto *Globe.* Robert's family nearly didn't make it, he now recalled. Their ship, the SS *Lafayette,* got caught in a storm and delayed. But his father and mother had prayed, and the storm subsided in time for the ship to dock and the family to join the rest of their kinfolk at Gravenhurst for Christmas.

"Christmas!" the boy thought out loud.

"What's that, Robert?" his mother replied.

"Oh, nothing. I was just thinking about Christmas."

One of the seaman overheard the remark. "Let's hope we're off this raft by then! I don't hope to see no Santa Claus and reindeer in the middle of the ocean!"

"I don't believe in Santa Claus," said Carol Shaw. "I don't believe in anything anymore."

"You do too!" her brother, Richard, rebuked her.

"No, I don't. I don't believe in Santa Claus and I don't believe in the tooth fairy and I don't believe in God. Most of all, I don't believe in God."

"But, Carol, you must believe in God," Ethel Bell cautioned her. "Only God has kept us alive, and only God can rescue us."

"He didn't keep my mommy and sister alive!"

"No, he didn't. He took your mother and sister to be with him in heaven."

"By way of the sharks!" said a cynic.

"Mr. Owen, that's a dreaful thing to say to a child! You ought to be ashamed!"

The fury in Ethel Bell's eyes might have burned through most men's stare. But the bosun simply looked back at the woman and smirked. Ethel Bell turned toward Carol Shaw and tried to shield the child from the man's cruelty, but she knew in her heart that the damage had already been done.

"Owen," said Joe Greenwell through clenched teeth, "when we get off this rig, you'd better run for cover, 'cause I'm gonna take special pleasure in beating the crap outa you once and for all!"

"Anytime you want to try!" the cocky little man replied.

"Please, Mr. Greenwell," Ethel Bell urged, "no fighting. No more threats."

The woman could feel her energy draining away. Three nights without sleep and the constant watching over the four children in her care had left her with no reserve for tension and quarrel. For the first time she felt a wave of weakness, a floodtide of discouragement and self-pity sweeping her away from her strong moorings in hope. She seemed so helpless, so outnumbered, in the face of such overpowering hostility and hopelessness. How much longer could her supposed faith hold out before it too cracked and gave way to the realities of their circumstances? They were lost at sea! Now the men were threatening to fight among themselves. The captain had lost his strength. How long would it be before ultimate disaster struck and they all found themselves devoured by the sharks? It could happen! What could prevent it?

She buried her face in the nape of her life jacket, searching for a word, a phrase, some passage memorized from Scripture, to hold her mind at peace and stave off her panic. Her thoughts spun out of control. Could Carol Shaw be right? Was faith in God all a delusion, like belief in Santa Claus or the tooth fairy? Had her husband's life been worth no more to God than to end in a stupid collision between a bus and a parked truck? Had her infant twins meant nothing to the God she worshiped? Were her prayers so ineffectual?

Ethel Bell raised her head slightly and saw the streaming sunrays glancing off the ocean's surface, bright as an angel's splendor. Suddenly to her mind came an obscure Old Testament figure, a woman named Hagar, mistress of Abraham, mother of Ishmael. Sent away by Abraham's jealous wife, Sarah, Hagar too had seen an angelic vision. Ethel Bell recalled the story from Genesis 16. Alone in the wilderness, abused by human faithlessness and endangered by her condition, this woman had nonetheless believed in the God who was her only hope. Hagar had prayed and named the place of her assurance, "Thou God seest me." Now Ethel Bell spoke those words, at first inwardly, then quietly formed on her lips, then with volume, clearly and distinctly projecting them across the raft.

"Thou . . . God . . . seest . . . me! Thou . . . God . . . seest . . . me! Thou God seest me! Thou God seest me!

It was her prayer of affirmation, her credo repeated for all to hear, especially the speaker herself.

"What's with the lady?"

"Ah, who knows? She's a religious fanatic."

"Let her be. She don't do no harm."

"Yeah, every one of us is gonna be looney by the time this trip's over."

"Well, I don't care for all that preachin' and prayin'. It gets on my nerves."

"That so? Well, that's sorta silly, if you ask me. Since you don't believe in it, how can if affect you?"

"Whaddaya mean?"

"You don't believe in Mother Goose, right?"

"Of course not."

"So then, suppose I say 'Hickory dickory dock,' or 'Little Jack Horner sat in a corner.' Does that make any difference to you?"

"It don't mean nothin'. It's just words."

"So, it's just words that Mrs. Bell's sayin'."

"Yeah, but there's a difference. Those are Bible words,

and they get on my nerves, I tell ya."

"Well, we're all entitled to free speech, and we're all entitled to disagree with what's bein' said."

"Yeah, nobody's forcing you to believe in God or whatever."

"And the lady's entitled to pray and all that. After all, she's a missionary."

"She *was* a missonary. Right now, she's on this raft, like the rest of us."

"Oh no. She's a lady first, then she's a mother. And she's also a missionary. I don't want to see nothing happen to her."

"Why so?"

" 'Cause I have a feeling she may be my ticket off this raft. There's something special about her. So I say, let her pray and sing and quote the Bible and even preach, for all I care. Just don't get in the way of her and her God."

That night following the evening rations, Ethel Bell drew the children as close to her as possible.

"How are we doing on our memory verses?"

"I've been saying Psalm 46, Mother," Mary replied. "I think I know most of it now."

"Let's hear it, dear."

Mary Bell wrinkled her forehead and closed her eyes to concentrate. Then she began in a slightly whispered, self-conscious voice, reciting the words of the psalm:

> *God is our refuge and strength, a very present help in trouble. . . .*

When the child faltered ever so slightly, her mother smiled encouragingly, urging her on.

*He maketh wars to cease unto the end of the earth;
he breaketh the bow, and cutteth the spear in sunder; he burneth the chariot in the fire. Be still and
know that I am God: I will be exalted among the
heathen, I will be exalted in the earth. The LORD
of hosts is with us; the God of Jacob is our refuge.*

"Wonderful, Mary."

Sitting across the raft, Woodman Potter began to clap
his hands in applause.

"That's good, little girl. You done real good. Now, Mrs.
Bell, lemme ask you something. You think that psalm
means anything today? I mean, that part about wars ceas-
ing? Don't look like to me this war has ceased!"

"Mr. Potter, that's a good question, and I'll try to answer the best I know how. I think that this entire psalm
is a promise. It's not true that we never have any trouble
in this life, but the psalm promises that, when we do find
ourselves in great trouble — like on this raft, for
instance — God will be our strength. With that promise,
we can believe that there's no reason to be afraid, even
if all sorts of terrible things seem to be happening to us."

"OK, Mrs. Bell" — Rodriguez joined the discussion —
"so it's only a promise that someday God is going to end
all wars?"

"That's right, Mr. Rodriguez."

"Some good it's going to do, to take away everybody's
bow and arrow!" Robert McDaniel scoffed.

"I don't think we have to limit God's intelligence quite
that much, Mr. McDaniel," said Mrs. Bell. "I think we
can use our imagination and our common sense. When
David wrote this psalm, the conventional weapons of war
were bow and arrow, spear, and chariot. But David

wouldn't expect to fight a battle with those weapons today."

"You mean, it's OK to bring the Bible up to date?"

"Of course it is. We can do that right here and now. Let's see . . . instead of saying, 'He breaketh the bow, and cutteth the spear in sunder,' what could we say?"

"How about, 'He jams the rifle and clogs up the machine gun'?"

"No, it's more like this—'He disarms the infantry, and he orders the artillery to cease fire.' "

"That's very good," said Ethel Bell. "And what about this phrase—'He burneth the chariot in the fire'?"

"That might be tanks, Mrs. Bell," said Richard Shaw.

"Or bombers . . ."

"Or subs."

"I'm for that! I'd like to see a few subs burn in hell!"

"Ours as well as theirs, Mr. Greenwell?"

"Just theirs, Mrs. Bell."

"But when God makes all wars to cease, there'll be no more *us* and *them*. Don't you see, it's only when we are delivered from our hatred of each other, our envy and fear of each other, that God can bring us into everlasting peace. And I'm afraid that won't be until we're all changed in our hearts through the power of Jesus Christ."

"There she goes again, preachin' as usual!"

"Shut up, will ya! The lady's OK. I like the way she talks. She makes the Bible make sense to me for the first time."

"Yeah, well, it don't make no sense to me. I can do without it."

Later that night, while the men moaned in restlessness and cursed their misfortune, Ethel Bell watched the moon passing among the silhouttes of clouds. It had been a more difficult day than any since the shipwreck—perhaps the most difficult she had faced since George's death six and a half years before. But in spite of her own discouragement and seeming lack of faith, she had somehow been able to restore faith for others. Out of her emptiness had come forth fullness; out of her weakness, strength.

She heard herself speaking words from Psalm 34:

> *I sought the LORD, and he heard me, and delivered me from all my fears. They looked unto him, and were lightened; and their faces were not ashamed. This poor man [and woman, she edited] cried, and the LORD heard him, and saved him out of all his troubles. The angel of the LORD encampeth round about them that fear him, and delivereth them.*

Ethel Bell smiled at the inspiring confidence these words brought. Just then, the moon broke through an open space in the clouds, lighting the woman's countenance.

"My God, look at that lady's face! It's like an angel!"

"Like you say, maybe she's got something special to her."

"I wouldn't bet against her!"

Thursday, September 3
FOURTEEN
SEPARATION AND SHADE

"I can remember waking on the fifth day," says Bob Bell, "with the feeling that something important was going to happen. I didn't know what it might be, and I was too afraid of being disappointed to hope for rescue. But I knew something was up."

From the first hour after the *West Lashaway* sank, the forty-two survivors had been linked by ropes holding the four rafts together. It had seemed like a wise decision by Captain Bogden, keeping the entire party together. Because three of the rafts were damaged, only the captain's raft could hold more than a half dozen or so. But even in their discomfort, the nineteen survivors on the fourth raft felt better, knowing that they were not alone. Furthermore, the collection of four rafts tied together made a somewhat larger object, more visible from either the air or a surface vessel than would be a single raft drifting across the trackless ocean.

But as each day passed, the connected rafts seemed to be doing as much harm to each other as good to the survivors. Every swelling wave jerked the rafts apart or threw them against each other in broadside collisions or glancing rebounds. Men gripping the slats behind them had to guard against injury to their hands as one raft crunched against another. After all, these boxes weighed a half ton empty, far more with the added weight of their passengers. The constant jarring and bumping, the side-swipes and head-on jolts, were charging a heavy toll on the stability of the one undamaged raft and on the morale of every survivor.

After the morning rations the captain, who had been silent since Tuesday, spoke for the first time:

"Mr. Greenwell."

Joe Greenwell bent over and leaned in as close to Captain Bogden as he could reach. The captain said a few words, inaudible to the rest of the raft; then Greenwell sat upright.

"I agree, Captain."

"Give the men my orders, Mr. Greenwell."

"Aye, aye, sir."

Joe Greenwell raised his voice to be heard by every raft. "Listen up, everybody. Captain's orders."

"Before you give your speech, Mr. Greenwell," the bosun interrupted, "why don't you try to get the rafts closer together?"

"Good idea."

It took some effort and a lot longer than Robert Bell would have imagined before the rafts could be drawn side by side.

"Wouldn't you know," observed George Marano, "when you want them together, you can't get them. When you don't, it's like the Dodge 'Em cars at Coney Island!"

At last the rafts were aligned, but not before one of the

seamen, Elliott Gurney, had been pinched between two rocking rafts. It was the first time all the rafts had been so close since that first transfer of survivors on Sunday afternoon.

The formation of rafts brought one of the other three rafts close to where Ethel Bell and the children sat. On that raft Robert could see the huddled figure of Harvey Shaw, sitting with head bowed, never once looking up.

"Mother, look, there's Mr. — "

"Hush, Robert!" she cut him off sharply.

Richard Shaw turned his head just enough to follow Robert's line of vision, but the boy said nothing to his father, nothing to his sister.

"It was clear," says Bob Bell, "that Richard knew his father was in poor shape. Nothing was to be gained by trying to attract his attention. Nobody wanted to cause Carol any more grief. My mother knew this intuitively, and that's why she stopped me when I blundered into naming Mr. Shaw."

When the four rafts had been drawn as close together as seemed reasonable, Joe Greenwell stood, holding on to the nearest upright oars that made a mast for the sail.

"Captain Bogden's decided it's best for us to cut the lines and go our separate ways. That way, we've all got more of a chance. Woodman, you got your knife handy?"

"Yessir, Mr. Greenwell."

There was no discussion, no questioning the decision, no protest. Everyone seemed content with the captain's wisdom, even though they all knew what separating might mean.

One by one, the lines connecting the captain's raft to each of the other three were cut by Woodman Potter's knife.

"There were calls of 'Good Luck' and 'See you in New York,' " Bob Bell remembers. "One of the hopes we had, of course, was that, with four drifting rafts, one of them might be spotted in its location and could inform the rescuers about the other three."

"I remember a sad, sinking feeling," says Mary Bell Whitbeck, "when we separated from the last raft and began drifting apart." She can still see the several rafts, rising and falling on the crests of the waves, out of synchrony with each other. "We'd go up and down at different times, flowing through a trough and entirely out of sight from the other rafts. Then, suddenly, we'd pitch upward, and there we'd see one or another of the rafts. But each time they came back into view, we were farther and farther away. For me it was very depressing to watch the other rafts disappear."

And disappear they did!

"It's astonishing how quickly each raft simply evaporated from our sight," says Bob Bell. "Almost as if they'd been swallowed up. We were tied together; then we cut apart. They became three little specks on the top of a distant wave, and then they were gone."

"I was numb," Richard Shaw recalls. "I knew what was happening—perhaps my sister Carol did too—but not with full realization. I remember watching Dad's raft drift away, watching it get smaller and smaller, until it was gone, and he wasn't there anymore. It happened so fast."

Such speedy pulling away offered some encouragement to the survivors now left alone on Captain Bogden's raft. Prior to the separation, they had had no means of judging their rate of drift. Now it was clear that the ocean currents were powerfully at work and might be carrying them as fast as two or three nautical miles per hour. Both speed and direction were topics for fresh discussion, and the men occupied the next several hours, off and on, with their exchanges of opinion. But no one knew for certain where they were drifting or how fast. Anywhere would do, and the sooner, the better! On that principle they all agreed.

By the middle of the afternoon on this fifth day, the sun seemed especially unbearable. James Owen sat on the food box, squinting at the sun, then checking on a large sheet of canvas still being dragged along behind the raft, a relic from the unsuccessful mattress experiment.

"I've got an idea I want to try," Owen announced and stood up. "Some of you guys move so that Chico and Seremos can help me."

"What's up, Owen?" Joe Greenwell asked. The edge in his voice could not disguise his suspicions.

"Oh, you'll like this one, Mr. Greenwell. It'll remind you of your rocking chair on the front porch back home. You know, nice and shady and cool?"

"What you talking about, Bosun?" Levi Walker whined. "No place shady and cool on this rig."

"No, but there will be!" said Owen confidently.

Quickly he ordered Pacheco and Seremos to help him drag closer the useless mattress and its frame.

"Dump that friggin' thing," said Owen, pointing to the soggy mattress. "Probably kept us from making the speed we might. Now, Chico, latch on to that sheet of canvas. Careful, it's heavier than you are."

Isabelino Pacheco reached over the raft and took hold of a corner of the tarpaulin. Coated by the grease of palm oil and latex—even after five days in the water—the sodden canvas resisted any one man's efforts to bring it aboard the raft. First Servior Seremos, then the bosun himself joined Chico in hauling and straining to pull the canvas. It was an unsteady business.

"Somebody hold on to me," cried out Pacheco, "or I'll be shark bait!"

Gradually, an inch at a time, the canvas slopped over the edge and onto the raft.

"Now what, Owen?" George Marano asked.

"It's too big and clumsy," said Rodriguez Rosibrosiris.

"You'll never get that thing dried out," Levi Walker added.

"We don't need the whole piece. We only need a part of it," the bosun retorted. "Potter, give me your knife."

The bosun began scraping the jackknife through the canvas, trimming it to a rectangle a little larger than the area of the well. Into the corners of this sheet he now cut holes.

"Now, Seremos, grab some of that framing."

The seaman leaned out to where the ladder and its extra lumber had served as a makeshift support for the mattress. He cut and loosened the ropes, tying several sturdy lengths of wood, then handed them back to Chico.

"OK, Flavor, stand these up at the other end of the well and secure them good," the bosun ordered. "Somebody help him, will you? Use the line we salvaged when we cut from the other rafts."

"I get it!" declared Robert McDaniel. "We're going to have a canopy!"

"A beach umbrella," said Owen triumphantly, "just like a bunch of sunbathers on Miami Beach!"

With enthusiasm, two or three men began to assist Servior Seremos to erect the pair of poles at the base of the well, opposite the two masts supporting the sail. Then came the tricky part, fastening the piece of canvas at its four corners to the four uprights.

"It's wet, and it'll stretch some," said the bosun, "but don't pull it to pieces."

"And don't pull so hard that you fall overboard!"

Bits of rope were laced through the punctures the bosun had cut in the canvas, then knotted around the posts. The canvas drooped and dripped, sagging under the weight of its sodden condition.

"That's OK," said Owen. "Give it a couple of hours in this steam room, and that tarp will be as dry as the desert. You watch."

The bosun resumed his seat on the water keg. The sun had shifted in its course so that it beat down directly on those survivors seated on the bow and port side of the raft. But the bosun, seated in the stern, under the fringe of canopy, enjoyed the shade.

Late on the afternoon of September 3, the British destroyer HMS *Vimy,* accompanied by the Royal Navy's *Quentin* and *Pathfinder,* steamed toward Port of Spain, Trinidad. Having delivered the damaged battleship HMS *Queen Elizabeth* safely to Norfolk, Virginia, for repairs, the *Vimy's* skipper, Lieutenant Commander H. G. de Chair, had next been ordered to Trinidad. There *Vimy, Quentin,* and *Pathfinder* would provide escort protection for a convoy of tankers and freighters leaving Trinidad for Gibraltar. None of them could know that their cargoes of fuel and other supplies would be needed for Operation Torch, the planned invasion of North Africa by the Allies a few weeks later.

As the trio of British destroyers moved into the area off Barbados, lookouts suddenly spotted torpedo tracks in the placid waters. Douglas K. Stott, then a nineteen-year-old specialist in the new technology called radar, recalls the action.

"Our ships were able to take evasive action in time to avoid being hit, and an immediate counterattack began, using depth charges." But, Stott says, "There was no apparent sign that we'd hit anything."

So the three destroyers resumed their course for Trinidad. But as soon as darkness fell, Stott remembers, the ships abruptly changed course. "We made a return sweep of the area where we'd been attacked, each destroyer ten miles apart. Our tactic paid off because, around midnight, our radar picked up an object. It was a U-boat, surfaced and badly damaged."

Although the term *radar* had been coined by the United States Navy in 1942, the British were well ahead of any other Allied or Axis nation in the development of radar as a sophisticated weapon. Furthermore, Britain had been at war far longer than the United States — three years as against only ten months — and in that time Britain had gained considerable experience in combatting U-boats. Thus, the radar system onboard the *Vimy* exceeded anything available to either American or German vessels. Even so, the *Vimy*'s radar was like an imperfect toy by today's technological standards.

Stott sent word of his finding to the *Vimy*'s bridge. Sub-lieutenant R. B. Venables read the message and informed Commander de Chair that a German U-boat had been located.

"What's the sub's identity, Venables?" de Chair asked.

"U-162, Commander."

"Ram it and sink it!"

The destroyer wheeled about and came at flank speed

head on into the helpless *U-162*. The submarine sank, although all of her crew and officers, including the commanding officer, Heinz Wattenberg, survived and were taken on by the *Vimy*—except for the chief engineer, whose responsibility to scuttle the U-boat and prevent the capture of anything of value to the enemy kept him down below until it was too late. But the sub did not yield without costing the *Vimy* a damaged propeller and a gash along its port side.

"Damn!" grumbled Commander de Chair. "Now we'll be laid up in Port of Spain until they can repair us."

"Sorry, sir," replied Venables with just a trace of a grin. "Can't be all bad, sir. A few extra days on a tropic isle?"

"Mr. Venables, there's a war on!"

"Aye, aye, sir!"

"Children," Ethel Bell said when all the evening rations had been eaten and the food box tied down, "Mr. Owen's work today reminds me of another psalm we ought to learn."

"Oh, Mother," said Robert Bell in exasperation, "not another psalm. All we do is memorize Bible verses!"

"Got anything better to do, kid?" asked George Marano.

Mrs. Bell smiled at the seaman, then turned to her son. "I know it's tedious, Robert, but learning Bible verses is good for you in a number of ways. First, it does help to pass the time. And Mr. Marano's right, we don't really have much else to do with ourselves."

"Besides, Robert," his sister said petulantly, "If you're such a good Christian, you ought to want to learn Bible verses."

"Well, who said I'm such a good Christian!"

"You'd like everybody to think you are!"

"Children! I will not have you speaking to each other like this!" Ethel Bell lowered her voice to a harsh whisper. "I'm thoroughly ashamed of both of you — Mary and Robert. You see how every word we say is so easily overheard by the others. And there you sit, cheapening our faith by bickering with each other over who's the better Christian!"

The woman sank within herself.

"Go ahead, Mrs. Bell," Woodman Potter spoke up. "What was you 'bout to tell us before them chil'ren peeved you?"

She gathered herself and spoke. "Thank you, Mr. Potter. I must apologize to you all. I don't like conducting my family business — especially the disciplining of my children — in public. But as you can see, I don't really have much privacy."

"You could always take them out behind the courtesy curtain," said James Owen.

She ignored the remark and its innuendo. "What I was going to say was that, thanks to Mr. Owen's ingenuity, I was reminded of one of the most beautiful psalms of all. May I say it, Mr. Owen, as my way of saying thanks?"

The bosun made no response. Ethel Bell waited.

"Sure, Mrs. Bell," Woodman Potter broke the awkward silence. "We'd all like to hear the psalm."

"This is Psalm 121, and it's really a song."

She clasped her hands tightly in front of her knees. as if to strengthen her concentration. Then tilting back her head, she recited:

> *I will lift up mine eyes unto the hills,*
> *From whence cometh my help.*

*My help cometh from the LORD, which made
  heaven and earth.
He will not suffer thy foot to be moved:
He that keepeth thee will not slumber.
Behold, he that keepeth Israel shall neither
  slumber nor sleep.
The LORD is thy keeper:
The LORD is thy shade upon thy right hand.
The sun shall not smite thee by day, nor the
  moon by night.
The LORD shall preserve thee from all evil: he
  shall preserve thy soul.
The LORD shall preserve thy going out and thy
  coming in from this time forth, and even for
  evermore.*

"That's good, Mrs. Bell, that's real good!" said Potter. "I like that part about God not takin' any naps, you know? 'Shall neither slumber nor sleep.' I like that!"

"I like the shade part," Robert McDaniel said. "Just like you said, Mrs. Bell, it fits right in with what the bosun did for us, putting up that canopy." Then addressing Owen, he added, "See that, Chief? You're in the Bible, and you didn't even know it!"

"Cut the crap, McDaniel!"

The younger man persisted. "No, I mean it, Chief. Maybe God gave you the idea to put up the canopy as a way of helping us."

"God—God—God—God! That's all I hear, is *God!* What are you guys—a bunch of Holy Rollers? We're stuck out here in the middle of the ocean, and all you and this fool woman and her brats can blab about is God! Well, let me tell you something once and for all. There is no

God! I'm the only God I'll ever know or need. You want to be alive when this raft is found? Go on singing and praying, and we'll all be dead! Act like men, use your heads like I do, and we've got a chance."

For a long, nerve-rending moment, no one replied to the bosun's outburst. Then, very quietly, Ethel Bell began to sing a hymn, a paraphrase of her psalm:

> *Unto the hills around do I lift up*
> *My longing eyes.*
> *O whence for me shall my salvation come?*
> *From whence arise?*
> *From God the Lord shall come my certain aid,*
> *From God the Lord, who heaven and earth hath*
>   *made.*

As she sang, her voice growing stronger, Joe Greenwell leaned over toward the bosun and said ironically, "See, Owen? You just can't win with these women!"

The bosun swung away from Greenwell in rage.

"From that time on," Bob Bell recalls, "the bosun sat on the food box with his back turned to us as much as possible. It was his way of telling us that, for him, we didn't exist. Out of sight, out of mind—or, at least, so far as further conversation was concerned. He had other ways of communicating his disgust with us."

Friday, September 4 —
Saturday, September 5
FIFTEEN
NOTHING HAPPENED

Friday — their sixth day on the raft — was the first day of which Bob Bell's only recollection is that nothing happened.

True, the same routine prevailed, that same schedule. Morning rations were served, then the food box tied fast. His mother, ignoring the bosun's hostility, continued to lead her children in morning prayers and conduct drill work in minimal Scripture memorization.

After this, they sat.

Perhaps the men had too much on their minds to make idle conversation.

Perhaps they needed to conserve their energies.

Perhaps their fears were too insurmountable to be disguised by banter.

Perhaps John Vargas had run out of Latin love songs to sing, accompanied by his tattoo on the water keg.

Perhaps Rodriguez Rosibrosiris could no longer

remember the tantalizing recipes he had mastered as a chef.

Pehaps there was nothing left to say.

And so they sat.

Until close to sundown, when it was time to break open the food box again and pass around the same rations. Portions remained as before; one tin of pemmican shared by two persons; a morsel of chocolate, a single graham cracker, one malted milk tablet, and a sip of water from the greasy tin cup. Of course the food supply was diminishing, but no one had yet considered the prospect of reducing daily rations. That thought would have been unthinkable!

Then, after the evening meal, they sat.

The sun dipped beneath the rounded horizon, and immediately the night's chill set in.

"Remember," says Joe Greenwell, "some of us barely had any clothes on. Me, I had only my skivvies and a burlap bag that itched me all day and did little to warm me all night. It was like an ice box out there."

So, with the coming on of darkness — the rising moon behind them, the brilliance of stars — these survivors tried to sleep.

"At night," George Marano now recalls, "it was if we were in a coma. You knew where you were, and yet you didn't know. It was like a blankness of the mind, or maybe a way of easing up on the reality of our situation. Otherwise, we all might have gone crazy. In the daylight it was somehow different — as soon as the sun came up. But in the dark, semisleep.

"I say semisleep," Marano continues, "because no one slept soundly, that's for sure. I fell backward one night, but I managed to straighten myself up in a hurry before

I hit the water. The first thing I had on my mind was those sharks."

"Something else kept us awake," says Joe Greenwell. "Subs. German U-boats were thick in those parts, and at night they'd surface to run their generators. One time we passed so close to a sub that we could hear conversation and laughter from the deck. Another time there were two tied up together. We could hear their iron hulls grating against each other, and see the string of lights — blue or green, I can't recall — that marked the walkways. But they never saw us in the dark."

"Another time," Mary Bell Whitbeck remembers, "we knew there was something out there, and so somebody lit a couple of flares from the food box. I was so frightened. I was sure it was a U-boat that would open fire on us. But the flares sputtered out before anyone could see them."

Joe Greenwell says, "I don't know about Mrs. Bell and the children — they all seemed huddled together, so maybe they kept each other under control. But among the men, most of us would go nuts for an hour or two every night. It just seemed like we'd lose contact with reality. There'd be a lot of moaning and men talking to themselves. Every now and then, Flags Croons would let out a cry of pain. But not Captain Bogden."

Bob Bell agrees. "How Benjamin Bogden held back what he was feeling is a wonder to me. His pain must have been excruciating. Nobody knows how much he suffered. Yet never once did he allow himself the normal man's expression of agony or frustration. He was a superb example of personal courage on behalf of us all."

So Friday, September 4, came and went, a day on which nothing happened.

Of course it is far from true that nothing happened on this day. All over the world, events were occurring worthy of note in subsequent history books. In the Pacific theater of war, heavy fighting continued at Milne Bay in New Guinea, where the Japanese faced strong opposition from Australian and American forces. At sea near the Solomon Islands, two American destroyer-transports, USS *Little* and *Gregory,* were sunk by Japanese warships.

In Egypt, some sixty miles west of Alexandria, the newly appointed commander of the British Eighth Army, General Bernard Law Montgomery — later to be known as Viscount Montgomery of Alamein — was leading his forces against a respected enemy, "the Desert Fox," Germany's Field Marshal Erwin Rommel. In a little over two weeks Montgomery had begun to turn a seemingly certain disaster for British and New Zealand troops into possible victory. Just two days before, Rommel had ordered his German-Italian Axis army to execute a staged withdrawal after failing to take the Alam el Halfa ridge. Now, on September 4, Monty's men had Rommel in retreat to a new position beyond the British mine fields. Two months later to the day — on November 4 — Rommel would retreat altogether, and El Alamein would forever belong to Montgomery.

On the eastern front of Europe, the German Sixth Army, commanded by General Friedrich Paulus, had arrived at the western edge of Stalingrad. Over the next few days the city's collapse would seem imminent; but as days stretched into weeks, and Stalingrad did not fall, the Russian Army prepared itself for a devastating maneuver, begun on November 19, that completely encircled a quarter-million German troops.

While these battles were being fought with weapons

of war, another kind of struggle was going on this same day. In Stockholm, Sweden, Gunder "the Wonder" Hägg set another world's record in middle-distance running, his seventh in slightly more than two months. Having previously run 4:06.2 for the mile, Hägg lowered that mark to 4:04.6, running a pace that left his nearest competitor nearly ten seconds behind. Before the war finally ended, Gunder Hägg would lower that time to 4:01.3, running in the luxury of a neutral nation and living like one of today's ostensibly amateur world-class athletes.

All these and other events occurred this same day, Friday, September 4. But on a raft congested with nineteen bodies, adrift somewhere between Trinidad and Barbados, no one knew of these triumphs or defeats, no one cared. Their lives had been stopped, as when a motion-picture projector freezes the action of a single frame. For them, nothing would ever happen again until they were delivered from that raft. So, like many other victims of the sea's uncertainties, they spent the whole long night wishing for the day to come.

And then it was daylight again, another day. Saturday, September 5. Their seventh day on the raft. Another day when, again, nothing happened.

CHURCH SERVICES

As Sunday morning dawned, the eighth day on the raft, the lethargy of the previous two days seemed to dissipate. A week had passed since the *West Lashaway* went down — and they had survived! They had proven themselves to themselves and to each other. They had earned the right to be proud of their survival.

After morning rations, the first conversations in two days broke out among groups of men.

"This is Sunday, right?"

"Sure is."

"Let's see, that makes it September 5."

"Sixth. September 5 was yesterday."

"That so? I musta lost a day somewhere."

"Oh, that's easy when you're as busy as we are!"

"Yeah, what is it they say? Time passes when you're having fun?"

"Yeah, maybe so, but it's not passing quick enough for me."

"What were you doing a week ago today?"

"Right about now?"

"Whenever."

"About now—what time do you suppose it is, anyway?"

"Sun's been up about four hours or more, so it's probably between ten and eleven."

"Naw, it's closer to noon."

"Maybe."

"Well, last Sunday morning, I went to the worship service on deck. Mr. Shaw—those kids' father—was the
preacher."

"Whatever happened to him?"

"He was on one of the other rafts we cut loose from."

"Yeah, don't you remember the little girl over there with
her arm in the sling? Spent the whole first night cryin'
out for her father. Got on my nerves."

"Well, you can understand how she felt, can't you? Her
mom and sister killed, and her dad on a different raft?"

"Funny she didn't say nothin' when we separated."

"Oh, kids are better at adjusting than most of us are.
She'll let it out in time."

"So you went to church last Sunday?"

"Yeah, I used to go regularly at home, before I went
to sea. Figure it's a good thing I did last Sunday morning."

"How's that?"

"Probably why I'm on this raft today instead of catchin'
crabs down below."

"I didn't go to no service last Sunday morning, and I'm
here!"

"Well, I don't know how it works. I just know I'm glad
I went when I did."

"Maybe we oughta have a service right here on the raft.
Mrs. Bell could lead it."

"Naw, bosun would never stand for it."

"Bosun ain't in command!"

"Well, it's clear that Captain Bogden isn't!"

"Let's ask Joe Greenwell."

That same Sunday morning, at their home, Ethel Bell's parents, Alfred and Mary Roffe, and her sister Nell were preparing to attend worship services at the Christian and Missionary Alliance Tabernacle. They had concluded breakfast with their usual morning devotions, reading a passage from the Bible and praying together for many people on a list of name faithfully maintained by Mary Roffe. The list, of course, was headed by her children's names.

All week long the Roffes had waited for word from Ethel. Not knowing precisely her expected date of arrival at the port of Fall River, Massachusetts, her parents nonetheless hoped to hear some word through the New York City office of the Christian and Missionary Alliance.

"I remember praying last Sunday, Alfred," Mrs. Roffe said, "that this week we'd have Ethel and Mary and Bobby with us."

"That's right, dear," her husband replied, "and I remember adding 'The Lord willing' to that prayer. We'll hear from the Alliance headquarters soon, I'm sure."

"Now we'd better get moving," said Nell Roffe. "It's a long ride on the streetcar and a longer wait if we miss one."

Together the elderly couple and their daughter, each with a Bible in hand, left the house.

By Sunday morning, September 6, the *West Lashaway* had been formally reported as delayed, perhaps missing.

Authorities in Port of Spain, Trinidad, had so informed the Barber Line's headquarters in New York. A copy of this report had also been forwarded to the United States Naval Air Station and its VP-31 commander, Lieutenant Donald Gay. It was one of many such reports.

Just such a report brought out the best in these PBY pilots. "To my mind," says retired Rear Admiral Donald Gay, "one of the most beneficial services we provided was our air-sea rescue work. Our job, after spotting survivors with our fledgling radar equipment and confirming our find visually, was then to vector surface ships to where they could rescue lifeboat and raft personnel. We'd drop a string of smoke lights on line from a surface vessel to the survivors. Then the vessel would set course at high speed down that line. We used the same technique in partnership with destroyers to team up against an enemy submarine.

"There were a great many unsung heroes," Admiral Gay goes on, "with whom I was proud to serve — men who flew thousands of hours over that open water and never saw a single submarine or raft in need of rescue. We flew a hundred and eighty hours each month *at night* in unimaginable weather, horrible weather! Some of us had cases of stomach ulcers and couldn't figure out why. You see, terms like 'combat fatigue' hadn't been invented yet, and it never crossed our minds. These U.S. Navy pilots were in the war until victory was ours, and we had no thought of being relieved."

Lieutenant Gay handed the new report to Lieutenant Tom Evert.

"Do we know anything about a ship called *West Lashaway?*"

"What kind of vessel?" Evert asked, now glancing at

the message. "I see. Small American freighter. Headed here. Supposed to make port September 1. That's last Tuesday, right?"

"Yes. Of course, in these waters a day or two's delay is common. But hardly more than that. See, this report is as of 0600 hours this morning, and that makes it five days late."

"So what do we do?"

"As if you didn't know!" Gay replied. "Let's get a couple of more men and go searching."

"We got anything to go on — something as elementary as the *West Lashaway's* last reported position?"

"Yes, it says right in the report," and Gay pointed to the place on the page where Evert read:

"Last message received 29 August, 1200 hours.
'WREA, official registry number 217002.
Position, 11° 20′N/53°30′W.'
Expected Port of Spain 1 September."

"Well, that gives us some idea of where to look — like, say, the whole western Atlantic!"

"Let's do it!"

"Sure, I'll ask Captain Bogden," said Joe Greenwell.

He bent over to address the captain.

"Captain, some of the men would like to ask Mrs. Bell to conduct divine worship this morning, if that's OK with you."

"Benjamin Bogden opened his eyes and gave the slightest nod of his head. It seemed to be the only effort he could muster at that moment.

Turning back and facing across the raft, Greenwell said, "OK, Mrs. Bell, if you're willing."

"Mr. Greenwell, I'm willing, but I don't want to force a worship service on anyone, and it's a little hard not to offend. I can just speak quietly to the children, if you prefer."

"Oh no, Mrs. Bell! We all want to be a part of the meeting."

Sitting immediately next to the bosun, Robert Bell could see his jaws tighten to a grimace, but the man said nothing.

"All right, then, if you wish. I'll conduct a service just the way my late husband might have."

"Only keep the sermon short." George Marano laughed.

"I promise, Mr. Marano."

"That Sunday morning," Bob Bell now recalls, "was like no church service I ever attended, before or since. True, Mother had a captive audience. Not even the bosun could escape. But the way the other men entered into the service was remarkable."

Ethel Bell proceeded unself-consciously, just as though she were in some great sanctuary—although, as a matter of fact, in her church affiliation, few if any women at that time ever took leadership roles in worship services. She began by affirmatively declaring, "This is the day the Lord hath made. We shall rejoice and be glad in it."

Then she announced a hymn, hoping that she had chosen one known to most of the men. "Let's sing, 'Onward, Christian Soldiers.' "

Several of the men nodded in acknowledgment, and she hummed a note as close to the starting B flat as she could guess. Little by little, the group of men joined the woman and children, until almost all were singing:

> *. . . With the cross of Jesus*
> *Going on before.*

When the song ended, she prayed briefly. "Our heavenly Father, we thank Thee for giving us life this day. Help us to be good soldiers of Christ, to endure our hardship, and to follow our Lord. In Jesus' name. Amen."

Then Mrs. Bell said, "You've all listened while the children and I have been trying to remember or learn for the first time some verses from the Bible. Let's see how well we've been doing. We won't ask anyone to say the verses individually; that might be too embarrassing. So let's say them together, beginning with Psalm 23."

As before, the woman conducted the recitation with her head bobbing in rhythm with the words and phrases, turning from side to side to keep the four children in tempo together:

> *Yea, though I walk through the valley of the shadow*
> *of death, I will fear no evil; for thou art with me;*
> *thy rod and thy staff, they comfort me. . . .*

When the psalm concluded, Ethel Bell said, "Are we ready for Psalm 46 yet?"

A general shaking of heads among the children indicated their lack of confidence in being able to repeat that psalm.

"Well, let's try as much as we know."

> *God is our refuge and strength . . .*

Remarkably, the children arrived almost at the end of the psalm before they stumbled over any words at all.

"That's very well done!" she said. "I'll finish just to round it off.

> *Be still and know that I am God.*
> *I will be exalted among the heathen; I will be ex-*
> *alted in the earth. The Lord of hosts is with us . . .*

"The God of Jacob is our refuge!" burst in little Carol Shaw. "See, Mrs. Bell, I do so know it!"

"Wonderful, Carol!"

"After we'd recited our Bible memory work," Bob Bell remembers, "my mother spoke to the men about life and death, the danger we were in, the fears we all were trying to overcome. She told them about her own experience as a young woman stricken by tuberculosis, about the sorrow of losing her twin sons, and then her husband."

As she spoke, the men seemed to listen intently.

"I believe in a God who not only created each one of us," she told them, "but who also wants to preserve us and give us the joy and satisfaction of life. Listen to what God says in the words of the prophet Isaiah:

> *But now thus saith the LORD that created thee, O*
> *Jacob, and he that formed thee, O Israel, Fear not:*
> *for I have redeemed thee, I have called thee by thy*
> *name; thou art mine. When thou passest through*
> *the waters, I will be with thee; and through the*
> *rivers, they shall not overflow thee: when thou*
> *walkest through the fire, thou shalt not be burned;*
> *neither shall the flame kindle upon thee.*

"You see, men, God wants to bring us to safety so that we can give Him praise, so that we can serve Him. I'm sure that, for anyone trusting in the will of God, nothing can touch our lives except that which comes through the hand of God."

Drained by her efforts at speaking, the woman leaned back against her daughter, Mary. Immediately, Joe Greenwell sensed her weariness and took charge.

"Thanks, Mrs. Bell, for the sermon. I'm sure that's an encouragement to us. Maybe we oughta finish up this Sunday go-t' meetin' with another song, or somethin'."

"How about the collection? They always take a collection in church, don't they?"

"How would you know? You never go to church!"

"That's why. I don't like them collections."

"Well, we ain't takin' no collections here, so just slam it shut!"

"Yes, let's sing something. I'd like to hear 'Home on the Range' or 'Deep in the Heart of Texas.' "

"Those aren't church songs!"

"Mrs. Bell, how 'bout that pilot song you sang before?"

She tried to clear her dry and cracking voice and, nodding to the children, began in little more than a whisper to sing:

> *Jesus Saviour, pilot me,*
> *Over life's tempestuous sea . . .*

"Now we'll close with the Lord's Prayer," said Joe Greenwell.

Alfred and Mary Roffe and their daughter Nell got off the Long Branch/Lake Shore streetcar at Superior Avenue in Mimico and walked to the Missionary Rest Home at 119 Lakeshore Road. They had spent the morning at church. Now, as they approached their house, a teenaged boy on a bicycle came toward them.

"You live here, mister?"

"That's right."

The boy reached in a leather pouch slung over his shoulder and leafed through a packet of envelopes.

"Reverend A. W. Roffe?"

"Yes?"

"This telegram's for you."

"Oh, Alfred! Perhaps it's news from Ethel!"

"Sign here, please."

The old man took the telegraph delivery boy's pencil and scrawled his signature. Reaching in his pocket, he found a coin and gave it to the boy, who sped off on his bicycle.

Fingers trembling, Alfred Roffe unsealed the envelope and took out the message:

ETHEL'S SHIP DELAYED, NO CONTACT.
ALL HERE PRAYING WITH YOU.

The telegram was signed by the Reverend A. C. Snead, Foreign Secretary in charge of overseas missionaries, and sent from the Christian and Missionary Alliance headquarters at 260 West Forty-fourth Street in New York City.

Taking his wife's arm, Alfred Roffe said, "Let's go in the house and pray. That's all we can do now."

"Now can we sing 'Home on the Range,' Mrs. Bell?"

"Of course!"

Throughout the early afternoon, the raft came suddenly alive with the sound of men's and children's voices.

Ethel Bell was too hoarse to sing at all; in fact, her mouth was sore and her tongue seemed to be swollen. But the men sang heartily, going from one song to another—folk songs, popular songs of the thirties and early forties, and patriotic songs. John Vargas led the other Spanish-speaking seamen in a few Latin American favorites, like "La Golandrina."

Two or three times, however, some one would say, "Let's sing the pilot song again." So they did.

Lieutenant Donald Gay, commanding officer of VP-31, could only guess at how many search missions went out that Sunday, looking for the *West Lashaway* and any other ships in distress. Pilots kept coming back to base to refuel, then going out again to try a different sector of the compass. They flew high, they flew low. They circled and dived and did all other maneuvers called for when searching for something on the surface of the ocean.

Each time a pilot returned to the Naval Air Station he filed the same report: "Nothing sighted." Two or three pilots had dipped low enough to skim the ocean, thinking they had spotted some sign of life. But each time the pilot climbed away, having found nothing more than a mass of flotsam or, perhaps, just a shadow.

A song had just ended when the bosun, who had refused to join in the singing, turned suddenly to face the raft:

"Shut up, you guys!"

"Easy, Owen! Nobody's buggin' you!" Joe Greenwell answered.

"Yeah, nobody's askin' you for a solo, Chief!"

"I'm not talking music, you silly sons o' bitches! I'm talking airplanes! Listen!"

In an instant all commotion ceased. Every muscle locked in place. Even breathing stopped as the survivors strained to hear what they feared not to hear. For an unbearable moment they sat in crazy positions, titling heads this way, cocking shoulders that way, half falling overboard in their anxiety to catch the fainest sound. They heard nothing.

"You dreaming, Owen?" George Marano asked.

"Be quiet, I tell you! There's planes up there, at least two of them, revving at different speeds."

Again a hush.

Then from somewhere beyond the space immediately overhead, the dull drone first of one, then another set of airplane engines registered on their ears.

"Jeez! The bosun's right!"

"It's a plane."

"Two planes! Hear 'em?"

"Where the hell are they?"

"One's off to the west, I think."

"Naw, they're both off our starboard."

"I only hear one."

"There's two, I tell ya!"

"Wave somethin'!"

"Quick, get that canopy down!"

"Keep it tied to one mast. You can wave it like a flag."

"They'll never see that tarp. It's too dark. We need something light."

"Here's my shirt, it's white."

"Should we try shouting?"

"Naw, save your energy. Them flyboys can't hear

nothin' but what comes through their headsets."

"Where's the sound now?"

"Everybody shut up so we can listen."

The babel of voices switched off like a radio. Nobody dared so much as to breathe.

Then it was there—out of nowhere—directly overhead—the sound of aircraft. But nothing visible.

"Where is the damned thing?"

"Right above us."

"Can you see it?"

"No, but I can hear it real good."

"Keep wavin' that shirt!"

The roar grew louder, then faded to a buzz, a drone, a hum, a memory.

"Do ya think they seen us?"

"No, but . . ."

"There's your answer."

"They gotta seen us."

"Why?"

" 'Cause we're out here, dammit, we're sittin' right here!"

"Well, maybe so."

"They saw us. We'll be picked up soon."

"I heard that one last week!"

"Remember what Mrs. Bell said . . ."

"Aw, to hell with Mrs. Bell. That's OK for her kids. Let her God show up in a friggin' PBY, and maybe I'll believe!"

"Easy does it, Mac."

"Sorry, Mrs. Bell."

Lieutenant Jack Hillman parked his plane and climbed down to the tarmac, waiting for his partner, Lieutenant

Ray North, to do the same. Together the two navy pilots walked to their command post. Inside, a weary commanding officer waited for this last patrol to return.

"See anything?" Donald Gay asked.

"If it's out there and we missed it, I'll eat a swastika for supper!" Hillman vowed.

"No sign of life at all?"

"Not that I saw," North agreed.

"Probably the currents carried any wreckage or survivors out of our range," Hillman suggested.

"Maybe so. Well, that's it for now. We'll try again another day," said Gay. "Sign in and get some rest. We may be busy again soon."

Monday, September 7—
Wednesday, September 9
SEVENTEEN
DEATH

Everyone knew that something was seriously wrong with Earl Croons, but nobody expected him to die.

The navy signalman had been lying curled up in the well almost from the first moment aboard the raft. His outbursts of rage, his foolish act in gulping salt water had all been explained by his unknown injuries. But several people seemed to be injured or depressed, and Flags Croons was hardly any worse off than, say, Captain Bogden. So the others simply let him be. Besides, what else could they do? The first-aid kit provided no miracle cures: only some skin ointment, a bottle of iodine, and some bandage strips.

Everyone, however, began to share the effects of physical deterioration as this second week commenced in earnest.

"I remind you," says Bob Bell, "that six or more inches of water constantly was washing through the well. For

Captain Bogden and Flags Croons—and me, too, the first couple of days—who were sitting in the well, that meant being soaked in salt water from head to foot. The discomfort—and at night, the cold—of that hardship is unimaginable to anyone who hasn't suffered it.

"But even those of us sitting on the rim of the raft or perching on the two water kegs—or, from time to time trailing along behind in the doughnut—had our share of discomfort, too. After a couple of days of inactivity, our feet had swollen so badly, none of us who had shoes could wear them. We took them off, but believing we'd be needing them again soon, we tied them to the slats. Of course, these few pairs of shoes took up space far more precious than shoes! So, with some reluctance, we tossed our shoes overboard.

"That left us," Bell continues, "with swollen feet immersed in seawater. The raft's slats weren't smoothly polished; we'd get scratches or slivers in our feet and ankles. It wasn't long before every one of us had festering sores which then grew into ulcers the size of an egg yolk."

Some people had five or six sores on each foot. Scabs could never form because of the constant soaking. Every unintentional nudge from a neighbor's foot, every touch by some other object felt like a fresh wound. In the overcrowded circumstances of the raft, such bumps and knocks were frequent.

Now that the canopy had been raised, there was even less room for nineteen people to avoid contact with each other. The uprights opposite the oars holding the sail occupied a few inches of room for thighs and knees, reducing the already minimal comfort even more.

"Why is it so often true," says Joe Greenwell, "that somebody's brilliant idea—the floating mattress or the canvas roof—has its sour side as well as its benefits? It's what today we call trade-offs, I suppose. To get something, you have to give up something else. In our case, to get some relief from the sun, we gave up a little more space. I guess that's life!"

"Nights were the most difficult in every respect," says Bob Bell, "but particularly where our ulcerated feet were concerned. In our restlessness or in our fitful sleep, someone would barely move a foot, which inadvertently would touch somone else's foot. Always the pain created the same chain reaction. The person touched would move quickly, thereby hitting up against someone else, who'd try to get out of the way, and thereby hit someone else, who'd try to get out of the way, and thereby hit someone else; and so on, around the raft, like dominoes."

The anticipated pain kept men on the edge, irritable over the slightest carelessness, ready to lash out verbally if not physically, and only because they were so enervated and lethargic, too weak to fight.

"Their recriminations against each other were sharp," Bell recalls, "especially at night. Under cover of darkness, when they couldn't see my mother distinctly, the men often spoke abusively to each other, using profanities and obscenities that would have shamed them and caused them to apologize in broad daylight.

"By the beginning of our second week," says Bob Bell, "the bosun's hostility toward my mother and us four children was apparent to everyone. As I've said, he tried to intimidate her by ridicule. When that didn't work, he treated her with contempt, sitting on the food box in a position half turned away from our side of the raft. But from time to time, he had to turn back, and sitting next to him, I was the closest member of our party to him.

Therefore, I received most of his little acts of cruelty."

According to Bob Bell, the bosun seemed to delight in aggravating the boy's injuries, stepping on his foot or bumping against his leg. Was he merely thoughtless? Or was his clumsiness deliberate? Was he expressing his spite?

"He never once apologized, the way other men did when they accidentally hurt one another. Sometimes he'd be looking me straight in the eye, then step on my foot," says Bell. "There wasn't much I could do, except try to stay out of his way as much as possible and watch out for his next attack."

To make matters worse, the bosun had now established himself on the food box, where he alone of all the survivors could sit with his feet raised out of the water. So he never shared the painful ulcers with those whom he tormented.

Long after midnight, but before the morning star appeared, Flags Croons grew more restless than usual, twisting his upper body from side to side as he sat in the well of the raft, scratching and tearing at the acid burns on his chest. George Marano tried to hold his head still and speak comfortingly to him. But the youth would not respond; instead, he raved in his delirium:

"I've got a cup of coffee! I've got a cup of coffee!"

"Quiet, Flags. Be still," Marano cautioned him.

"More coffee, Mrs. Bell? I want more coffee!"

The navy signalman kept up his monologue, rousing the rest of the men from their stupor and antagonizing several of them.

"Make him shut up, Marano!"

"Yeah, stuff a rag in his mouth!"

"He doesn't know what he's saying," Marano defended Croons. "Let him be. He's real sick."

For a short while Flags quieted down; then he began to speak again, his voice strained and peculiar, as if speaking words not his own:

"That's it, Mrs. Bell, that's it. Say it again. Valley of the shadow of death. No fear. No evil. Valley . . ."

"What do you think, Rodriguez?" George Marano asked the cook. "Should we give him some food?"

"Sure," replied Rosibrosiris. "We'd better do something."

A tin of pemmican was handed to the cook.

"Flags, try a little food."

Rodriguez Rosibrosiris took a finger and scooped some of the sticky paste into Earl Croons half-opened mouth.

"Come on, Flags. Grub time."

"What's with Flags?"

"How come they're feedin' him now? Ain't time for rations till after dawn."

Robert McDaniel reached out and touched the signalman.

"My God, I think he's dead!"

"Don't be crazy!"

"He's just sleepin'."

"Flags! Flags!"

Bob Bell recalls his first close encounter with death. "I clearly remember the sight of Flags lying opposite me, his head in George Marano's lap, his lips parted, and the food still in his mouth. He died just as the first slants of dawn came over the raft."

The funeral service was simple. The body of Earl Croons had been pulled out of the well by four men and laid momentarily on the edge of the raft nearest to the sail masts. To accommodate the corpse, the bosun had to move off the food box.

"Shove over, kid," he said to Robert Bell.

Captain Bogden would ordinarily have been responsible for any last rites. But he sat looking dazedly at the scene, offering neither comment nor direction.

"Mrs. Bell," said Joe Greenwell, "maybe you'd just say a prayer for Flags."

She nodded ever so slightly.

"Certainly, Mr. Greenwell."

Ethel Bell attempted to clear her throat so that she could speak loudly enough to be heard; instead, her throat seemed clogged with sand. "Men," she spoke in a voice like gravel, "I'm not able to pray for Mr. Croons. His soul is in God's hands and in God's destiny. But I can pray for each of us. Let us pray."

"Our heavenly Father, as we commit the body of this departed comrade to the deep, we ask you for your help and support. We are troubled by his death, and we must trust in Thee for added strength. Help us all this day. In Jesus' name. Amen."

"Amen."

Several men made the sign of the cross on their foreheads and chests.

Before the body was buried at sea, Joe Greenwell and George Marano stripped off Earl Croons's clothes as gently as possible and handed his shirt and pants to someone else to wear.

Ethel Bell knew what would follow. Eveyrone knew. But the woman wished to protect her children against the horror of the next few minutes. She could hold only the two girls' eyes, pressing them shut with her enveloping arms and hands.

"Robert, Richard," she addressed both boys, "I want you to close you eyes and cover your face."

"Aw, Mrs. Bell," Richard Shaw protested, "I want to see. I'm old enough."

"Richard, please! Robert, put your head down here." She pointed to the small of his sister Mary's back.

Reluctantly, Robert obeyed. From behind the mask of his closed eyes and buried face, he saw nothing. But what he heard filled him with cold terror. The movement of men at his feet told him that the signalman's body was being pushed overboard. There was no splash, but all at once a violent thrashing exploded in the water just beyond the raft. From beneath, gray forms converged to tear at the flesh. The sharks had discovered the body.

Few men had anything to say during the rest of the morning. The unspoken horror had occurred, removing any necessity for speech. There were no eulogies for Flags, no attempts at recalling happier memories, no references to the youth's folly or fate. He was dead, and that was it. The living had to concentrate on remaining alive. Furthermore, yesterday's episode with the unseen airplanes remained to be dealt with. Men who were certain they had heard the planes had decided against repeating last week's disappointment. Men who were certain that they had all participated in an instance of mass delusion contented themselves with waiting for the moment to say "I told you so!" Still others had no opinion at all. So they sat, mulling over their circumstances, waiting for the day to pass.

Their lack of sleep had begun to tell on the survivors' attitudes and outlook, as well as on their physical well-being. While their daily diet was certainly less than adequate, the rations they received twice each day would sustain life. No one as yet seemed in any mortal danger due to starvation. Everyone would have enjoyed more to drink, but no one seemed to be dying of thirst. Yet their fatigue, mentally even more so than physically, had no means of respite. Men's eyes, once clear and dancing, now gave off a glassy and doltish stare, red-rimmed and bloodshot, sunk deeply into shadowed hollows. Nervous tics and twitches, drooping jaw and lolling tongue became the marks of human beings who no longer cared about social appearances. Their digestive systems had long since begun to absorb every atom of food and water, making the elimination of body wastes unnecessary. But had they needed to do so, the men were far past any point of delicacy. Most of them were almost naked; the few clothes they might have been wearing when pulled onto the raft had disintegrated in the salt water or fallen slack about their skinny loins. They no longer even commented on each other's fetid body odor. To them, the niceties of etiquette were no longer important. Sleep alone mattered, and sleep, they knew, could come only after rescue. Of that much reasoning, their minds were still capable.

So the survivors sat in their torpid state, while at home Labor Day parades and speeches, Labor Day beach parties and picnics, Labor Day baseball doubleheaders happened as usual.

"What day's today?"

"Well, that's easy. Yesterday we had church, no?"

"Yeah. Remember, the bosun made a stink."

"To hell with him. He's a sourpuss anyway."

"Like I say, yesterday we had church, so that meant it was Sunday."

"So today's Monday."

"That all? Seems like three days since we had church."

"What's the date?"

"Woodman's been scratching lines with his knife to keep count."

"Hey, Woodman, what date we up to?"

The second cook looked at the slats between his legs and counted nine gouges in the wood.

"We went down on August 30, right?" Woodman Potter checked for accuracy.

"Never forget that date!"

"Got it circled in red on my calendar!"

"OK, we been floatin' nine days."

"Counting August 30, or since then?"

"Countin', 'course."

"Well, what's today's date?"

"August 39, right?"

"Very funny."

Robert McDaniel counted on his fingers, starting from his left thumb. "August 30, August 31, September 1–2–3–4–5–6– and today is September 7."

"So it's Monday, September 7?"

"Hey, that's Labor Day!"

"How do you know?"

"It's always Labor Day—"

"What is? September 7?"

"No, the first Monday of September."

"I thought the first of September was last week."

"No, the first *Monday* of September, I said."

"That so?'

"Always been the first Monday of September."

"Big baseball day, I remember."

"Oh yes, lots of doubleheaders today, I suppose."

"You a baseball fan, Joe?"

"Not much. I pay attention, but I don't live and die over it."

"Me, I'm a Yankees fan."

"I hate the damned Yankees! I'm a Dodgers fan."

"The Bums of Brooklyn? You gotta be kiddin'!"

"Better than your Giants!"

"The New York Giants will beat the Brooklyn Dodgers every time."

"Well, not this year."

"That so?"

"Last time I looked, the Giants were trailin'."

"That so? Well, they'll probably sweep the double-header today, and they'll be in first place by tonight."

"Come off it! Both you guys is wrong. The Cards are gonna win this one. Then they'll go on and cream the Yankees or whoever the American League puts up."

"The St. Looie Cardinals! What makes you so sure?"

"Pitchin' and hittin', what else?"

"So, lots of teams got pitchin' and hittin' – "

"Not like the Cards. We got ol' Mort Cooper throwin' that screwball to his brother Walker Cooper, and we got this new kid, the rookie—what the hell's his name?— Brewster or Beebe or some such name . . ."

"You mean John Beazley?"

"Yeah, that's his name! How'd you know, Levi? I didn't reckon you to be no major league baseball fan."

"I read the papers," said Levi Walker.

"Yeah, well, this kid can really pitch."

"Who else you got?"

"Well, hitters, of course. We got 'Country' Slaughter and Stan Musial for a start."

"The Yankees got Joe DiMaggio. That's all we need."

"Can't win the pennant with one man."

"How 'bout DiMaggio last year?"

"Could you believe that? Hittin' safely in fifty-six consecutive games!"

"And he woulda kept on goin', iffen Keltner hadn't of made those plays against him in Cleveland."

"Levi, you really do know your baseball. And you ain't even got any of your people playin'."

"Someday we will."

"Don't count on it, Levi. Baseball's a white man's game. Always has been."

"Things could change."

Levi Walker's blasphemy—the idea of a colored man playing major league baseball—ended the conversation.

Robert Bell had listened but not understood much of the men's talk. As a child of missionaries, born in distant Africa, living most of his young life there, Robert had not yet become the sports fan he would subsequently be. Names like Musial and DiMaggio as yet meant little to him. For now, all the eleven-year-old boy could wonder at was why there would be no Negroes playing baseball. At Bouaké and at school in Mamou, the American and Canadian missionary children often played their games with African children. Why should it be any different in North America, where grown men played their sports for money? It was a question that Robert would want to ask once he got home to Nyack. As near to New York City as it was, maybe someone would offer to take him to see the Yankees or the Giants or even the Dodgers in faraway Brooklyn. The he would find out for himself why only white men could play baseball.

By Tuesday, September 8, their tenth day as derelicts at sea, Woodman Potter made it his job to lift everyone's spirits.

"You know what we gotta do? We gotta sing!"

"Sing!"

"Potter, you crazy?"

"No, man, I always feel better when I sing. So do you too!"

"Not me. I can't carry a tune."

"No matter. You can say the words same as the rest."

He began to hum quietly within himself, then louder, until he had settled on a song, and it burst out of his wide mouth.

> *You are my sunshine, my only sunshine!*
> *You make me happy when skies are gray.*
> *You'll never know, dear, how much I love you.*
> *Please don't take my sunshine away.*

Woodman sang his solo a second time, but on the third repetition he was joined by two or three others. On the fourth, more sang, until almost everyone was singing. The song now carried itself. As one man or group of men tired of singing, others took responsibility. The singing might diminish to a single monotone growling out his lines, then swell to full chorus again in a matter of phrases.

"The men kept at the song for what seemed like hours," Bob Bell says. "I'm sure it was far less than that, but time meant nothing to any of us. What would have been utterly boring—dull and tedious beyond anyone's ability to bear—offered us a challenge, to keep the song alive."

Now the raft had two theme songs: "You Are My Sunshine" and "Jesus, Saviour, Pilot Me" — the pilot song, as the men called it. By Bob Bell's recollection, scarcely a day went by thereafter without the singing of both songs, over and over.

"Just as the food game had helped to sustain us during the first week," says Bell, "so now it was singing that became our topic."

Wednesday, September 9, the eleventh day, and still no sign of rescue. Ever since the previous Sunday, when the first aircraft had been heard, the men's ears seemed able to hear even the most distant reverberations from above. Furthermore, many planes passed overhead, or so the incidents of hearing seemed to indicate. Every so often, several times each day, one or another of the men would point aloft; the rest of the raft would wait in anticipation for the sound of a plane en route to somewhere. Perhaps this would be the one that would finally look down and see the raft. Before it was too late.

In Sea Cliff, Long Island, Matilde Koop put her hand on her daughter Ruth's head and prayed, "Lord, bless Toots as she begins a new school term, and help her to be a good girl in school and learn well. Amen."

A kiss on the cheek sent the little girl in bangs and a gingham dress off to Miss Smith's fifth-grade class at the Sea Cliff Public School.

Early in the morning, Joe Greenwell, who had taken upon himself the care of Captain Bogden, noticed how restless the captain seemed. Bogden had been lying in the same position for days, semi-propped in the well, his shoulders resting against the side of the raft. His elevation was barely enough for him to eat and drink, but his vast bulk was constantly soaked by the water filling the well. He had not spoken in several days; not even when Flags Croons had died and was buried at sea. So Greenwell was surprised when suddenly he heard the captain call him by name, in a voice strangely colored by anxiety.

"Mr. Greenwell?"

"Yes, Captain?"

"Mr. Greenwell, our secret is secure with you, right?"

"What secret, Captain?"

"The gold, Mr. Greenwell."

Joe Greenwell's mind had been filled by many thoughts since the first torpedo struck. Never once, however, had he given any thought to the secret cache stored on the *West Lashaway*. Now wearied by insufficient sleep, his mind fuzzy from lack of nourishment, Greenwell struggled to remember the gold bars hidden in the captain's own quarters and elsewhere on the ship.

"What gold, Captain?"

"De Gaulle's gold? The Free French gold!"

Greenwell slid down off the edge of the raft to speak more quietly to the disturbed captain.

"It's all right, Captain Bogden. The gold went down with the ship."

"With the ship! The ship's sinking, you say?"

"The ship's been sunk for more than a week, Captain. Don't you know where you are?"

"We've got to save the ship! Save the gold!" the agitated captain whispered.

"It's too late to save the ship, Captain Bogden." Joe Greenwell tried to calm the man. "We've got to save ourselves now. Just relax, sir."

But Greenwell spoke to no avail. Looking out of eyes in which shone no light of understanding, the deranged captain muttered on about his ship and its secret cargo.

"Mr. Greenwell, did they get the gold?"

"No, Captain Bogden. It went down with the ship."

"All of it? All 50 million dollars' worth?"

"Yes, sir."

"But I didn't have time to scuttle the ship."

"You didn't have to, sir. It sank all by itself, very quickly."

"But you know the regulations, Mr. Greenwell."

"Yes, sir."

" 'From the Secretary of the Navy. Subject — Instructions for Scuttling Merchant Ships. Date — 30 March 1942.' "

"Yes, Captain, I know—"

" 'One. It is the policy of the United States Government that no U.S. ship be permitted to fall into the hands of the enemy.' "

"The *West Lashaway* didn't fall into Jerry's hands, Captain. They shot it out from under us. It went to the bottom in less than two minutes. Now, sir, you just rest."

" 'Two. The ship shall be defended by her armament, by maneuvers, and by every available means as long as possible.' We tried, Mr. Greenwell. Tell them that we tried, but there just wasn't any time."

"Of course, Captain, but nobody's gonna ask us anything. We got sunk, that's all."

" 'When in the judgment of the Master, capture is inevitable, he shall scuttle the ship. Provision should be made to open sea valves and to flood holds and compartments adjacent to machinery spaces, start numerous fires and employ any additional measures to insure certain scuttling of the vessel.' You see, Mr. Greenwell, I didn't have time to follow my orders."

"The ship was scuttled for you, Captain. Don't you remember?"

"I remember my orders, Mr. Greenwell. 'Three. In case the Master is relieved of command of his ship, he shall transfer this letter to his successor and obtain a receipt for it.' "

"But you weren't relieved of command, Captain. We're still under your orders."

"But if I am relieved, Mr. Greenwell, I want you to take command."

"Yes, sir. Now, you just rest easy."

"You're sure they didn't get the Frenchman's gold?"

"No, sir, nobody got it. It all went to the bottom, I'm sure."

"They mustn't get the gold, Mr. Greenwell. Don't tell them where we've hidden it aboard the ship. Not even the bosun knows about the gold, Mr. Greenwell. Just you and Mr. Pearson and I."

"Yes, sir."

"It's General de Gaulle's gold, you know, Mr. Greenwell. The Free French. The Germans mustn't get the Frenchman's 50 million in gold."

"Shh, Captain, don't talk any more about it. The other men are listening."

"Then close the wardroom door, Mr. Greenwell. We can't have every member of the crew listening at the door. Close the door!"

Joe Greenwell squeezed down into the well to cradle the raving captain and muffle his cries.

"What's going on, Joe?" George Marano asked.

"I dunno, George. I think the captain's gone looney."

"What's this about gold?"

"Aw, nothin'. He's just not talkin' sense, is all."

"He going to make it?"

"Sure. He's just hurt inside. Losin' the ship and all, it's busted him up pretty bad, what with the burns, too. He'll be OK."

By this time, everyone's attention had zeroed in on Joe Greenwell.

"Is there anything I can do, Mr. Greenwell?" asked Ethel Bell.

"Sure is, Mrs. Bell. You can pray."

Benjamin Bogden died later that morning.

"For all of us," says Bob Bell, "the death of our captain was a serious blow to our morale. Not that he had been a strong leader. Ever since the second or third day at most, he had declined physically, until he hardly spoke at all. The major responsibilities had been taken over by Joe and the bosun. But the presence of Captain Bogden meant something. We were sure that as long as he was aboard the raft, the men would obey any command of his; there'd be order and routine. Now, with him dead, we worried what might happen with the captain gone."

Once more the men removed the body from the well, placing it on the end of the raft opposite the courtesy curtain that Captain Bogden had ordered for Ethel Bell's privacy. Once more, Joe Greenwell asked Mrs. Bell to conduct a funeral service.

"Before I pray," she began, "I want as many of us as are able to say together Psalm 23. I know many of you men have heard it with the children."

"The Lord is my shepherd . . ."

Their voices rose and fell with the waves, swept by fear, cracking with emotion.

"Yea, though I walk through the valley of the shadow of death . . ."

Which of them would be next? The kid had been a weakling, not the sort with any spine to stand up in the face of hard times. But Captain Bogden? Who would have supposed him to be a victim? And if Captain Bogden had been so vulnerable, which man could presume to be stronger?

"Now let's say the Lord's Prayer," Ethel Bell continued.

" . . . but deliver us from evil, for thine is the kingdom and the power and the glory forever. Amen."

Deliver us? There could be only one deliverance that mattered. A sea plane, a ship, even a friendly submarine. Deliverance! After that happens, lots of time for religion and prayer. Deliver us!

"Our heavenly Father," the woman prayed, "we commit to you and to your loving grace the soul of our captain, Mr. Bogden. We are troubled by his death. We are frightened. Now we ask you, Father, to watch over us especially. Keep us from harming each other. Keep us from being unkind to each other. Help us to know how to help the person sitting next to us and across from us. And, please, dear God, bring us to safety soon. In Jesus' name. Amen."

"The captain must have been injured internally," said Joe Greenwell many years later, "because he had no external wounds that would have amounted to anything. He was one of the finest men I ever knew—certainly the best I ever worked for on a ship. He was the type of man who could have gone through a disaster such as ours with the best of the crowd. Benjamin Bogden was no quitter; that's why I'm sure he must have been hurt far worse than any of us knew or he let on. He was a very fine man."

In spite of his mother's attempts to keep him from watching, Robert Bell was determined to see what the sharks would do.

"The men slid the captain's body into the ocean as quietly as possible so as not to attract the sharks," Bell remembers. "But they might as well have made an announcement to the sharks. Almost as soon as the body hit the water, the sharks were at it. It was the most destructive, humanly agonizing moment of my life—far more terrifying than the sinking of the ship or the German submarine firing off their weapons.

"Here was a man I had known, almost as kind to me as my own father. Now I watched as his body was slashed and torn to shreds by the omnivorous sharks. I watched in spite of my horror, unable to take my eyes away from the scene, while the sharks shook the body as a dog shakes a rat. His blood discolored the foam created by the sharks, and it even seemed that they were turning on each other in their frenzy. I have never been so immobilized by fear, and still I couldn't do anything but watch."

"Robert!" His mother's limp and weak hand scarcely grazed his cheek as she attempted to slap him. "I told you to close your eyes!"

"Yes, Mother."

"Listen up, you guys," said James. Owen. "Captain Bogden was a good man, and all that, but he was too hurt to give us the kind of leadership we need. Now that he's dead, I don't propose that we should be without a leader any longer. So I'm declaring myself in command of this raft. I'm the best organizer here, and from the looks of things, I'm also in the best shape. So, from now on, you take your orders from me."

"Says who, Owen?" Joe Greenwell retorted. "I'm the senior officer on board!"

"Yeah, but you haven't done nothin' but play nursemaid to the captain. I'm the real leader here, and everybody knows it."

The bosun's will, like steel tempered in a Pittsburgh foundry furnace, could not be broken. He had determined to take charge of the raft, and he did.

Robert Bell felt a new chill of fear as the bosun spoke. From the beginning the boy had been frightened of this coarse and bitter man; but as long as Captain Bogden had been alive, Robert believed that the bosun was under his control. As the first few days passed and the captain's health declined, Robert had come to believe in Joe Greenwell and George Marano, the two men after Captain Bogden whom the boy could trust to protect his mother and the children. Now with the captain gone, the boy's worst fears loomed before him. James Owen in command? The bosun whose every word and every gesture communicated hatred for all that Ethel Bell represented? The man who never missed an opportunity to cause Robert physical pain? The bosun giving orders!

"OK, Mrs. Bell, I want you and the kids to get into the doughnut."

Owen indicated with his thumb the cork dinghy still tied to the stern of the raft.

"You must be kiddin', Owen," said George Marano. "That's hardly big enough for two men. You're not putting a woman and four children in it! Can't be done!"

"Shut up, Marano! You heard me, Mrs. Bell."

"Mr. Owen, I refuse to move. Mr. Marano is right."

Woodman Potter leaned over and said to Ethel Bell, "Don't never get in that doughnut, Mrs. Bell. Bosun, he don't care what he does. He'll get you all in that doughnut somehow, and sure 'nough, he'll cut you loose without rations!"

The bosun glared at Potter, then at the woman; but he said no more at the moment. Clearly, he was biding his time. His opportunity came with the distributions of the second rations. Mrs. Bell had shifted her position slightly, which caused the children on her right to fall against the oars serving as a mast for the sail. The makeshift mast fell inward, loosening the piece of canvas and causing the sail to fold.

"Damn you and your clumsy kids!" the bosun shouted. "You got no business being on this raft anyway. You oughta be with the other passengers!"

"Careful, Owen," Joe Greenwell warned.

"Oh, shut up, Greenwell! These rafts were made for officers and crew, not for friggin' women and children! You mark my words, you'll regret the day you let these five take your rations and your space!"

"Don't pay any attention to him, Mrs. Bell," George Marano cautioned. "He's all talk."

"Oh yeah, Marano?"

"That's right, Owen. The lady and her kids are safe, so long as you're the only threat. The other men and me, we'll take care of them."

That Wednesday evening, after tempers had calmed and the rations had been eaten, Mary Bell cried for Captain

Bogden. Her mother bent her face into the young girl's hair, trying to comfort her.

"Don't cry in sorrow, Mary. I'm sure the captain's far better off right now than we are."

"You think he's in heaven, Mother?"

"That's not for me to judge, Mary. But we do know that he was a very good man, especially kind to all of us."

"I want to die, too, Mother!"

"No, Mary, no! God has important work for you to do. For me, too. There's still time for Him to rescue us. You must believe that!"

Once more, a rainbow in full magnificence arched the sky.

"See, children," said the woman to the girls and boys on either side of her, "that rainbow is God's message of hope to us. God takes our tears, like raindrops, and by the sunlight of His love, He turns them into something beautiful."

EIGHTEEN

LOOKING BACK, LOOKING AHEAD

Throughout that night and for the next three days a sort of madness infected many of the remaining seventeen survivors. Twice death had visited their raft. The young signalman, the mature captain. Death, it seemed, was no respecter of persons. Their deaths had come surprisingly, without any violent symptoms, without obvious and slow demise, without warning. Now a pall of fear enshrouded the raft. Not just the fear of dying. For some of the men, in their increasingly demoralized state of mind, dying might even have seemed to be a wise option. Better to die quickly, apparently almost painlessly, like Flags and the captain, than to sit and waste away. But the thought of those sharks! That was something else. Death was one thing; being torn apart by those ravenous monsters was quite another matter.

And how could anyone feel sure and safe anymore? Each death, each burial at sea, had been followed by an unspoken benefit: more space, more leg room, more food and water for those yet alive. Who could tell when someone might decide to throw overboard not a corpse but a living comrade, just to make the raft more comfortable! Who would be the first victim? Or could there be a mass slaughter? Would the two blacks be forced off the raft? Would the five Latin Americans be ditched next? Would, at last, the woman and children be fed to the sharks? Was anyone safe? Would anyone survive?

On Thursday, September 10, U-boat *69*, in the same class as *U-66*, infiltrated the defenses of Chesapeake Bay. Commanded by Karl Metzler, who later earned the Knight's Cross, *U-69* deposited twelve mines in the Chesapeake channel off the United States Navy's most important home base, the yards and ways, the docks and piers of Norfolk, Portsmouth, Newport News, and Hampton, Virginia. Then *U-69* slipped away and out once more to prowl the open Atlantic. This mission was the last German submarine attack in American coastal waters.

Looking back four decades later, Bob Bell can trace the beginnings of character traits developed as a result of his ordeal on the raft. To those who come to know him and his story, the correlation between childhood experience and adult behavior becomes apparent. All indicators point to an indelible stamp of memory upon his character. Details of his rescue and its immediate aftermath remain to be told. But at this point in the narrative, it may be appropriate to look beyond the raft story and see how the events of this man's life seem to flow from his one transforming experience as an eleven-year-old boy.

Following their dramatic rescue, recuperation and recovery from the trauma of their suffering were of first importance to the Bells. After eventually arriving in New York, then spending some time with her anxious parents and sister in Toronto, Ethel Bell settled with her children in Nyack. But as soon as she was able, the missionary heroine began to travel throughout the United States and Canada recounting the saga of the raft and God's providence. For the welfare of Mary and Robert, she sought a boarding school where her children would receive the benefits of Christian nurture in a setting marked by caring.

When someone recommended a home and school for missionaries' children in Batesburg, South Carolina, Ethel Bell believed this to be the very place she had been looking for. So Robert and Mary arrived in South Carolina in the late summer of 1943 to continue their schooling at the Westervelt Children's Home, which occupied the campus of an abandoned junior college. But from the outset the Bell children recognized that their mother had made a mistake. Their year there can be summed up as one unmitigated misery after another. Of the 120 children in the home, most were anxious and rebellious at having been left behind by parents who were pursuing their own missionary vocation overseas. Furthermore, the staff seem to have been drawn straight out of *Oliver Twist*.

A spirit of meanness seemed to govern the adults supervising the children's home. They set up absurd social regulations intended to keep the sexes apart; their rigidity even extended to separating sisters from brothers and treating with suspicion any desire of family members to spend time together. Bizarre methods of discipline, including forced public repentance for the most insignificant acts of childish folly, kept the children in cowering fear.

"We lived under such stress," says Mary Bell Whitbeck, "that girls my age and older, well into our physical maturity, found our menstrual cycles disrupted."

Food served to these children at Batesburg tasted little better that the diet the Bells had known on the raft. Because of the war, quantity was limited.

"Grits, grits, and more grits," Bob Bell winces as he recalls the staple at every meal. "Even if the food had been tasty, there wasn't enough, and you had to be thirteen years old to be granted second portions. There was no such thing as a snack, and the rules of the home denied the children all rights to personal property. I sometimes lay awake nights at that 'concentration camp' in South Carolina wondering why my life had been spared on the raft if only to come to this dreadful place."

No parents could have known the truth about the Westervelt Children's Home; else, they would have never have sent their children nor required them to remain. Certainly Ethel Bell had no understanding of her children's plight. The few pieces of mail she had received — children's letters were routinely read and censored by the staff before allowed to be mailed — had indicated homesickness, nothing more. But at Christmas of 1943 Ethel Bell went to South Carolina to be with her children, breaking off her itinerary of deputation meetings. She was dismayed at what she found.

"Mother ought to have taken us away from there without delay," her son says, "but her options were limited. She felt obligated to the Lord and to her mission society to continue on her itinerary. You must understand how much in demand she was to tell our raft story, and it was effective in motivating audiences for mission support. Mother may have been wrong in her priorities, but that's how she saw them. She could scarcely send us to live with her parents, Grandpa and Grandma Roffe in Toronto, or with her sister Nell, whose health wasn't strong."

Instead, Ethel Bell informed the proprietors that she would be removing her children at the end of the school year.

"You've trusted God, my children, through far worse circumstances than these," she told Mary and Robert. "Now trust Him again. Make the best of your hardship, and try to be an encouragement to other children who may not have your spiritual strength."

"We accepted Mother's decision to leave us there for another six months," says Bell, "even though we would have much preferred to go anywhere, just so we left the Westervelts."

"Looking back, Bell can now say that the oppression and psychological brutality he experienced in that unwholesome environment were made bearable by the realization that he had indeed endured far worse — and had survived!

On June 6, 1944 — D-day on the beaches of Normandy — Mary and Robery celebrated their own "Deliverance Day" from a year of misery. Ethel Bell returned and took her children to Nyack, where she settled the family while she made her plans for the future. Her brother Paul Roffe and his family were on furlough from Peru and living next door to the Bells in the compound of homes maintained at Nyack by the Christian and Missionary Alliance.

In September 1944 Robert enrolled with his sister at

Nyack High School—he in grade eight, Mary in grade ten. A family named Woodberry, missionaries to China, were also on furlough and living nearby in Nyack. The Woodberrys had sent two older sons, Earl and Fred, to boarding school on Long Island; their youngest son, Dudley, would be enrolling the following year. Ethel Bell investigated The Stony Brook School and found it to be quite unlike the previous boarding institution. She applied for her son's admission to ninth grade. On September 10, 1945, he enrolled at Stony Brook.

The Stony Brook School is a college-preparatory school set in a historic village on the North Shore of Long Island. Founded in 1922, Stony Brook remains a Christian school, balancing a rigorous academic curriculum with concern for teaching its students to love the Lord their God and their neighbors as themselves. Now co-educational, in the fall of 1945, when Bell arrived in grade nine, it was very much a boys' school, dominated by strong men who served as mentors and models. Stony Brook was a small school, with only twenty-two boys in Robert Bell's ninth grade. One of these, Bruce C. Dodd, Jr., became a lifelong friend.

"For me, Bob Bell represents what Stony Brook is all about," says Bruce Dodd, now president of Rabun Gap School in Georgia. "He was—and is—the genuine article. Even as schoolboys, his classmates knew Bob as utterly honest, utterly dependable. I never saw anyone more caring about others, especially the underdog.

"Sure, he got into the same mischief as the rest of us," Dodd continues. "But whenever it came time for a significant decision, a real moral choice, we knew what side Bob would be on."

At Stony Brook, Robert Bell found what had been

267

missing in his life since his father's death nine years before: men whose example he could emulate. Men like Dr. Frank E. Gaebelein, Stony Brook's founding headmaster, and Pierson Curtis, the school's senior master, set a tone of devout Christian commitment blended with concern for academic rigor and appreciation for sports, camping, the arts, and fine converation.

Frank Gaebelein had gathered to work with him a faculty of earnest, industrious men who enjoyed the atmosphere of a boys' boarding school with its close relationships among classmates and between teacher and pupil. Of these men, none stood higher than Gaebelein's long-time associate Pierson Curtis. Like Bell, he was the son of missionaries, accustomed to being sent away to school. He had a special place in his heart for boys like the Woodberrys and Robert Bell, and he worked especially to help such youngsters in readjusting to American life, in overcoming homesickness, and in reaching out for independence.

In his four years at Stony Brook, Robert Bell grew from a scrawny adolescent, still bearing some signs of his malnourishment, to a broad-chested young man. He loved sports and never missed a season of participation. In the fall of his first year, another newcomer to Stony Brook was a young teacher of science and mathematics, Marvin W. Goldberg. Looking back over four decades, Marvin Goldberg, now Stony Brook's senior master recalls Bob Bell.

"When The Stony Brook School opened that September 1945, the news was still full of excitement. In the summer months one dramatic event upon another had filled newspaper and radio reports. Hitler, a suicide; Berlin surrenders; V-E day; the first atomic bombs; Japan's surrender exactly one month before the new term's registration day. And so it went.

"Of all the war stories," Goldberg continues, "nothing seems to stir Americans like adventures on the high seas. People talked endlessly about Captain Eddie Rickenbacker's long difting voyage alone in a raft. Now in the midst of all this news and notoriety comes a celebrity of our own, a freshman named Robert Bell. He came, as it were, right out of history into our dormitories, our classrooms, and onto our playing fields."

Marvin Goldberg makes it clear that young Robert Bell did not seek to attract attention to himself with his story. "People requested it—churches, other schools, Rotary Club, all clamored for the opportunity to share the excitement of this miracle.

"But through it all, Robert retained a serene stability, a mature composure. He was an extraordinary young man in so many respects. His confidence in God was so deep-rooted that it took him far beyond what a teacher or coach would have expected from his native ability. I never taught a more receptive student; I never coached a more team-conscious athlete."

Goldberg pauses to choose his words carefully. "It has been my observation that Bob Bell's character has not deviated one iota in almost forty years. He is still cheerful to be around. It's an uplifting experience just to be with him."

Bell's Latin and history teacher was a former GI named Val Harto. "What I liked about Val," says Bell, "was his ability to see right through the baloney. We never could get away with any nonsense in his classes. I enjoyed babysitting in the Hartos' apartment. They always kept something in the refrigerator for me to eat.

"What I got from Stony Brook," says Bell, "were strong academic standards—I really had to study!—vigorous athletic participation, close supervision by the teachers living right there among us, and a wholesome Christian atmostphere. It wasn't sanctimonious or pious. We were boys and our teachers were men—just plain human beings—but we knew that there was something special about the school that affected us. That something was the person and teachings of Jesus Christ.

"For the first time in my life," Bell goes on, "I felt like I belonged! I was important to other people because I was part of a team. Our teachers made us feel worthy, and that encouraged us all."

From Stony Brook, Robert Bell matriculated in the fall of 1949 at Nyack College, where his parents had met nearly thirty years before. There, too, Bob Bell met his wife, Ruth Martha Koop, also known as "Toots." Young people whose lives have been disrupted by culture shock or by personal cataclysm often seek security in early marriage. So it was not surprising that Bob Bell should ask Ruth Koop to marry him midway through their college years. The wedding took place on August 30, 1952, the tenth anniversary of the sinking of the *West Lashaway*.

Upon graduation from Nyack College, Bob and Ruth Bell accepted positions on the ministerial staff of the First Alliance Church of Atlanta, Georgia. Bob was to be the assistant pastor for youth ministries and director of music; Ruth would be church organist. Presumably they were both in final preparation for missionary service overseas. It was everyone's expectation, including Bob Bell's.

But while in Atlanta he began teaching as a substitute in Atlanta's inner-city schools.

"I hadn't thought of myself as a teacher," he says. "I'd received all my education with the intention of finding my vocation in some area of full-time Christian ministry—the pastorate, perhaps, but more likely in foreign missions. How could I not become a missionary!"

For two years Bell substituted on a regular, though not quite daily, basis. He found teaching to be highly enjoyable.

"I also learned," he says, "that there are frequent opportunities to be of help to students and parents. That, too, can be a full-time Christian ministry."

As time went on, Bell began to seek opportunities to begin formal graduate studies in education. Thus an enormous internal struggle began.

"I didn't want to leave the pastoral work unless it was to become a missionary. For a time I assumed that the pleasure I found in teaching was no different from other kinds of temptations that might take me out of God's will for my life. But it just seemed that I couldn't get away from teaching as a profession. Finally, I quite literally gave up struggling. I simply said to the Lord, 'I'm not going to wrestle over this choice anymore.' "

Within a week of reaching that decision, Bell received in the mail a flyer announcing summer graduate courses leading to a master's degree in education being taught at Farmingdale, Long Island, fairly near Ruth's parent's home. As if from nowhere someone presented the Bells with a gift of money sufficient to pay the summer school tuition. Taking these indications as a message from God, Bob Bell resigned from his Atlanta church position in

June 1957 and began summer classes a few days later.

Midway through the six-week course, he was in the library of the State University of New York at Farmingdale when he saw a familiar face. It was the wife of his former teacher at Stony Brook, Val Harto, who had become principal of the local public elementary school in the village of Stony Brook. Bell told her his story and the fact that he had no position to go to when his summer course ended.

"Within a week," he says, "Val Harto had hired me to teach third grade, starting that September! Ruth and I could hardly believe how God had worked things out for us! I was so wet behind the ears. Fortunately for my first pupils and me, the school was on double sessions, and I'd been assigned to teach only in the afternoons. Marjorie Lathham, a master teacher, taught the morning class. I would spend four hours each morning watching her teach — then I'd do the same lessons in the afternoon. What a student-teacher experience! Every teachers' college should offer some similar training."

For eight years Bob Bell taught elementary classes in Stony Brook's public schools, soon to be known as the Three Village Central School District. In 1965 he moved from the classroom to an administrator's office, becoming assistant principal to his own former teacher, Val Harto.

"I had admired Val Harto since I was a boy; I do so still today," says Bell. "His standards of excellence, his desire for self-improvement, helped to shape me. He has always been fair, forward-looking, eager to develop a strong staff of teachers. I respected him so highly, it took twenty years of working with him before I was able to call him anything but Mr. Harto!"

In 1975, Bob Bell received the appointment as principal of his own school, the Setauket School in the Three Village Central School District. He opened his first faculty meeting by announcing that he would do so with prayer, simply because it is his custom to pray for guidance and to give thanks to God. In a secular community and in the state whose regents'-approved prayer had been waived as unconstitutional by the Supreme Court, Bell's forthrightness in declaring his spiritual dependence took some of his colleagues by surprise. But he prospered as principal, winning the enthusiastic support of parents in his constituency.

Yet something was about to happen in the professional career of Bob Bell that many men would have found crushing. A series of changes within the school district's hierarchy resulted in Bell's reassignment from school to school, almost on an annual basis. One year he would be principal of a certain elementary school; the next, principal of another; the year following, he was back at the first school, now serving as assistant principal. All these changes and maneuvers were quite legitimate and above board, tied to a system of seniority and local necessity; nonetheless, they subjected one man to extraordinary chagrin and self-doubt.

How did he manage to overcome the humiliation, the frustration of being regarded as an administrative utility player, the first man off the bench?

"I won't deny the disappointment," says Bell, "but the facts speak for themselves. I've always known that these changes were caused neither by political scheming nor personal and professional failure on my part. Family—especially my wife, Ruth—friends, and colleagues have been most reassuring.

"Then there's past experience to rely on. I know at first-hand how God sometimes chooses to place us in difficult circumstances, not to punish us but to give us a chance to be what St. Francis of Assisi called 'an instrument of Thy peace.' So, whatever the circumstances of our lives, they become a challenge. As we meet those challenges, those difficulties, they become the means of blessing for other people."

Bell pauses for a moment to reflect. "The raft experience is an example. In one manner of speaking, I wouldn't wish such an ordeal upon anyone; sometimes I can hardly believe that we endured what we did and survived! But in another respect, I wouldn't have missed it—not just because of the adventure but because of all the people I know personally who have been encouraged to persevere in their own tough times, simply because they heard our story of God's deliverance.

"God has blessed Ruth and me," Bob Bell affirms, "in spite of any apparent setbacks in my career. We've been able to establish a stable home here in Stony Brook. We are active in the fellowship of the Three Village Church. Both our daughters, Carol and Kris, have graduated from the Stony Brook School; I've been able to serve as president of the Stony Brook Alumni Association. We've been able to contribute in small ways to the life of the community. It's a good life, and I have no regrets, only thanksgiving."

Without spirit, without appetite, merely from force of custom, the seventeen survivors ate their Saturday rations. Ethel Bell prayed her customary prayer, whispered hoarsely over the children's bent heads. Her prayer seemed almost as mechanical as the act of eating that followed. Neither could now be more than a gesture, a concession to some lingering measure of hope. The food would not sustain them, the prayer could not deliver them. Nonetheless they ate while the woman and children prayed.

While the *West Lashaway's* survivors were welcoming the coming on of dawn on Saturday morning, September 12, in the Greenwich time zone, four thousand miles away, it was already midmorning. Five hundred and fifty miles south of Cape Palma on the Liberian coast of West Africa, Admiral Dönitz Polar Bear group of submarines, led by Kapitänleutnant Werner Hartenstein's *U-156*, swept in a curve across the surface, heading for the Indian Ocean. Precisely at 9:37 A.M. a watchman spotted a wisp of smoke on the horizon. Hartenstein turned his boat to pursue the telltale smoke.

All day his *U-156* stalked the still-unknown ship, waiting for the cover of night. By 8:00 P.M. he could hear music from the ship's salons. At exactly 8:07 P.M. Hartenstein recorded his position as 5° 0′ south, 11° 8′ west, and then fired two torpedoes. Within fifteen minutes the 20,000-ton HMS *Laconia* had disappeared, spilling into the sea its nearly three thousand passengers.

Built in 1922, the *Laconia* had been a commercial liner, pride of the Cunard White Star fleet. In fact, in 1938, when Ethel Bell and her children returned to Africa, she had booked their passage on the *Laconia*. Since 1939, however, the ocean liner had been coverted to troopship duty, though still commanded by a Cunard captain, Rudolph Sharp.

In addition to wounded British soldiers being repatriated, the *Laconia's* manifest included many women and children, British dependents returning home after having been stranded in Egypt and East Africa since the war began. A few moments earlier they had been enjoying their evening meal and the relief of cooler darkness after a torrid day in the equatorial sun. Now they floundered in the ocean while a shoal of barracuda attacked. Like Ethel Bell, their sister in misery, these women prayed, "O God, help us!"

Cruising through this scene of ruin, Werner Hartenstein was troubled by the plight of these helpless women and children. But he was soon more deeply struck by the realization that his quarry, HMS *Laconia*, had also been carrying some eighteen hundred Italian prisoners of war. By accident, by random bad luck, Hartenstein knew he could be blamed for the loss of Axis comrades-in-arms. Hartenstein was no novice commander; at age thirty-two he had already sunk ten ships, amounting to almost 100,000 tons. But the knowledge that he was responsible for hundreds, even thousands, of helpless victims was more than he could ignore. To abandon them would be inhumane.

Acting unilaterally, Werner Hartenstein ordered a wireless message, plain and uncoded, in both English and German, requesting help from any potential rescue vessels in the area. He also promised all ships safe passage. Then he began loading onto *U-156* as many people as the U-boat could hold.

In his Paris headquarters, Admiral Dönitz, informed of the *Laconia* mishap, ordered *U-507*, commanded by Harro Schacht, and two other U-boats to proceed to the aid of *U-156*. Upon arriving, these submarines found *U-156* overloaded and attempting to tow lifeboats crowded with more victims. Then further catastrophe. An Allied

B-24 Liberator spotted the surfaced subs and attacked the mission of mercy, damaging Hartenstein's boat. When Dönitz got word of this latest irony, he wrote an order against any future attempt "of any kind . . . at rescuing the crews of ships sunk." His order continues:

> *This prohibition applies to the picking up of men in the water and putting them in lifeboats, righting capsized lifeboats and handing over food and water. Rescue runs counter to the primary demands of warfare for the destruction of ships and their crews.*

Dönitz concluded his order with these telling words:

> *Be harsh, bearing in mind that the enemy takes no regard of women and children in his bombing attacks on German cities.*

In the first week of May 1945, after Hitler had disappeared and was presumed dead in his bunker, Admiral Karl Dönitz reluctantly filled the role of Fuhrer. On May 5, 1945, he sent his comrade-in-arms, Admiral Hans von Friedeburg, to Allied headquarters to negotiate Germany's surrender. At the Nuremberg Trials, concluded in October 1946, Dönitz was found guilty of war crimes for having "deliberately ordered the killing of survivors of shipwrecked vessels, whether enemy or neutral." Sentenced to ten years' imprisonment, Karl Dönitz served until his release in 1956. To his dying day, Christmas Eve of 1980, the grand admiral denied that he had ever ordered the slaughter of shipwreck survivors.

But on Saturday, September 12, 1942, Ethel Bell and

her children knew nothing about the fate of the *Laconia*, on which they had once voyaged. Nor could they presume to judge the guilt or innocence of their enemies. Instead, on this the fourteenth day of their agony, all the Bells could do was pray. And hope. And daydream. And pray.

Sunday, September 13 —
Thursday, September 17
NINETEEN
AT THEIR WIT'S END

Another busy Sunday for the Roffes in Toronto.

All week, since receiving the telegram from the Alliance headquarters in New York, Ethel Bell's parents and sister had attempted to learn more information about Ethel and the children—their whereabouts, their condition. But long-distance phone calls to New York City were restricted for private citizens because of wartime conditions. Besides, even if Alfred Roffe had been able to reach the office of his friend Alfred C. Snead, foreign secretary of the Christian and Missionary Alliance, what else would he have been able to communicate? Nothing. Nobody knew anything, except that the *West Lashaway* had been officially listed as "missing"—not yet "lost at sea," but that status certainly would soon follow.

All they could do was pray and enlist the support of others who would pray with them. Thus all across the city of Toronto—a city of churches, a city known as "Toronto the Good"—on that Sunday morning, September 13, ministers such as Dr. Oswald J. Smith, pastor of The People's Church on Bloor Street, and the Reverend Robert Gordon at Oakwood Baptist Church—as well as Christian and Missionary Alliance pastors throughout the Province of Ontario—led their congregations in praying specifically, fervently for an unknown woman and her children.

At the Roffes' own church, Alfred Roffe himself stood before the assembled audience and spoke:

"As many of you know, Mary and I expected to have the joy of worshiping today with our younger daughter Ethel and our grandchildren, Mary and Robert. But God, in His providence, has chosen to delay that joy and to test our trust in His love and grace. Ethel's ship is missing and has been for at least a week, probably longer. We don't know what has happened, but we do know that our God is faithful.

"I want to read a passage from Psalm 107. Then may I ask you to join in singing a hymn of prayer and praise?"

The seventy-five-year-old man adjusted his glasses and bent his white head to read the text.

> *They that go down to the sea in ships, that do business in great waters; These see the works of the LORD, and his wonders in the deep. For he commandeth, and raiseth the stormy wind, which lifteth up the waves thereof. They mount up to the heaven, they go down again to the depths: their soul is melted because of trouble. They reel to and fro, and stagger like a drunken man, and are at their wit's end. Then they cry unto the Lord in their trouble, and he bringeth them out of their distresses. He maketh the storm a calm, so that the waves thereof*

> *are still. Then are they glad because they be quiet;*
> *so he bringeth them unto their desired haven. Oh*
> *that men would praise the Lord for his goodness,*
> *and for all his wonderful works to the children of*
> *men!*

Tears streaming, the father read the words again: "Oh that men would praise the Lord for his goodness!"

Then, setting down his Bible, he reached for the hymnal. "I want us to sing for our encouragement and hope a great hymn, number 356. While you're turning to it, let me tell you something about this hymn.

"The words were written by William Whiting in 1860—that's eighty-two years ago. He dedicated his poem with this citation—'For those at sea. These men see the works of the Lord, and His wonders in the deep.' As you can tell from what I've just read, William Whiting had in mind the description of Psalm 107. But in his poem, the hymn writer takes each element of danger at sea and directs a prayer to each member of the Trinity.

"Something else to note about this hymn. Its music was composed by John B. Dykes, one of the great composers of hymn tunes such as 'Holy, Holy, Holy' and 'The King of Love My Shepherd Is.' Dykes gave names to his hymn tunes, and as you can see, he called this one 'Melita.' That's the ancient name for the Island of Malta, where St. Paul landed safely after his shipwreck in the Mediterranean.

"So," Alfred Roffe went on, "this hymn has come to be known as 'The Navy Hymn.' It's still sung by our sailors, who face storms at sea. But nowadays, they also face the possibility of danger from the guns of other ships, from airplane bombs, and from submarine torpedoes.

Many persons at sea need our prayers — not just Ethel and our grandchildren — so let us lift up to our Father all those who may be in desperate need right now."

He nodded to the church organist, who struck the C major chord; then the congregation sang all four stanzas of "The Navy Hymn."

> *Eternal Father, strong to save,*
> *Whose arm hath bound the restless wave,*
> *Who bidd'st the mighty ocean deep*
> *Its own appointed limits keep:*
> *O hear us when we cry to Thee*
> *For those in peril on the sea.*
>
> *O Christ, whose voice the waters heard*
> *And hushed their raging at Thy word,*
> *Who walkedst on the foaming deep,*
> *And calm amidst its rage did sleep:*
> *O hear us when we cry to Thee*
> *For those in peril on the sea.*
>
> *Most Holy Spirit, who didst brood*
> *Upon the chaos dark and rude,*
> *And bid its angry tumult cease,*
> *And give, for wild confusion, peace:*
> *O hear us when we cry to Thee*
> *For those in peril on the sea.*
>
> *O Trinity of love and power,*
> *Our brethren shield in danger's hour;*
> *From rock and tempest, fire and foe,*
> *Protect them wheresoe'er they go;*
> *Thus evermore shall rise to thee*
> *Glad hymns of praise from land and sea.*

"Let us pray," the father said.

The third Sunday—their fifteenth day, the beginning of their third week on the raft—passed in a much more somber mood than had the previous Sunday. With the bosun in command, there was no thought of a public worship service; if asked, he would not have allowed one. Knowing this, Ethel Bell confined herself to speaking only to the children. They sang more softly than before; they recited their Scripture passages more tentatively, with a flickering glance every so often in the bosun's direction, as if hoping to avoid some unpleasant word from him.

By late afternoon the second round of rations had been distributed. James Owen had been quiet throughout the day. Now he spoke.

"Listen, everybody. We're getting low on food. Starting tomorrow, it's one meal a day, so eat up now. We won't have rations again until sundown tomorrow."

His words—so stark, so real—cut through any fantasy. For two weeks, the survivors had been floating along on a regular routine of two meals each day. True, the diet was restricted, the quantity limited; but it had been there without fail. Now a new regimen had been ordered. How long before it too would be revised? How much longer before one meal a day reduced to one meal every other day? How much longer?

As dusk approached, each survivor sat in silence, slowly coming to grips with the truth. This morsel of food—so unpalatable, so bland, so much taken for granted until now—seemed like a precious jewel in the hand. It must be treasured; it must be examined and appreciated before it disappeared into the parched mouth. It would be the last food consumed for the next twenty-four hours.

"I don't remember who saw it first," says Bob Bell, "but all of a sudden, that Sunday evening, there was a PBY directly overhead — in plain sight, this time. We saw the pilot, and best of all, he saw us."

Jubilation! Men almost past the point of hope seemed suddenly revived. Weak as they were, they jumped up and twisted their necks to peer past the canopy and see the United States Navy star. In their excitement, the survivors forgot all about balancing the raft.

"Easy does it!" the bosun warned. "Let's not dump this damned thing! We still got company out there in the water!"

The pilot had tipped his wings to acknowledge the frantic waving of burlap sacks and any other article of clothing the men could rip off their backs.

"He's seen us all right!"

"You betcha!"

"I knew one of those navy flyboys would come through!"

"Sure took 'em long enough!"

"Who cares? They've found us now!"

"God bless America!"

"God bless Mrs. Bell and her prayers!"

The plane circled the raft at an altitude of about two hundred feet.

"What's he doin' that for?"

"Checkin' on us."

"What for? He's seen us, ain't he?"

"Yeah, but he's tryin' to identify us. See if we're Yanks or maybe Jerrys."

"We're Yanks! Can't he tell we're no Krauts?"

"Not from up there."

"Probably also checking on his coordinates. He's got

to get an accurate reading, or else he'll never find us again."

"Find us again? Watcha talkin' about?"

"Well, stupid, he's not about to land and take us all aboard at once! He'll get his bearing, then go back to his base and bring out some buddies to help."

"Or maybe he'll guide a ship our way. They do that, you know. Navy calls it 'Air-Sea Rescue.' "

Now the pilot aimed his seaplane in a pass over the raft, no more than fifty feet about the sail.

"Get the lady and kids in line where he can see them."

With a burst of power, the plane shot away. Then banking steeply, the pilot brought his aircraft back over the raft. A door opened and out fell a package, a simple cardboard box. It struck the water like a brick, collapsing the box and spilling its contents across the surface of the water, not more than twenty feet from the raft.

Ham sandwiches!

"Imagine our disappointment," says Bob Bell, "as we saw that food floating for a fraction of a minute before the sharks gobbled it up!"

Men cursed the sharks and wept openly in frustration.

But within minutes the PBY had circled and was heading back in another dive over the raft. With engines roaring, the plane again dropped a package, wrapped this time in a yellow, waterproof canvas. This container held together as it smacked the water.

"Chico," the bosun ordered, "go get it in the doughnut."

Isabelino Pacheco moved from the raft to the dinghy and rowed a few yards to the slicker.

"Heads up! Here they come again!"

A third time the navy plane passed by, so close that the crewmen's faces were perfectly visible.

"They were smiling," Bob Bell remembers. "They'd done their job well, and they were satisfied. We were laughing and crying for joy, waving our arms, hugging each other. We knew our rescue was certain, probably that same evening."

The third drop fell close to the second, a smaller container tied to a life jacket. Pacheco retrieved both drops and rowed back to the raft.

"Here, give 'em to me," said the bosun. "OK, Rodriguez, you and me, we'll take charge."

Together the bosun and the cook opened the two packages. In one they found not more ham sandwiches, but extra cans of pemmican! Even so, these additional rations were passed around the raft and devoured by the starving. The other package contained a tin of Spam, a tin of hash, several bottles of malted-milk tablets — some broken by the impact — and four cans of condensed milk.

"What a banquet you could make out of this, Rodriguez!"

"Hey, Woodman, where's that knife? Let's break open this stuff!"

The canned food was washed down by a beverage concocted from the mixture of condensed milk and the remaining supply of water.

"Do you think we ought to use up all the water?"

"Why not? We're not gonna need it tomorrow!"

"That's for sure! Tomorrow by this time, we oughta be in a British pub in Barbados!"

"Drink up, shipmates!"

"Here's to the United States Navy!"

"Here's to Chico for pullin' in the drops!"

"Here's to the bosun for grabbin' the doughnut in the first place!"

"The doughnut!"

In the excitement of opening the packages, nobody had bothered to make fast the dinghy. Now it floated free, beyond reach.

"Damn!"

"Ah, what the hell! We got no more use for it."

"Say, what's this?"

Rodriguez Rosibrosiris had found something else in the third package. He held it up.

"Hey, it's a dress! A woman's dress!"

"Where do you suppose them friggin' flyboys would get a dress!"

"Wouldn't you like to know!"

"Here, Mrs. Bell," said the bosun, tossing the garment to her. "Looks like it's just about your size."

"Thank you, Mr. Owen." Removing her life jacket for a moment, Ethel Bell slipped on the dress over the tatters she wore.

The fresh supply of food and drink was all consumed by the time darkness enveloped the raft. As on the first Sunday night, some of the survivors paid for their overindulgence with intestinal cramps. But no one cared. In spite of their weakened condition and the energy expended by excitement, almost nobody thought of sleeping. Rescue at night may have been unlikely but not entirely impossible. So they waited, knowing that the dawn would bring the inevitable return of a PBY to guide some rescue ship their way.

Years later, when Bob Bell attempted to track down the pilot responsible for first sighting the raft, then dropping the welcome supplies, he found a cold trail. The Navy Department kept no such records; instead, the navy gave

Bell the names of two retired commanding officers, Rear Admiral Allen Smith, Jr., commander of VP-31 headquarters in San Juan, Puerto Rico, and Rear Admiral Donald Gay, commanding officer of VP-31's Trinidad Detachment.

"I regret that I can't tell you specifically," says Donald Gay, "the name of the pilot who spotted you and dropped the supplies. Many of us were involved in such missions; it could even have been me, but I can't say for sure I did it. Our VP-31 squadron, with fifteen officers and seventy-five men, flew so many similar missions, and we never really had a way to record those we'd found and made drops to."

Rear Admiral Gay continues, "There were no medals for things we did in those days. We did get letters similar to yours, which were certainly appreciated, heartening for us to read even long after the fact. Such encouragement as we received gave us all we needed to do the very best we could for survivors such as you and your shipmates.

"As for the man responsible for dropping supplies to your raft, he's probably one of the many who were later killed in action. They were my most dedicated officers, and such men are proof of my thesis about war—the best never come back!"

In the full sunlight of Monday morning, September 14, the seventeen survivors never gave a thought to the bosun's order the previous day. They ate their rations as usual, remarking on the contrast to last night's collation of food. While they ate, their eyes were fixed on the sky and horizon, scanning the distance for signs of the expected Air-Sea Rescue team—a PBY to locate the raft once more and vector the vessel that would pick them up.

But the plane never returned. Somehow the navy must have assumed that, given the pilot's report of the raft's location, a ship could find the raft on its own.

"I can't remember the exact hour," says Bob Bell, "but soon after Mother's morning prayers and our final meal on the raft—or so we thought!—a ship appeared. Our watch identified it as a U.S. destroyer."

Once more the survivors rose as one in ecstasy. Their ordeal would be over in just another few minutes. All that remained was for the destroyer to cover the two or three miles separating the raft from deliverance. Steadily the ship rose higher as it approached. On board the raft, a spirit of giddiness overtook some of the men. Their laughter became childish, even silly, with delight.

Then the ship turned and began to sweep in a wide arc, seeming to take a course away from the raft.

"Hey, what's goin' on?"

"Must be changing course to come at us from a better angle, that's all."

"Never mind the angle! Let's just get here."

"Take it easy. You don't want her to run us down, do you?"

"Come on, baby! Come to papa!"

Just when the destroyer seemed closest—not more that a mile away—another sudden turn of the hull, this time directly away from the raft.

"What the hell!"

"Hey, I'm tired of these games!"

"Over here!"

"This way!"

"Damn you, open your eyes! Can't you see nothin'?"

Another change of course, and the ship circled the raft, drawing another round of jeers and pleas from the merchant seamen.

"That's what's wrong with this navy. They got nobody on the bridge with twenty-twenty vision!"

"Send 'em back to Annapolis!"

"Send 'em down to Davy Jones!"

"God, if they don't find us, I don't think I can make it another night!"

All morning and into the afternoon, the survivors agonized while the ship tacked back and forth, turning upon its own course, retracing its own wake.

"We could tell that the navy was looking for us," says Bob Bell, "and we couldn't believe how small a speck our raft must have been. The ship paced back and forth. We were so certain of being seen, we never made an attempt to wave until it was too late."

The smoke disappeared below the horizon. The ship was gone.

With it evaporated the survivors' last hope. Not until then had they known the true meaning of panic. They had emptied their water kegs; they had eaten all but a few remaining tins of their rations. They had counted on rescue and had been cruelly deceived. There was no more reason to hope.

On Monday, September 14, Joe McCarthy's New York Yankees clinched the American League championship, beating the Cleaveland Indians by a score of 8-3. For the Bronx Bombers, it was their sixth pennant in seven years and qualified the Yankees to face the St. Louis Cardinals in the World Series.

On this same day in Washington, D.C., a feisty little

man from Independence, Missouri, Senator Harry S. Truman, accused the American military brass of impeding the war effort by refusing to cooperate with each other. Truman called upon army generals and navy admirals to stop their childish competitiveness among themselves and to put their energies together in defeating the enemy.

Meanwhile, on this same September 14, at Guadalcanal's Bloody Ridge, 143 United States Marines died, along with 600 Japanese fighting, as Shakespeare put it,

> *for a plot*
> *Whereon the numbers cannot try the cause,*
> *Which is not tomb enough and continent*
> *To hide the slain.*

Late in the afternoon, about the usual time for eating, the bosun made his expected announcement.

"There's no second rations from now on. We ate this morning, so that's it for today. We'll eat again tomorrow at this time — if we're still here! But from now on, we go on split rations. That means one tin of pemmican for every *three* people, and we'll divvy up on the crackers and chocolate and malted-milk tablets too."

The men heard and accepted his statement in stolid silence. Then the bosun added, "I don't suppose I have to remind you that we're out of water. We drank it all yesterday."

To this the men responded with groans and anxious curses. Then, looking across the raft, Robert McDaniel said, "Mrs. Bell, if this God you believe in really hears your prayers, you'd better pray for rain."

The late afternoon sun shone as brilliantly as it had

throughout the sixteen days. In spite of the time of year and the regularity of tropical storms spawned in those latitudes, hardly enough rain had fallen on the raft to fill the single cup. There had been rainfall somewhere in that region; the frequency of the afternoon rainbows told that fact. But the raft had remained essentially dry. On diminished rations, the survivors might exist for an indefinite number of days. But without water? Especially in that heat? Their chances of lasting another whole day seemed minimal. "Water, water, everywhere," the Ancient Mariner had intoned, "Nor any drop to drink." Each of them had recalled Earl Croons's desperation; each of them hoped to avoid being driven by thirst to his solution.

Ethel Bell's lips were cracked and swollen; her tongue had become enlarged so that speech, even to the children was difficult. Yet, challenged by the young seaman to pray for rain, she nodded and spoke for them all.

"Our heavenly Father, if it is Thy will that we should survive to be rescued from this raft, please turn the clouds in our direction and send us the rain we need. We thank Thee. In Jesus' name. Amen."

On the eastern horizon a small cloud hovered. The men sat watching it, studying it, measuring it, as if in a test of faith. Gradually the cloud drifted closer and closer to the raft until its billowing blackness shadowed the raft, blocking out the sun.

Then the rain came. In church the Bells had often sung

> *There shall be showers of blessing:*
> *This is the promise of love;*
> *There shall be seasons refreshing,*
> *Sent from the Saviour above.*

> *Showers of blessing,*
> *Showers of blessing we need:*
> *Mercy-drops 'round us are falling,*
> *But for the showers we plead.*

Never before had they known the real fulfillment of that prayer, that promise.

"The rain came down in torrents," Bob Bell remembers. "I had seen tropical rains in Africa, but never anything like this. The rain collected in the canopy so that it sagged under the weight of the water. Woodman Potter took his knife and tore a hole in the center. Men crouched underneath the canopy to catch the water that poured through the hole. They used anything they could — a hat, a shirt, their cupped hands, our communal drinking cup — to hold the water and transfer it to our water kegs.

"Occasionally, the tin cup was filled and passed around for everyone to enjoy a drink. Most of us just tilted back our heads and let the rain stream right into our mouths."

While the cloudburst continued, one of the men called out, "One barrel full!" An entire keg had been filled, and still the rain fell without letup.

"It rained steadily until the second keg was nearly full," says Bob Bell. "Then it stopped just as suddenly as it had begun. The cloud was gone, and the sunshine returned."

When the squall had ended, Ethel Bell made no point of preaching to the men. For those who believed, the connection between her prayer and the rain was already self-evident; to disbelievers, a mere coincidence. But now that the rain had passed and the evening was coming on, their drenched clothing made them all even colder than usual in the night's chill. So in her evening prayers with the children, Ethel Bell thanked God for sending showers of blessing and asked that they might now be kept from further, unnecessary rain. That Monday night, at least, it was so.

Tuesday, September 15 — another day during which hope declined, the seventeenth day on the raft.

Woodman Potter spoke up, "If there's no rations from the food box this morning, why not get us some rations from the sea?"

"Oh yeah? How you gonna do that, Woodman?"

"By fishin', that's how!"

The second cook took out his precious jackknife and cut away a piece of line salvaged days before when the rafts had separated. Patiently, painstakingly, he began to unravel the rope; then he tied together its several strands.

"Now we need a hook and some bait, Chief," he addressed the bosun, "if you'll just get off'n your perch on the food box for a minute, maybe we can get a safety pin outa the first-aid kit."

Owen complied and found the pin.

"Now let's look right here in the well and see if anything washes through that we could use as bait."

A hapless sea minnow was soon caught and handed to Potter.

"I've seen better fishin' lines, and I've seen worse," he said as he dropped the improvised bait and hook over the side.

"It took a while," says Bob Bell, "but Woodman caught two pilot fish that morning. Rodriguez filleted them with Woodman's knife, and we all had a small bite of raw fish."

Neither Woodman Potter nor anyone else tried fishing again. Perhaps the concentration required to string a line and find a minnow demanded more than the men could sustain. Besides, for the next several hours they had other matters than eating to think about.

For by late afternoon of that Tuesday, September 15, a new danger threatened them. A tropical storm seemed headed toward the raft in fury untrammeled. Until then, the ocean had been essentially calm. For more than two weeks only its groundswell kept the raft rocking. Yet even the normal rise and fall of the waves had not been sufficient to trouble anyone with seasickness; no threat of being pitched overboard worried those who sat on the raft's slats. But on the seventeenth day adrift, the survivors suddenly realized the weather's terrifying force. Almost without warning, the sky darkened to an ugly amber. Vicious-seeming clouds swirled into a vortex as atmospheric conditions worsened, changing from a tropical disturbance to depression, to storm, to hurricane. With no land objects — buildings or trees — to block their view for miles in all directions, the survivors could watch with increasing apprehension while the killing power of wind and water came steadily toward them.

Such tropical storms, born in the equatorial belt of lowest atmospheric pressure, sweep across the Atlantic from West Africa. Late each summer, these storms intensify, often to hurricane proportions — with winds reaching seventy-four miles per hour and more. By mid-September, the storm season is at its peak as winds attack the West Indies, the vulnerable coasts of Florida, the Gulf states, then Mexico. Or sometimes, in a meteorological whim, a storm will turn northeast, raking the Carolinas, strafing the Middle States and New England before dissipating its strength or swinging eastward again out to sea. In recent years, September had recorded the shocking violence of hurricanes: In 1935, 414 people had died, another 600 in 1938.

The 1942 hurricane season had been relatively placid. Only four tropical storms had been elevated to official hurricane status by the United States Weather Service. Two of these had reached the American continent. A total of seventeen people had died as a result of wind and flood. A relatively mild season. But no one on the eight-by-ten-foot raft that mid-September afternoon could have been convinced by such statistics.

Lurching and leaping through wave after wave, the raft tossed like a cork. From crest to trough the raft fell thirty or forty feet, careening down its uncharted course like a runaway bobsled. At the bottom of each watery chasm, great breakers swept over the raft, tearing apart the grip each survivor struggled to retain, blotting out the sky.

"Grab that water keg!"

"Hold tight to the food box!"

"Mrs. Bell, you'd better hang on to those two girls or they'll be swept over!"

The raft had become a roller-coaster car, bound to its tracks, with no end to the ride in view.

"Each time we were swallowed up in a trough between the waves," says Bob Bell, "I was sure that we'd never come through the next crest. One wave seemed to piggy-back on the other. They came so fast, so incessantly. Spray felt like buckshot against our bodies."

For twelve hours — from Tuesday afternoon until early Wednesday morning, September 17, the raft buckled and spun, tilted and reeled, while its riders clung to the fragile frame.

"It may not have been a full-fledged hurricane," admits

Joe Greenwell, "but it sure was one helluva tropical storm!"

Miraculously, everyone survived. Once again, these derelicts from the *West Lashaway* had been stretched beyond all endurance; still, they had not broken. Nature's battering had done its worst; nonetheless, they had faced the storm and could say, "We're not licked yet!"

Riding out the storm's fury, the British destroyer HMS *Vimy* wallowed through the eastern Carribean escorting a small but highly important convoy of tankers. These ships had left Port of Spain, Trinidad, bound for Gibraltar and the secret Allied invasion of North Africa, to be known as Operation Torch.

Tagging along with the convoy chugged a Dutch cargo ship named *Prins Willem van Oranje*. Only 250 feet long and a mere 1,300 tons, this tiny merchant vessel carried cargo among Allied colonies in the Lesser Antilles. Several days earlier, the ship had left its home port at Oranjestad, capital of Aruba, heading for Kingstown, St. Vincent, in the Windward Islands. But because of U-boats threatening that course, the *Prins Willem* had been happy to accept the protection of the *Vimy* until near Barbados, when the Dutch ship would have to part company with the convoy.

Because of the storm, the entire convoy had been slowed, making it unlikely that the *Prins Willem* would reach St. Vincent before Friday, September 18.

Physically, the storm caused no further damage to the seventeen desperate survivors. Emotionally and psychologically, it marked the point at which some men's nerves became too frayed. They had struggled so long against hunger and thirst, exposure and exhaustion. Now they had battled for their lives against the monumental forces of violent weather. Winning that contest, however, had cost some men their last degree of morale. By Thursday afternoon, September 17, they had arrived at their wit's end.

The first sign of emotional collapse had come early that morning, before dawn. In the darkness, Joe Greenwell recalls, someone was mumbling and cursing.

"There was nothin' unusual about that," says Greenwell. "Somebody was always sayin' somethin' in the dark. Lots of one-sided conversations goin' on all over the raft. But this guy—I won't say who he was—had gone completely crazy. In his mind he thought the rest of us had eaten all the food while he was asleep. He was cursing us out royally.

"Then he suddenly stands up and says, 'Ah, to hell with it! I'm gonna go down to the corner and get me a beer and a hamburger.' I swear, those were his exact words! And this guy takes one step right off the raft and into the water!

"Well, that woke him up pretty smart, lemme tell you!"

Why the sharks did not attack the live body, Bob Bell does not understand. "They were still close to the raft. In fact, they never were more than an oar's length away on both sides. Yet they let that sleepwalker—if that's what we can call him—back into the raft unscathed."

Later in the morning, another man, momentarily deranged, shouted, "I want to get out of this place!" Grabbing Carol Shaw, he tried to take her with him over the side. But the canopy, the masts holding it up, and the crush of other bodies created too much interference. As one, the rest of the crew wrestled him to the floor of the well and might have killed him if Ethel Bell had not screamed at them to stop and let him be.

By judging the sun's angle, the bosun decided that noon had passed. He had also read the signals coming from the men. He knew that they were at the breaking point. How much longer even his forcefulness could control them, he could not tell. James Owen decided to break his own disciplined routine and give out the day's only rations several hours early.

"Many of us were dozing in the terrible afternoon heat," Bob Bell remembers, "and those of us who weren't partially asleep may have been too emotionally spent to think clearly anyway. We weren't aware of what the bosun was up to. He was passing out the food to some and not to others, especially not to Mother and us children."

Mary Whitbeck recalls the incident. "I guess I must have been more awake than some of the others because I started crying that we weren't being given our share of the food. I remember shaking Mother and telling her to do something, but she was almost in a daze."

George Marano and Joe Greenwell realized what the bosun had intended and protested. "If anybody eats, we all eat!"

"If they're not awake when we eat, that's too bad!" the bosun retorted.

But the moral conditions on the raft had not sunk to such a low level that men could allow another man to deprive a woman and four children their minuscule portion of food. As one man, the crew rose against the bosun, threatening mutiny, bringing him back to his senses.

Later that night when a cloud covered the moon and the raft seemed enveloped in darkness, Robert Bell thought he smelled chocolate.

"Nobody kept any food beyond our eating time. Although we ate slowly, what we were given we ate, saving nothing for later," he says. "There could be only one explanation for the smell of chocolate late at night — someone had gotten into the food box."

With the bosun seated on the food box, no other man could have access to it without removing Owen from his place. But the bosun himself occasionally changed his position, seating himself slightly behind the food box on the rim of the raft.

"I remember that he seemed frequently to be checking on the box, as if to make sure that it was securely tied down. Could it have been the bosun who, all along, was stealing from our food supply?" asks Bell.

Others must have smelled the telltale contraband, but nobody said a word about it at that time. The showdown with the bosun was still to come.

Friday, September 18
TWENTY
RESCUE

As Thursday night passed into Friday morning, the raft became a danger zone. For almost three weeks the dozen remaining men had fought their own worst tendencies toward selfishness and self-preservation at any cost. Most of them had tried to behave as gentlemen before the woman and children. Gaunt from near-starvation — weight loss of fifty and sixty pounds was common — these men had struggled nonetheless to keep clothes on their ravaged bodies as the last semblance of decency. But by Friday, September 18 — the twentieth day since the sinking of the *West Lashaway* — the men no longer cared about such matters. Who had energy to concern himself with whether or not his ragged shorts would stay above his extruded pelvic bones? Most of the men had also aimed at being honest and fair with each other. Now they were prepared to abandon themselves to animal impulses, to fight over the last scrap of food — if necessary, to kill for their own survival. The pilfering of their food had been the straw that broke their resistance. By morning's light

Robert Bell wondered how long before someone accused someone else and the killing would begin.

Robert's gaze swept around the raft. To his left sat Mary, his mother, Carol, and Richard. Then came Robert McDaniel. John Vargas sat on a water keg in the corner. George Marano, whose makeshift pants had fallen off in shreds the night before, was now wrapped in a burlap diaper; he sat next to Joe Greenwell at the bow. Woodman Potter and Levi Walker leaned into Rodriguez Rosibrosiris, crowding against Frank Flavor and Servior Seremos. Near the corner diagonally opposite from Vargas stood Louis Vega and Isabelino Pacheco, on watch. Last in the ring came James Owen, seated now on the other water keg, his feet resting on the precious food box.

"There was a different spirit among us that Friday morning," says Bob Bell, "a hostility so obvious and pronounced, you could see it in a man's eyes as he looked at you, just briefly, then quickly looked away."

A new mood of pessimism also prevailed in the side remarks and glances of the men.

"I'd sure like to be in an alley in Hoboken with that sub commander!"

"I'd settle for just being in Hoboken!"

"You'll get there."

"Yeah, sure thing."

"Who you guys think you're kiddin'? We're done for, and that's a fact!"

"Don't talk like that!"

"What am I supposed to say? *Any day now?* We ain't got that many days left! Look at us!"

"We'll make it."

"Keep convincin' yourself, Greenwell!"

Suddenly, Frank Flavor, one of the Hispanic deck-hands, jumped to his feet, lunging at the cook.

"Rodriguez, I want some more chili! I smell the chili you make, and I want some more!"

Louis Vega and the others nearby dragged Flavor to the bottom of the well, murmuring to him in Spanish.

Had hunger become so extreme—that men were now smelling the aromas of their imagination? What about the odor of chocolate last night? Could Robert be certain that he, too, was not being victimized by a maddened craving for food?

Across the raft from each other, Robert McDaniel and the cook were talking.

"Well, you've been helping him pass out the rations, Rodriguez."

"I tell you, I don't know how much we got left," Rosibrosiris replied. "Little of this, little of that, not much of anything."

"I want to know, is all."

"Well, ask him."

"You ask him. You got more standing with him."

"I'm just the cook!"

In the silence that followed Robert Bell heard the rhythmic tattoo of John Vargas's fingers on the water keg. Then the conga drum stopped, and a new voice spoke:

"I'll ask him," said Vargas.

The pantryman slid off the water keg and squeezed in next to McDaniel. He would need to feel the moral support of others.

"Chief," he began, "some of us want to talk to you."

James Owen had been looking off into the morning sunlight. He now turned on his water keg to face the speaker.

"What's up, Vargas? You sure haven't had much to say, except with your mitts on that keg."

"It's about the food, Chief."

"Shoot."

"We want what's left passed around now."

"Why's that, Vargas?"

The pantryman dropped his head for an anxious moment.

Here it comes, Robert Bell thought to himself.

John Vargas looked up and fixed his eyes on Owen's. "Because we don't want nobody left short, Chief."

"What makes you say that, Vargas?"

"We smelled food last night."

"Yeah, chocolate," added McDaniel.

"I smelled chili," said Frank Flavor.

"You guys are nuts!" Owen retorted. "Chocolate? Chili? What was it, Flavor? Con carne or just with beans? Did you have it in a bowl or with a *tostada?*"

"Lay off, Chief!" Vargas warned. "Flavor may have been dreaming, but we weren't. We smelled chocolate, and we know where it came from. So we decided—"

"Who's this *we?*" the bosun threatened. "I'm in charge here!"

Vargas shook his head from side to side. He would not be intimidated.

"So, like I say, Chief, we decided—the men, all of us— that we want all the food distributed right now."

"Just so there's no more shoplifting after hours, Chief," the cook added.

The bosun's eyes never blinked as he looked his accusers right in the face.

"You know what'll happen?" Owen asked rhetorically.

"Some of you damned fools will eat everything you're given all at once; then you'll sit there pleading for handouts, like Bowery bums."

"That's up to each person to decide for himself, Owen," said Greenwell philosophically.

"Yeah, well what about the woman and children?"

"They're Mrs. Bell's responsibility. She'll take care of them."

"Well, I don't like it," said the bosun.

"You haven't got any choice," replied Vargas.

"I smell chili," said Flavor in a pitiful voice. "Who's got the chili?"

"What's happening, Mrs. Bell?" Carol Shaw asked.

"Mr. Owen is going to give us the rest of our food, Carol," Ethel Bell answered.

"How will we hold it all?"

"Well, Carol, there won't be that much to hold, I'm afraid. You'll just have to put it on your lap and try and not let the water splash on it."

"I dreamed last night about food, Mother," Mary Bell said, "just like that man over there."

"Mr. Flavor, Mary. You must refer to people by their names."

"Mr. Flavor. Only I didn't dream about chili. I hate that stuff."

"What did you dream about, Mary?" her brother asked. "Cream puffs, I bet."

"No, not cream puffs, Robert. I dreamed about a big Virginia ham with lots of glaze and white fat running all through it!" The girl's eyes lighted up with her fantasy. "And there were yams and mashed potatoes . . ."

"Yams! Yuk!" Her brother gagged. "We ate too many

yams in Africa! I never want to see another yam!"

"Shut up, you kids!" the bosun bellowed, taking out his humiliation on them.

"OK, you want the food? You got it! But, remember, this is it. No begging for more from somebody else," Owen warned.

"Rodriguez!"

The bosun called the cook's name and gestured to him for assistance. Together they bent over the food box and passed around the last cans of pemmican, the last crackers, malted-milk tablets, and pieces of chocolate.

"Where's the rest of the food?"

"That's it."

"That's all there is?"

"That's all," Owen replied. "I hope you know what to do with it."

Robert looked at his cupped hands. Two crackers, three malted-milk tablets, some crumbs of chocolate. In her skirt his mother held two tins of pemmican, to be shared among the five of them.

"Only then did I realize how close to death we were!" Bob Bell declares. "We had less than a full day's rations among the five of us."

While he sat looking at his portion, he heard, then saw his mother's dismay.

"Oh, no, Carol!" The little girl had swallowed her handful of rations.

"Richard did it first," said the little girl.

"Oh, Richard!"

"Why not, Mrs. Bell?"

The teenaged boy had made a man's decision. He had eaten the last of his food. Now he would simply settle back to die.

"That was pretty dumb, Richard!" said Mary Bell.

"Quiet, Mary!" her mother rebuked. "We'll just have to pray even harder now. And we'll have to be prepared to share what we have."

"Then we'll all die, Mother!"

"Hush, Mary. There's a good girl."

With one propeller still damaged, the HMS *Vimy* proceeded at only seventeen knots or so, all its remaining screw could generate. Its convoy of five ships, plus the little Dutch *Prins Willem van Oranje,* still along for protection, had passed the 60° longitude. Soon the *Prins Willem* would turn away to continue on its own to St. Vincent.

Precisely at 9:50 A.M., Douglas K. Stott, working at his radar station in back of the upper bridge, picked up a signal.

"Object bearing three hundred and thirty degrees," he called out, "about five miles."

His partner wrote the message, adding these words, "U-boat on the surface."

Receiving this message, Lieutenant John D. Craven, a member of the bridge watch, reacted instantly.

"I grabbed my binoculars and swept the ocean. There it was," says Craven, "and I thought, of course, that it was a sub. I hadn't the slightest doubt."

Craven relayed his confirmation of the radar's finding, and Lieutenant Commander H. G. de Chair gave the order.

"Attack at all possible speed!"

The call to general quarters sounded.

"Convoy," Louis Vega, on watch, called listlessly.

No one responded. Already that same morning a plane had crossed the sky in range of the raft without any sign of recognition whatever. Why bother to get excited over ships on the horizon? They had all seen ships before, but none of the ships had seen them. Besides, there probably was no ship, no convoy, just the watchman's mirage.

"Convoy! They're coming our way!"

"How far away?"

"Close. Maybe three, four miles."

"How many?"

"Look and see for yourself!"

"One—two—three—four—five . . ."

"Six. See that little one off to port?"

"What are they?"

"Looks like tankers to me."

"Then there's a destroyer with 'em. No tankers cross these waters alone."

"Look, you're right. See that one break away from the formation? That's a destroyer, for sure!"

"She must see us!"

"We're saved!"

"Praise God!"

"Hold your fire until we get in range!" the *Vimy* commander ordered. "I don't want that U-boat to get the jump on us."

Through his binoculars Lieutenant Commander de Chair could make out what he was sure was the tower of a submarine. "Cheeky bastard, what?" he commented. "Must see us coming, yet doesn't dive."

"Perhaps Jerry's damaged, sir," offered Sublieutenant Raymond B. Venables.

"Let's find out," said de Chair. "Lieutenant Craven, give the order to fire."

"Fire A gun!" shouted Craven. "Fire B gun!"

Two four-inch cannons opened fire on the raft.

To the seventeen eager watchers on the raft, the first flash from the destroyer's deck seemed like an exploding light bulb. But the thunder reverberating behind it and the screaming shell that burst just beyond the raft revealed the truth. A second shot, then a third, a fourth, and more. Volley after volley zeroed in on the presumed target, all just barely missing.

"Shells landed on both sides of the raft," says Bob Bell, recalling this final horror. "One smacked down just in front of the raft, then ricocheted over the canopy, taking down the sail."

"Oh God, not now! Not this way!" lamented Robert McDaniel.

Ethel Bell rolled with the children into the well, and several men threw themselves down on top of them as the bombardment continued. A total of fourteen rounds had been fired before James Owen grabbed the canopy in both hands and began waving its shreds. The *Vimy's* guns ceased firing, but as the destroyer continued toward the raft, great cataracts of water churning up threatened to swamp the tiny box.

Douglas Stott says, "Our intention on board the *Vimy* was certainly to force the supposed submarine to dive so that it couldn't use its deck artillery against us. Fortunately, this was not one of our gunners' best days! The bridge watch—our skipper, de Chair, his officers Venables, Craven, Moore, and the rest, signalmen and other lookouts — all with their binoculars took the object to be a U-boat. Not until they saw the waving canvas did they realize what the target really was."

The destroyer slowed and idled to a position less threatening to the raft. At its rails stood British sailors, mouths agape in astonishment at the sight below.

"Who are you?"

"We're Americans!" the survivors shouted back.

Douglas Stott, now residing on the island of Anguilla, West Indies, remembers seeing numerous sharks around the raft. "One of our boys ran for a machine gun," says Stott, "and sprayed bullets at those sharks." Soon the water turned crimson as the sharks tore into each other, leaving the *West Lashaway's* survivors with one last token of what might have been their common doom.

Rope ladders streamed over the side of the *Vimy*. But most of the men were too weak to help themselves up the ropes, so a netting was thrown over, and Royal Navy men scampered down to help gather everyone to safety.

Robert McDaniel refused to move.

"You sons o' bitches! You sons o' bitches! You fired at us! You coulda killed us!"

"Come on, laddie. You're all right now," a Scot comforted him.

But the young messboy refused to budge. At last a line was lowered and slipped over his head and under his arms so that he could be lifted onto the ship.

Meanwhile, the bosun had made his way up a ladder and straight to the bridge. "I saw him later at our mess," says Douglas Stott. "He seemed surprisingly fit, a dark curly-haired young man, who I remember sat chatting with us around the table. Others of the party weren't even able to stand; they lay on their cots without saying much."

In all the excitement of the rescue, somehow Ethel Bell broke a rib. Perhaps it happened on the raft, when bodies piled up on each other to avoid the shelling; perhaps as she toppled over the rail to the deck of the *Vimy*. In any case, the woman and four children were quickly taken to the officers' lounge.

"I vividly remember the soft, plush chairs in that lounge. They seemed to be a foretaste of heaven!" says Bob Bell. "Sailors kept coming by and giving us candy bars and fruit. Everyone was so very generous and kind."

Ethel Bell's clothing and that of the two girls concerned her. She asked for bathrobes to cover them properly; three officers complied.

The ship's doctor and his medical staff came with basins to bathe and bandage the survivors' most serious wounds. Then they took each person to a clean bunk for a few hours' rest, until a transfer could be arranged. Just before he dozed off, Robert Bell asked the medic treating him, "What day is today?"

"Friday, September 18, son."

"Oh, that's good!" the boy said. "My sister Mary will get to have her birthday on Sunday!"

"So, Sunday's her birthday! And what would your sister like for her birthday?"

"Cream puffs!"

When every survivor had been taken off the raft, a British naval officer and an aide went down to scour the raft for any belongings. They brought back to the *Vimy* several life jackets, the last remaining tins of pemmican, and Woodman Potter's knife. The remaining engorged sharks were slaughtered and the raft scuttled by bullet holes in its flotation tanks.

For the Bell family and the others, the luxury of lying flat upon a firm mattress could not yet overcome the joy of being rescued—the thrill of being alive! These survivors were too excited to sleep. Furthermore, they had been told that they were to be transferred to another ship as soon as such a maneuver could be worked out on a choppy sea. Around 3:00 P.M. they were roused from their bunks and taken to the ship's rail. How different they now looked! Each of the men had been given a shower and fresh clothing—Royal Navy duds. The boys, too, were attired in seamen's garb. But the woman and two girls also had new wardrobes. Someone on the *Vimy* had remembered a collection of women's dresses worn at a recent masquerade party in Trinidad. Moreover, Ethel Bell received a generous favor. An officer, taking home to England a gift of delicate lingerie for his wife, gave the underwear to the lone woman survivor instead.

"The British were so good to us," says Bob Bell, "and we were so in need of their compassion and care, the last thing we wanted to do was leave the *Vimy*. But in time of war, we had no choice."

"Our skipper had orders to escort those tankers to Gilbraltar," Douglas Stott recalls, "so the best thing to do with the raft party was to pass them over to the Dutch freighter, *Prins Willem*. She was scheduled to leave our convoy just about the same time that all the midmorning action began."

Stott explains how the transfer occurred. "The *Vimy* nosed as gently as possible into the foredeck of the *Prins Willem*," he says, "and while the two vessels were bumping and heaving and grinding together, lines were attached. The raft's survivors were tied in slings and shot across on those lines."

But not without incident: "In the process," Stott continues, "part of our superstructure smashed into the Dutch freighter's starboard lifeboat, caving it in. I can clearly recall the Dutch captain—complete with bowler hat!— cursing our skipper, calling him a clumsy so-and-so. The two men were just a few feet from each other, across the rails. Our skipper apologized, saying that he could not maneuver any better because of our still-damaged screw. We drew away from the *Prins Willem* to the sounds of continuing sailor language, mostly in Dutch!"

Joe Greenwell also remembers. "Actually, it took quite a bit of seamanship to make that transfer. You've got to realize that we were in sub-infested waters. For any ship—not to mention an entire convoy—to shut down its engines and sit idling in the open ocean is like shooting fish in a barrel! The sea was moderate, with swells two to three feet, but even so, there was enough rise and fall between the *Vimy* and the *Prins Willem* to make our transfer a problem.

"The crews of both ships were very brave and risked their lives to go through with that transfer," says Greenwell. "I've always been very touched by their unselfishness on our behalf."

Extract from HMS Vimy's *Report of Proceedings*

18 September 1942

. . . Vimy opened fire from "A" and "B" guns. The object looked like a conning tower and 14 controlled salvoes were fired at it. Not until the sail had been shot away did it appear that what was in

*fact a raft with survivors could possibly be any-
thing but a U-boat's conning tower. The fact that
it did not dive was ground for suspicion, however,
and fire ceased. Mr. James Owen, Bosun of the
American SS* West Lashaway, *said when rescued
that he feared all along that they would be mistaken
for a U-boat. There was virtually standing room
only on the raft and the compact mass of 17 people standing up must obviously resemble a conning
tower. When I apologized for opening fire he said
that they were all delighted to see some action taken
and was complimentary about our shooting. They
all prayed and the children screamed. It was a
miracle they were not hit. . . . After a little food,
drink, medical attention and sleep, the survivors
were transferred at 1500 to the Dutch SS* Prins
Willem van Oranje *for Babados.*

H. G. de Chair
Lieutenant Commander, RN

Again, the new ship's crew could not do enough for the
survivors.

"I can remember particularly," says Bob Bell, "sitting
in the Dutch captain's dining room with Richard and
Carol and Mary, eating sandwiches of strawberry jam
on freshly baked bread. It was a great banquet!"

Each person was given a bunk, but once more the
shock of deliverance and emotional intensity combined
to make sleep impossible. Just after sundown, the Dutch
ship's whistle blasted several times. Robert Bell looked
out a porthole and saw land!

"There were lights and buildings and other ships at their

docks. I didn't know where we were until we stood on deck and learned that this was Bridgetown, the port and capital of Barbados."

A motor launch stood by to receive the survivors from the *Prins Willem* and take them to emergency medical treatment in the harbor area. By this time, however, exhaustion had begun to set in; stretchers were needed to carry them down the Dutch ship's ladders and onto the launch, then from the launch to the wharf. Once on land, Joe Greenwell insisted on walking. "I was the remaining senior officer and had the report of our rescue from the *Vimy*'s captain to deliver. So I was determined to walk to the car that would take us to the hospital. I remember taking two or three steps with the harbor master. Then I fell flat on the ground."

Picked up and placed on a stretcher, like all the other survivors, Greenwell waited for ambulances from the St. John's Brigade to arrive and take them to Bridgetown's Barbados General Hospital. There Ethel Bell and the two girls were separated from the men and boys, who were bedded down in a large ward. Immediately they began to receive proper medical and nutritional care.

Just before falling asleep at last that Friday night, Robert Bell was asked, "What would you like when you wake up?"

"Sunday is my sister's birthday. I'd like her to have some cream puffs for her birthday."

Then he slept.

Extract from letter from HMS Vimy
to the Senior British Naval Officer, Barbados,
dated 18 September 1942

Sir,

I have the honour to report that at 1020Q (GMT + 5 hrs) today seventeen survivors (see List) were rescued from a raft in a position 12° 45' N, 60° 24' W. They were from the American SS West Lashaway, Barber Line, left Takoradi 15 August for Trinidad, torpedoed at 1400 on 30 August in approximate latitude 11° N, some 500 miles East of Trinidad. . . . Fourteen out of fifty-six persons in the ship went down with her. The Captain and one male passenger died on the recovered raft. . . .

The courage and fortitude shown by these people after nearly nineteen days on an open raft in the tropics, surrounded by sharks, with virtually standing room only, was astounding. Except for Immersion Foot, they all appeared to be in good health. Food had been dropped to them by a U.S. plane on 13 September. . . .

It is considered that Bosun James Owen deserves great credit for the fine spirit and fettle in which his raft crew was found when picked up.

> *I have the honour to be,*
> *Sir,*
> *H. G. de Chair*
> *Lieutenant Commander, RN*

No one could have agreed more with Commander de Chair than the bosun himself. On Saturday, September 26, the local Bridgetown newspaper, *The Barbados*

Advocate, ran a feature story on the survivors, from which the following excerpts have been taken.

SURVIVORS 20 DAYS ON A RAFT
SAVED FROM THE SEA AND SHARKS

"God helps those who help themselves and I propose to help myself. If you don't like it, you can quit and step off this raft right now. We're going west, skipper! Don't argue!"

With these words of determination the thirty-two-year-old Boatswain of a torpedoed ship "set sail" without chart, compass or clothing and after 20 days at sea was shelled by mistake and then saved along with 16 others by an Allied destroyer protecting a convoy in the Caribbean. Boatswain Owen of 1400 Veto Street, Pittsburgh, Pennsylvania, the hero of the story, now lies a patient at the Barbados General Hospital after his harrowing experience. "I saw two of our men go demented and die after they had lost the will to win . . . we saw the sharks devour them . . . we were saved and saw the same sharks destroyed."

As the newspaper reported Owen's version of the story, Captain Bogden had been a weak man who soon went mad and did all sorts of things to hinder the raft's progress. But through Owen's ingenuity and Owen's fearless leadership, the survivors had been saved. The *Advocate* article concluded, "Mr. Owen is in high spirits and hopes to be out and about soon."

No doubt he was.

NAVAL MESSAGE

From: AMCON BARBADOS, B.W.I.
*   For Action: COMINCH (CAR)*
Date: 19 September 1942
TOR Coderoom: 1617
Decoded by: Rothaus
Paraphrased by: Kennedy
Text:
WEST LASHAWAY, *OPERATORS BARBER*
LINE, TORPEDOED AND SUNK 3 TO 4 HUN-
DRED MILES EAST OF TRINIDAD 1600 GCT 30
AUGUST. EXACT POSITION NOT DETERMIN-
ABLE. TWELVE CREW AND FIVE PAS-
SENGERS, OF WHICH ONE WOMAN WITH
FOUR CHILDREN, LANDED BARBADOS 18TH.
ALL PUBLICATIONS BELIEVED SUNK WITH
SHIP. INFORMATION FURNISHED BY FEMALE
PASSENGER. ACCURACY UNKNOWN.

CONFIDENTIAL

On September 23 a battered life raft bearing the in-
scription *SS West Lashaway* drifted ashore on the southeast beaches of St. Vincent. On board a single refugee
from the sea still survived, a man named Elliott Gurney.
His story matched his haggard looks and rattled mind.
Along with another half-dozen men, his raft had been cut
loose from three others almost three weeks before. By
that time the rafts had already been adrift for five days.
All of his companions had died, the most recent that very
morning.

After Gurney had been taken to a hospital in Kingstown, Allied naval authorities on St. Vincent tore apart

the raft to learn what made it so seaworthy, in spite of its damaged flotation tanks. Inside the otherwise empty food box they found an envelope containing an American Express money order and a certified check. Both were payable to Harvey Shaw.

> *General Hospital*
> *Barbados, B.W. I.*
> *September 28, 1942*

The Reverend A. C. Snead
Foreign Secretary
Christian and Missionary Alliance
260 West 44th Street
New York, N.Y.

Dear Mr. Snead:

Your cable reached me Saturday morning and I was greatly cheered by it. It is good to know that you, at that end, are cognizant of our need, and are praying. I don't know how much you know, but we'll be able to fill in details when we see you. God has surely worked miracles in bringing us through this experience; every day. He lovingly answered our prayers on the raft, and here we are overwhelmed with His goodness. The people of Barbados are exceedingly kind and have sent in more than enough to meet our needs (which were rather extensive, since we lost literally everything). We have had the best of care here at the hospital. Robert was able to leave after five days, and Mary after a week. Kind friends are opening their homes to us.

I suffered considerably from the reaction after coming here, but I am so much better now—almost myself again. Our worst trouble has been the sores on our feet caused by the salt water, but mine are healing nicely now, and I believe it won't be long before I'm up.

Thank you for sending the money. It ought to be sufficient, but will depend, I suppose, on how long we'll be here. The doctor has just been in and I asked him what I should tell you. He answered— "Getting along fine, no complications, and you'll probably be out of the hospital in about two weeks." Now I'll close. It's good to be in touch with you and to know that you are praying. We send greetings to all at headquarters, others at Nyack, and all in general.

Cordially and gratefully yours in His service,
Ethel G. Bell

Gradually each survivor regained health and strength, some more rapidly than others. In only three days Richard Shaw and Robert Bell were able to walk a little; after five days they were released from the hospital and taken together to a home high on a hill overlooking Bridgetown and the ocean.

George Marano, on the other hand, was much more seriously ill. To assist his recovery, he was removed from the hospital ward and placed in a closetlike room. "I was certain I'd been taken there to die," Marano remembers, "and I wanted out of there and back with the rest of the men—fast!" His request was granted. Soon followed a spaghetti dinner, and George Marano knew he would recover.

"They fed us as well as they could during wartime," says

Joe Greenwell. "Let's say there wasn't much variety, but we had plenty to eat. I must have eaten gallons of split-pea soup.

"Everyone in the hospital and throughout Bridgetown did all they could for us," Greenwell says. "We were there, most of us, for about six weeks. It was like being in paradise."

"What impressed the medical staff most," Bob Bell says, "was our remarkable absence of acute sunburn and sun poisoning. They'd seen other cases of people found on rafts in those waters, and after even a few days, their bodies had third-degree burns. But we were saved by that awful oil and sludge. It never washed off, and it gave us its blessing, even though it made us uncomfortable."

Mary Bell remained in the hospital for seven days, then went to stay with a different family. But her birthday, celebrated at General Hospital on Sunday, September 20, was memorable for one reason: cream puffs!

"There were cream puffs in abundance," she recalls, "far more than anyone could eat. When I asked how the nurses knew I wanted cream puffs for my birthday, someone said, 'Your brother told us.' I knew then how much I loved him, in spite of all our childish quarreling."

A missionary couple, Wayne and Anges Divine, stationed in Barbados, befriended the Bells and Shaw children. Agnes Divine was the daughter of Dr. M. E. Hawkins, president of Baptist Mid-Missions, the Shaw's sponsoring agency. She came frequently to the General Hospital and, as their recuperation progressed, she cared for the needs of Ethel Bell and the four children.

Once settled in her hospital room, with Mary and Carol in a room nearby, Ethel Bell slept as if in a coma for three days and nights. She had borne so much emotional as well as physical burden—days and nights of anxious wakefulness, daring not to doze—her system had nearly cracked. But she had also carried the spiritual weight for others, and in that regard she had proven unfailing. No wonder that, as the men began to recover and were allowed to walk about the hospital, some of them sought out her room and came to thank her.

"Mrs. Bell, one night when I was scared, I looked up and I believe I saw a light over the raft! That light was your faith, and it saved us!"

Woodman Potter told her that, as a result of her prayers and hymns and Bible verses, he had returned to his own boyhood faith. As a token he gave his jackknife to her as a gift, which she later presented to her son.

Joe Greenwell summed it up. "I guess Mrs. Bell was just about the best one there. Just her being there had a great effect on the rest of us, helping us to keep our heads, preventing us from doing things that might have been the end of us all.

"She is a great lady. God bless her!"

TWENTY-ONE
REUNION

On October 23, 1942, Ethel Bell and her two children arrived at LaGuardia Field in New York City. Their hospitalization and out-patient recuperation in Bridgetown had come to an end ten days earlier. Assisted by the American Consul in Barbados, Ilo C. Funk, the Bells and the two Shaw children had received sufficient funds, sent from their respective mission agencies, to cover all their medical and travel expenses.

"Imagine!" marvels Bob Bell today. "Our entire medical bill for the three of us at Barbados General Hospital was only a hundred and fifty dollars!"

From Barbados, Ethel Bell and the children in her care had flown to Trinidad. There they met Agnes Divine, who had gone ahead to prepare housing for them during the time they might have to wait for whatever scarce transporation might become available. They waited a week, living in a boardinghouse some miles from Port of Spain. At last, five seats were assigned them on a flight from Trinidad to Miami, by way of Caracas, Venezuela. On the evening of October 21, they arrived in Miami, met by the Reverend T. G. Mangham, Sr., a local Christian and Missionary Alliance pastor. The next day Richard and Carol Shaw were handed over to the care of Dr. M. E. Hawkins of Baptist Mid-Missions, who had arrived from headquarters, then in Mishawaka, Indiana, to meet the Shaw children. From Miami he took them to the infamous Westervelt Missionary Children's Home in South Carolina, while the Bells continued to New York on an overnight Eastern Airlines flight.

Arriving at LaGuardia on the morning of October 23, the Bells were met by Alfred Snead, foreign secretary of the mission, who took them to the Alliance headquarters building at 260 West Forty-fourth Street, just off Times Square.

"Quite a number of people had gathered to welcome us home," Bob Bell remembers. "Uncle Ed Roffe, Mother's brother, home from Indochina, was there. So was Dr. Harry Shuman, president of the Alliance, the Reverend H. E. Nelson, and many others."

The Bells were taken to Nyack, where they stayed for about a week. During this time Ethel Bell was summoned to Washington, D.C., for official debriefing by various government agencies. That duty done, she and her children arrived by overnight train in Toronto on October 30, 1942. "I remember Grandpa Roffe dressing up for Halloween the next night," says Bob Bell.

The months that followed Ethel Bell's return with her children seem almost cruelly hectic, even insensitive. Although her health was far from fully recovered — indeed, in the aftermath of her extended exposure on the raft, she suffered acute neuralgia — Mrs. Bell began an itinerary as rigorous as any door-to-door salesman. Everywhere she went audiences wished to hear the raft story at first-hand. The Alliance took full advantage of her celebrity—an article in *Good Housekeeping* had given her national notoriety—and her travels multiplied. During these early months Mary and Robert spent time, first, with Uncle Ed Roffe and his family at Gravenhurst, then in Toronto with their grandparents. Finally, Ethel Bell decided to place them in a boarding school. Someone had told her about the home for missionaries' children in South Carolina.

The lives of Mary Bell and her mother remained closely connected for the next forty years. After leaving the Westervelt Home, Mary lived with her mother at Nyack, while Robert was at The Stony Brook School. Ethel Bell continued extensive travel during those years, representing the evangelistic work of the Christian and Missionary Alliance, frequently telling the raft story to enthralled audiences. By 1947, Mary had graduated from Nyack High School and was ready to enter Nyack College. Two years later, with Robert having graduated from Stony Brook and also enrolled at Nyack College, Ethel Bell returned to French West Africa. Her work would be to begin a school for girls at Béoumi. She was there when, on January 27, 1950, her daughter married Elmer J. Whitbeck, a former Marine, whom Mary had met at Nyack College.

Together Mary and Elmer Whitbeck began their Christian ministry to rural congregations in the Badlands of South Dakota. Following seminary studies at Conservative Baptist Theological Seminary in Denver, Elmer Whitbeck joined the staff of the radio broadcast "Back to the Bible" in Lincoln, Nebraska. The Whitbecks have five grown children.

Meanwhile, Ethel Bell's missionary service continued, interrupted only by regular furloughs in 1954 and 1958. The girls' school at Béoumi flourished, and by the time of her retirement in 1962, Mrs. Bell could look back upon almost forty years of missionary labor, in Africa as well as at home.

She had been a missionary by intention and practice since the 1920s. She had helped her husband in pioneering for the gospel; she had founded a growing school for girls. But overriding all her other work had been the testimony of her faith during a period of extreme hardship and under the most severely trying conditions. For this, all who knew her honored Ethel Bell.

With her sister Nell, she retired to a colony for missionaries, first, in Glendale, California, then in Deland, Florida. By 1978 she was no longer able to care for herself independently, so she moved to Nebraska to live with her daughter and son-in-law. In the winter and early spring of 1983, Ethel Bell's health declined rapidly. On July 20, 1983, she entered the presence of the heavenly Father in whom she had believed all her life.

In poor health as a young woman — indeed, given up for dead — threatened by danger in Africa and on the high seas, she had nonetheless claimed as her own a promise in Psalm 91:16: "With long life will I satisfy thee and show thee my salvation."

As always, Ethel Bell had trusted and proven God true.

For more than twenty-five years Bob Bell lived quietly with his memories of that horrendous Sunday afternoon in August 1942 and the twenty days that followed. Although his mother told and retold their story to audiences throughout North America, her story grew increasingly to sound like the recounting of events from the past. The story lacked currency because the Bells had had only the most minimal contact with any of the other participants in their raft adventure. In 1943, Lieutenant John D. Craven, who had ordered the guns of HMS *Vimy* to fire on the presumed U-boat, contacted Mrs. Bell in New York. She had asked Craven directly, "Were you firing at us in earnest, or — as some in my audience have suggested — were you merely trying to get a reaction from us?"

"Mrs. Bell," the British naval officer had told her, "we were in dead earnest. In time of war, you fire first and ask questions later. We did our best to blow what we thought was a U-boat to kingdom come!"

More evidence confirming the providence of God, working through the unaccountable inaccuracy of skilled gunners!

Ten years later Robert McDaniel had turned up in New York, where he was working with The Salvation Army in alcoholic rehabilitation. Bob Bell, his wife, and mother spent a day with McDaniel, then never heard from him again.

As for the Shaw children, they seemed to have disappeared altogether.

By the mid 1960s, Bob Bell himself was beginning to receive invitations to speak to a variety of groups on Long Island. At first he, too, spoke solely from memory, without benefit of visual aids of any sort to help his audience, without reference to any up-to-date information about others than his own sister and mother. As such, his talk was interesting in itself; yet it left numerous questions in the audience's mind that Bell was unable to answer. But at a banquet in 1975 a member of the audience made a suggestion which awakened in Bob Bell his long-dormant curiosity. The man said, "Why don't you write to the

Mariner's Museum in Newport News, Virginia, and ask for a photograph of the *West Lashaway?*"

"That was the first step," says Bell, "toward my acquiring a half-dozen scrapbooks of photos, documents, and correspondence from anyone and everyone who could possibly offer me information about our story and its details."

Over the next four years Bell wrote to the British Admiralty and the Imperial War Museum in London, from which he acquired a photograph of HMS *Vimy* and copies of its proceedings for September 18, 1942; to the Naval Historical Section of the National Archives in Washington, D.C. From Dr. Dean Allard, head of the Naval Section, Bell found many leads to broad avenues of information, including declassified Naval Operations documents concerning the sinking of the *West Lashaway.* Allard also sent the name of Dr. Jürgen Rohwer, director of the Library of World History in Stuttgart, West Germany. The way now had been cleared for Bob Bell to begin making personal contacts with individuals significant to his story.

Bell began sending letters, identifying himself as a survivor from a torpedoed ship, requesting whatever information might be forthcoming. He placed a classified advertisement in periodicals such as the National Maritime Union's journal, *The Pilot,* asking other survivors from the *West Lashaway* to write. From these notices, he received no response at all.

Then one day, almost as if on a whim, Bell looked for a name in a telephone directory. "I'd remembered that George Marano was from White Plains, in Westchester County, just an hour or so from Stony Brook. On January 5, 1977, I call Directory Assistance for a listing. The family had kept its number listed under George's father's name, even though he was no longer living. I dialed, a woman answered, and I identified myself. She told me that she was George's sister-in-law and gave me his phone number in Florida.

"That same evening, I called the Florida number. Again a woman answered. I told her who I was and asked for George. I could hear her relaying the message to someone else in the room. Then I heard that person say, 'Bob Bell—I wonder if he's the one that was on the raft?' I knew my search had just taken a big step forward."

Four months later, Bob Bell met George Marano in White Plains; since then, Bell and Marano have met three additional times. George Marano's recovery from the ordeal took longer than most of the survivors. But by early winter of 1943, he was ready to enlist. No more sea duty! This time it would be as a foot soldier in the United States Army. Marano's company took part in the Italian invasion, and George was in Europe at the time of V-E Day.

Upon discharge, Marano returned to White Plains and married his girlfriend, Emily. They moved to Pinellas Park, Florida, bought land, and established a trailer park. Marano also owned a bar, serving a regular clientele of long-time patrons until his retirement in 1984. On one occasion, he told Bell, several British sailors came into his place for a drink. George began talking with them and discovered that some of them had served on HMS *Vimy*—in fact, they had been on board the very day of the raft's deliverance!

"I gave them all free rounds of drinks," says George Marano, "because I remember those Brits gave us their day's supply of rum when they pulled us off that raft. It was the least I could do."

Marano told Bob Bell another interesting fact. "For years I've read the weekend newspapers, especially the church ads, looking for your name. I was pretty sure you'd grow up to be a preacher or speaker."

In the summer of 1977, George and Emily Marano vacationed in Barbados. Somehow a local newspaper became aware of Marano's return to Barbados and published a story about his 1942 experience. Douglas K. Stott, the *Vimy's* radar technician, then living on St. Kitts, read the article and contacted Marano, who passed his name on to Bell. So one piece at a time, the puzzle of the raft story began coming together.

In 1978 Bell located Richard Shaw. Since the evening of October 21, 1942, when Richard and Carol were taken by their mission president to the Westervelt Home, there had been no communication between the Shaws and Bells. By the time Mary and Robert themselves arrived at the Missionary Children's Home, Richard had been expelled, and Carol had set out on an odyssey of her own.

"Some of the things that happened to me since we last saw each other," Dick Shaw wrote to Bob Bell on September 30, 1978, "were harder on me than what we went through together on the life raft, believe it or not. I'm sure it began at the Westervelt Home (ugh!). After being booted out of there, which didn't hurt me a bit, I lived in six different foster homes, attending seven different schools in five different states in two and a half years. I guess I was such a nice guy, everybody wanted to share me, huh? When I was seventeen years old, I ran off into the navy."

Shaw returned from World War II and headed for Burlington, Iowa, as he says, "to see the aunt and uncle that I did live with the longest of anybody, and who treated me like a human being." Called back into active duty by the Korean War, Shaw served a year in that conflict.

"All those years, from Westervelts' on, I really wasn't living for the Lord," Dick Shaw admits. "In fact, for a period of time no one would have suspected that I even knew who Jesus Christ was. I had tried to run away from everything, including Him, which turned out to be impossible to do.

"After I came home from Korea, there were more things I tried to run from, which was useless, and ended up with my spending six months in the V.A. hospital because of things I couldn't forget but had to learn how to face them and live with them."

But in 1957, Shaw says, he gave up fighting against the Lord in whom he had once, as a young boy, believed. The next year Evelyn, his wife, became a believer in Jesus Christ. After attending Moody Bible Institute, where his father and mother had also studied, Richard Shaw became an ordained minister in 1964. "You know, I even tried to run from that, too. The last thing," he says, "in the world I wanted was to be a preacher. But by this time I had already learned that it is a losing battle to fight God."

Shaw has been a pastor in Iowa, but his principal ministry is in conducting Bible study groups meeting in homes. "Would you believe," he adds, "I now have a Bible study in the Iowa State Penitentiary at Mount Pleasant—not exactly the same kind of *home* Bible study!" To meet expenses, Dick Shaw works as an electrician for the Burlington Northern Railroad. He and Evelyn have three children, now young adults, and grandchildren.

Like her brother, Carol Shaw's childhood was also affected by the Westervelt Home and the disruption of moving from one foster family to another. Brother and sister were in the same foster home for a few months during the winter of 1943-44, but after that, Dick Shaw says, "I never saw her for ten years. She had been nine years old, a knobby-kneed little girl. Now she was a nineteen-year-old young woman standing in front of me."

But Carol Shaw had changed in other dimensions than just her appearance. For one, she was no longer Carol Shaw. A new name, a new identity, had all but blotted out the past. Her story illuminates how some survivors deal with psychological trauma by burying its cause and thereafter disallowing the exhumation of memories.

A strange seqence of events, however, brought the story of Carol Shaw to the front page of the Chicago *Daily News*. The chain begins with Commander Raymond B. Venables, formerly sublieutenant in charge of navigation on HMS *Vimy*. In 1953 Venables was a master at the famous Harrow School in England. He still had in his possession a photograph of himself holding in his arms a small girl just rescued from a raft. In conversation with George R. Bent, an official in the American Friends Service Committee, Venables asked if that social service agency could possibly help him to locate the girl whom he remembered only as "Caroline."

Upon returning to Chicago, Bent asked the *Daily News* to assist, apparently not realizing at that time that Harvey and Vera Shaw had been students at Moody Bible Institute in Chicago and had also served in Chicago churches before going to Africa in 1937. The newspaper received calls from several persons recognizing the little girl named "Caroline" as Harvey and Vera Shaw's surviving daughter Carol. But none of the callers knew her present whereabouts, nor her brother's.

Someone, however, suggested that the American

Friends Service Committee might inquire of the Reverend Axel O. Odegard, former pastor of Galilee Baptist Church in Chicago, where Harvey Shaw had last been minister of music. Odegard was then pastor of a church in Albany, California. Contacted by George Bent, he too had no information as to where Carol or Richard Shaw might be found. He wished to know because Vera Shaw had entrusted to her pastor a box of keepsakes, telling him, in 1937, "if anything ever happens to me, please give this box to my children."

A few weeks later Odegard entertained in his home Dr. Richard Elvee, president of Northwestern College, now located in Roseville, Minnesota. During their dinner conversation, Odegard, an alumnus of Northwestern College, told Elvee this curious story about a pair of lost children—the young girl in particular—a British naval officer's photograph, and a mother's collection of precious possessions. Elvee recognized a connection between the story and the background of one of his own students, a freshman from Detroit, Michigan.

"But her name is Donna Hobson!" said Richard Elvee.

Mr. and Mrs. Lloyd L. Hobson, friends of Harvey and Vera Shaw, had learned of little Carol's misery, taken her into their home in 1944, adopted her as their own daughter, and changed her name to Donna Hobson.

So Axel Odegard traveled to Minneapolis to see once more the daughter of his late associates, to deliver to Donna Hobson her mother's treasures. Then, returning to California through Chicago, Odegard informed George Bent that the child in Commander Venables's photograph had been found.

On June 22, 1954, Donna Hobson came to Chicago and the offices of the American Friends Service Committee. Accompanying her were her adopted brother, the Reverend Robert G. Hobson, and his wife, Nina, of Kasson, Minnesota. In Bent's office Donna Hobson allowed herself to be interviewed and photographed for that day's lead story headlining the front page of the *Daily News:*

LOST CHILD FOUND,
END 12-YR. HUNT
Fulfills Last Wish of Drowned Mother
Chicago Minister Reunites Girl with
British Rescuer

Nina Hobson, sister-in-law of the reluctant celebrity, described her: "Donna hasn't been able to eat for a week, it's all been so exciting."

Two photographs accompanied the newspaper article, a copy of Venables's picture and a shot of Donna Hobson speaking by transatlantic telephone with Raymond B. Venables himself.

"You were a very little girl," Venables told her. "I remember you said to me, 'I'm so glad you picked us up!' "

For her part, Donna Hobson recalled "the man who gave me some tomato soup."

As far as Richard Shaw knew, that 1954 exposure was the last time his sister ever acknowledged her past. Writing to Bob Bell concerning the research for this book, Dick Shaw said, "Concerning my sister's being interested in any of this, I doubt it very much." Married and a grandmother, Mrs. William Taylor, formerly Donna Hobson, née Carol Shaw, has refused all attempts by this book's authors to communicate with her.

As years passed, Bob Bell began to assume that he had learned as much about his adventure as research and investigation could tell him. Almost four decades had elapsed. Undoubtedly death had removed most of those who — had he been able to reach them — might have contributed additional information. Then one day Bell received from the National Archives a newly declassified report from the Office of Naval Intelligence.

During the weeks of their recuperation in Barbados General Hospital, the men from the *West Lashaway* and Ethel Bell had been interviewed repeatedly by U.S. Navy personnel, who had pages of questions to ask: Type of ship? Particulars of ship and voyage? Ship's position, date, and time? Course and speed of ship when enemy was first sighted or attack commenced? Confidential documents, if any? What became of them?

The answers to these questions, filed by Lieutenant John W. Scott, Jr. USN, appeared in a confidential report dated December 9, 1942, and were delivered to the vice chief of Naval Operations. Reading the report, Bell realized how bland and unemotional the language of official records can be. The report had asked for "a brief, complete outline of extent of damage caused by each hit." The intelligence officer had recorded as follows:

> *1st torpedo* — to starboard deep amidships just forward of fire room. Detail of damage not observed.
> *2nd torpedo* — 20 seconds later close to waterline about where 1st torpedo struck. Broke generator housing, blew out #3 hatch, blew up bridges, damaged 2 starboard boats. Ship rolled over to starboard and sank within a minute.

On the navy document's final page, Bell found two names and addresses:

James Owen
1400 Veto Street
Pittsburgh, Pa.

Joseph Greenwell
206 W. Jefferson St.
Pulaski, Tennessee

"I wrote letters to them both," says Bell, "not really expecting to hear from either of them after almost forty years." His letter to each man identified himself and asked, "Were you on the SS *West Lashaway* that was torpedoed on August 30, 1942?"

From the bosun Bell received no reply, just his envelope returned and marked by the United States Postal Service "Not At This Address." But the letter addressed to Joe Greenwell had been forwarded to his current address. Less than two weeks later, on January 22, 1979, the *West Lashaway*'s first engineer, then eighty years old, answered by mail.

After reviewing their mutual experience on the raft, Greenwell filled in some missing details for Bell's benefit.

"The members of the crew and I remained in Barbados General Hospital for about six weeks, I think. When we all got out, I as the only officer in the group was more or less in charge. I chartered an old, beat-up, single engine seaplane to take us to Key West, Florida. But the pilot took us by way of Trinidad, where we were supposed to refuel. We got our fuel and started to crank up, when along came U.S. Navy brass and ordered us off the plane.

Some navy officer handed me papers, telling me that our plane was needed for the war.

"Well, we got loaded onto trucks and taken about ten miles out of Port of Spain to a jungle camp made up of hundreds of tents. We called it Torpedo Junction. It housed about three thousand survivors from various shipwrecks. There were people there from every nationality except Germans and Japanese. Conditions weren't much better than what we had on the raft! Food was in short supply, and we ate it off tin plates. Every night in our tents, lizards would crawl up out of the ground, inflate their bellies, and make their whistling noise. You could hear them for miles.

"The only good part about being at Torpedo Junction was the rum. It cost about sixty cents a bottle, and with nothing else on our hands, you can imagine that we had quite a picnic out there!"

For another six weeks Joe Greenwell and his comrades endured their second seemingly endless wait. Finally, in mid-December, they were herded onto a ship headed, first, for San Juan, Puerto Rico, then eventually to Norfolk, Virginia.

"When we got to Norfolk," says Greenwell, "a special train was waiting to take us to New York. We arrived at Penn Station at midnight on Christmas Eve — in the middle of a snowstorm! You have to imagine the sight: two thousand people from all over the world dressed in shorts, sandals, straw hats, straw suitcases! The Barber Line had a man at Penn Station to meet our crew and to furnish all of us with new clothing and with anything else we needed. I must say, they took good care of us. But the rest of the poor souls were on their own."

After a brief stay in New York, Greenwell went home to Pulaski, remaining there for only a month. Then it was time to get back to sea. For Joe Greenwell, there were no lingering fears, no second-guessing. "It was all part of the job," he says. "You can't give up in a circumstance like that. I don't think I'd ever give up. All the time we were on the raft, I always had a lot of hope. I knew we were going to be picked up sometime.

"When you've got nothing to eat," Joe Greenwell adds, "that's all you can live on—hope."

Greenwell served in the Atlantic zone until the Normandy invasion, then shipped to the Pacific theater. Three times his ships were hit but only minor damage resulted. When Japan surrendered, Joe Greenwell was stationed in the Marshall Islands.

Following the war, Greenwell continued to work on merchant vessels, shipping out of the Port of New York until 1962, when he retired.

"I live alone in the country," he wrote to Bob Bell, "and I'm a shareholder in a small lake development."

In July 1981 Bob Bell and George Marano traveled together to Pulaski, Tennessee, to meet Joe Greenwell.

"That was quite a get-together," says Bell. "Those two old salts had lots to talk about, lots to clear up in my mind."

One detail had always remained a mystery in Bell's memory: the captain's talk of gold. What was that all about? Bell asked Joe Greenwell.

Yes, Greenwell confirmed, there had been gold hidden on board the *West Lashaway,* belonging to General Charles de Gaulle's Free French Government, being spirited out of French West Africa before the Germans could capture it.

"But when the navy interrogated me in that Barbados hospital," said Greenwell, "I never mentioned De Gaulle's gold. As far as I was concerned, that secret belonged to Captain Bogden and me. I suppose that 50 million is down there at the bottom of the western Atlantic today, along with a lot of other treasure." Turning to his former shipmate, George Marano, he said, "Hey, Marano, how 'bout you and me go huntin' for it? Somethin' to do in our old age!"

Meanwhile, a far more remarkable reunion was being planned. As early as February 1978, Bob Bell had written to Jürgen Rohwer at the Stuttgart Library of World History requesting information about the German submarine *U-66* and its crew. Dr. Rohwer responded immediately with abundant information concerning *U-66* and with the names and addresses of the U-boat crew's survivors; he also sent the current address of Grand Admiral Karl Dönitz. In a subsequent letter Rohwer enabled Bell to locate microfilm copies of *U-66's* war diary, kept in the Military Archives in Freiburg.

Reading these official German records, Bell learned for the first time significant details about the commander and his crew, as well as information on the further adventures of *U-66*. Bell found that the SS *West Lashaway* had been Friedrich Markworth's seventh sinking on his first patrol as a submarine commander; two more ships had also been sunk before *U-66* returned to Lorient on September 29, 1942. Six weeks later, Markworth began his second mission, the U-boat's seventh patrol since its commissioning. This mission, however, was cut short. Markworth had barely begun to cross the Bay of Biscay when British airplanes attacked and damaged *U-66*. Two days after departure, *U-66* limped back to the home harbor at Lorient.

Repairs delayed Markworth and his crew until January 6, 1943. This time, in addition to its usual complement of men and munitions, *U-66* also carried a famous French sabateur, Jean-Marie Lallart. Off the coast of Cape Verde, near Dakar, the submarine surfaced and put out a rubber boat carrying the French agent and two German aides. These two were supposed to deliver Lallart, then return to the submarine. But nearing the shore, the rubber boat capsized. Lallart escaped, but the two Germans were captured by Free French forces. *U-66* observed their predicament but could do nothing to help them.

Instead, Kapitänleutnant Markworth proceeded with his assigned duties, teaming with six other submarines in the region of the Canary Islands. Along with commanders Bargsten *(U-521)*, Becker *(U-218)*, Schwantke *(U-43)*, Wolfram *(U-108)*, Schneider *(U-522)*, and Stiebler *(U-461)*, Markworth harried every ship in every convoy passing through those waters in the month of February 1943. Markworth's own boat claimed a destroyer and two other outright sinkings, as well as several more ships damaged. Not until a convoy including air support drove off the German submarines did Markworth return again to Lorient.

On April 27, 1943, Markworth took his boat to sea once more; however, diesel fumes forced *U-66* back to Lorient, and the eighth patrol resumed on April 29. This time Markworth's area of operation was to be the southeast coast of the United States, from Florida north to Cape Hatteras, North Carolina. On June 10, just north of Jacksonville, Florida, Markworth achieved his thirteenth kill, sinking the American oil tanker *Esso Gettysburg*. Three weeks later, on July 2, another tanker, SS *Bloody Marge,* sank after one torpedo had been followed by an artillery barrage from *U-66*'s deck guns.

Less than a week later, Karl Degener-Böning, the U-boat's chief radio operator, received a most important message from Submarine Service headquarters in Paris. The message, ordered by Admiral Karl Dönitz, greeted Friedrich Markworth with the news that he had been awarded the coveted Knight's Cross of the Iron Cross, the highest honor a submarine commander could be granted. Markworth and his men celebrated this distinction by attacking another American tanker, SS *Cherry Valley.* Two torpedoes scored direct hits; yet the *Cherry Valley* refused to fall. *U-66* opened fire with deck artillery, but when the tanker's own guns returned fire, the submarine was compelled to dive.

On its voyage back to Lorient, *U-66* encountered for the first time heavy aircraft presence all the way across the Atlantic. Much of the journey had to be conducted underwater, slowing the crossing and confining the men constantly to unbearable pressure and psychological tension. Finally, on August 2, 1943, Markworth decided to risk emerging and running above water. The day happened to be the twentieth birthday of Harald Nitsch, a torpedo mechanic. As a favor in honor of the occasion, the commander allowed Nitsch to go to the "winter garden" behind the tower for a cigarette. Shortly before 8:00 P.M., on a beautiful summer evening just east of Bermuda, an American fighter plane from the auxiliary aircraft carrier *Card* blazed out of the setting sun. The second watch officer, Schütz, saw the attacking plane too late. Almost before he could cry out, "Plane attack!" he was dead from the first bullet. Others on the tower—Markworth himself, his officers Klaus Herbig and Werner Fröhlich—as well as several crewmen were wounded. Markworth was shot in the stomach; Herbig's knee was shattered; Fröhlich took a wound in his heel. The young Nitsch, celebrating his birthday with a cigarette, lost both legs above the knees. Before the American plane had finished its attack, two bombs tore into *U-66*, setting off the motor of a torpedo within the boat itself. This torpedo had to be launched quickly to prevent its destroying its own boat.

Three men died as a result of the attack, including Nitsch, whose dreadful wounds claimed him the next day. Markworth had been gravely wounded. As soon as possible, a rescue boat, the submarine tender *U-117,* was dispatched to provide assistance. On August 6, four days after the air attack, a German Navy doctor came on board *U-66.* But before all of his supplies could be transferred from *U-117,* another air assault began. When the plane was sighted, *U-66* dived immediately; by the time the action had ended, *U-117* had been sunk. Dr. Schrenk performed emergency operations on both Markworth and another wounded submariner, using whatever medical supplies he could find at hand.

The fact that *U-66* survived such attacks and, in spite of its critically damaged condition, made it back to Lorient at all must be attributed in large measure to the skill of the engineering officer, Georg Olschewski. Upon their return to base, Olschewski, Degener-Böning, and Fröhlich received the German Cross in gold for their valor. Four and a half months later, on January 16, 1944, *U-66* set forth on its final patrol. But Markworth was no longer the commander. He would spend the remainder of World War II in Danzig and Travemunde as an instructor. He had much to teach.

In the spring of 1978, Bob Bell wrote to two of the German submariners, Karl Degener-Böning and Georg Olschewski. "It was a shot in the dark," says Bell. "I had no clear expectation that my letters would be well received or answered." Bell wrote as follows:

> *Dr. Jürgen Rohwer, Leiter of Bibliothek Für Zeitgeschichte in Stuttgart, has given me your name and address, indicating that you served in the German Navy on U-66, during World War II. My reason for writing stems from the fact that a freighter, the SS West Lashaway, was torpedoed by U-66 on August 30, 1942. I was a passenger on the freighter, and was eleven years old at that time. Following the sinking, seventeen of us drifted for twenty days until we were rescued by a passing British destroyer, the HMS Vimy. I wonder if you would be kind enough to answer some questions?*
>
> *I would appreciate hearing from you, for I have a great curiousity about events surrounding my experience. Thank You.*

Bell then asked a series of questions concerning the U-boat, its crew and officers, their duties, and any specific recollections his correspondent might have. He concluded with this statement:

> *Let me assure you that I carry no vindictive motive. Each side of the war was doing its duty, and all that is over.*

Two months went by, and Bell had resigned himself to the fact that his attempt to reach back into history and cross any remaining barriers of national or personal hostility had found its dead end. Then on May 31, 1978, another breakthrough: Karl Degener-Böning replied.

> *Dear Mr. Bell,*
> *Finally I am getting around to answering your letter of March 23, 1978. You can imagine my surprise upon hearing from a survivor of our wartime voyages aboard the U-66. I am very sorry that you, as a child, had to suffer such a terrible time. The long trip, I imagine, on the life raft, must have been a terrible experience for you. I can imagine that the experience cannot be erased from your mind, and the idea of it haunts you now and then.*

The U-boat radioman then went on to answer Bell's specific questions. Degener-Böning had been on *U-66* through every moment of its service, from commissioning to destruction, taking part "in every bit of military action in which the boat was involved, including the incident involving your ship." However, he confessed, "I do not remember the exact torpedoing incident." He then described his duties in the radio and sound rooms, as well as life in general aboard the submarine. "We were proud to be submarine crewmen," wrote Degener-Böning, "and the majority of us, I believe, were convinced that we were fighting for the protection and the freedom of our German people. Only with this firm belief in our cause was it possible to survive the physical and psychological stresses which accompanied the long and exhausting trips."

The radio operator briefly described the submarine's

sinking, on May 6, 1944, and spoke favorably of his rescue and treatment by his captors, the crew of the American destroyer USS *Buckley* and aircraft carrier USS *Block
Island*. "At that point our internment began, which ended
for me on September 23, 1947, and brought me to
America and later to England. But that is another story."

Karl Degener-Böning enclosed a photograph of *U-66*
entering its home harbor at Lorient. Then he concluded,
"If you are ever able to come to Germany, I would look
forward to meeting you personally, and I cordially invite
you to come."

Something in that letter spoke to Bob Bell's yearning
for a resolution to his story. "I liked the man who wrote
that letter," he says. "I liked his directness, his obvious
human compassion, yet his forthright manner of seeing
things as they are. Certainly, I was intrigued by his invitation and its more than merely courteous warmth." On
August 9, Bell replied in kind.

At the end of October 1978, Degener-Böning answered
with a lengthy letter.

> *The vivid description of your experiences on the
> raft after the sinking of the* West Lashaway *im-
> pressed me and at the same time affected me
> deeply. What tremendous fears and difficulties you
> had to overcome! The most unbearable must have
> been being at the mercy of the beaming sun while
> afloat in a desert of water and having to suffer
> thirst. After many years of peace and prosperity in
> our countries, one can hardly still recall the con-
> ditions of wartime. We can only hope that our
> politicans, who are in charge of such things, pro-
> tect us from any sort of wartime events.*

Then he proceeded with details of *U-66's* sinking and the crew's capture, expanding on his earlier references. "The conduct of your countrymen can only be called outstanding," he remembered.

In this same letter Degener-Böning presented Bell with another link to his past: the address of Friedrich Markworth in Detmold. "He is now a dentist." How perfect, thought Bob Bell. From submarine commander to dentist!

In ten days, Degener-Böning continued, he would be attending a convention of former submariners in Kiel. In the bottom corner of his letter's last page, he pasted an insignia. "The small symbol is that of the German Submariner's Club," he wrote. "Perhaps you will enjoy seeing it, despite the bad experiences which you have had on account of the submarines."

Once more Karl Degener-Böning repeated his invitation:

> *Mr. Bell, you will always be welcomed as a guest in our house. With the hope that you and your family are well, I now end this letter with good wishes and many greetings.*

Again Bell felt a quickening pulse as he read these words. The German Submariner's Club! An invitation reiterated to meet a crewman from *U-66!* He decided to pursue these possibilities. A letter to former Kapitänleutnant Markworth, written on November 7, 1978, began

> *Dead Dr. Markworth,*
> *May I introduce myself. We have never met, and yet our paths have crossed in a dramatic way. . . .*

On September 25, 1981, Bob and Ruth boarded Lufthansa flight number 409 from New York's Kennedy International Airport to Dusseldorf, West Germany. They had been invited as guests to a reunion of former comrades on *U-66,* a week-long vacation at a resort hotel near the Edersee in Westphalia. For Robert Bell it would be a different kind of reunion. For three years Bell had continued his correspondence with Karl Degener-Böning, their friendship growing with each exchange. But Bell had also written to and received replies from others in Germany; from the Grand Admiral himself, Karl Dönitz, Bell had received an autographed picture, mailed just two days before the *Befelshaber's* death; Dr. Friedrich Markworth, Georg Olschewski, and Werner Frölich had also replied. Their letters had increased his curiousity to meet these men who spoke with both compassion and detachment of their role in his life. The commander, for instance, had told him, "I was deeply moved by your letter, in which you described your experiences from 30 August 1942. I am happy that you were able to survive this horrible episode in your life." But in a subsequent paragraph, Markworth had also written, "Naturally, whenever we sank a ship during the war we would surface and try to help the shipwrecked people as much as possible." *Why not in our case,* Bell wondered, *and what about Admiral Dönitz' order following the* Laconia *incident?* These were questions he would want to pose to Dr. Markworth, winner of the Knight's Cross.

In one of Werner Frölich's letters, he had written:

> *Often, after the war, I thought about what happened to those who survived the ships which were torpedoed. Therefore, I was very happy to hear*

*that some managed to reach a harbor or were
saved. It must have required strong nerves, good
condition, and long-lasting strength to survive
twenty days long in a raft under the hot tropical
sun. Even if it has been so long ago, I would like
to congratulate you on being saved.*

For their part, the submarine veterans had questions
of their own. Olschewski had asked, "How come you,
as a child, were aboard the *West Lashaway* in spite of the
danger of submarines?" With all these questions on both
sides, no one need fear long lapses of silence in conversation. Bob Bell spoke no German, but his wife, Ruth,
had been rehearsing the German she had spoken as a
child; furthermore, several of the men had indicated in
their letters some grasp of English. Somehow they would
communicate.

Yet Bell was not without his qualms concerning this
journey. What if he had misjudged the correspondence — its fraternal cordiality mixed with objective,
matter-of-fact accounts of explosions, sinkings, and
death? The submarine veterans seemed to have put any
national enmity behind them; but what if, instead, they
turned out to be paradigms of those sterotypes of German enemies portrayed in movies like *The Train, A
Bridge Too Far, The Great Escape,* and others that feed
the American imagination? And what of himself? What
really were his motives in seeking out a face-to-face meeting with Markworth and his men? Could he be certain
that his emotions were sufficiently stable to remain under control? Or, to his shame, would he suddenly discover
a lingering, latent hatred of those who, in a legitimate act

of war—ignorantly, innocently—had nonetheless nearly destroyed his life? Soon he would have his answers.

Karl Degener-Böning met Bob and Ruth Bell shortly after seven o'clock on the morning of Saturday, September 26. "It was like greeting an older brother after a long absence," says Bell. "Karl was so warm, so hospitable, I knew that my intuition in trusting him had been right."

A two-hour drive on the *autobahn* brought the Bells to Karl's home in Bielefeld. There they met Hilde Degener-Böning, Karl's gracious wife. The remainder of that day was spent in broadening each couple's acquaintance with the other, admiring the host's splendid garden of late-summer flowers, leafing through photograph albums of their respective families, listening to recordings of the Bielefeld *Kinderchen*—a choir like those once conducted by Ruth Bell's father, Carl Koop. Then it was time to eat Hilde's sumptuous food while sampling Karl's collection of Germany's finest wines.

On Sunday their hosts took Bob and Ruth Bell to an Evangelical Protestant church in Bad Salzuflin, Hilde's parents' parish church.

"The first hymn we sang that morning," Bell recalls, "was *'Ich Bete an die Macht der Liebe'* [I Call upon the Power of Love]. In light of the purpose for our trip to Germany, I thought that hymn was like a benediction upon us."

Sightseeing, an afternoon concert, and dinner in a quaint restaurant occupied the day. That evening, for the first time, Karl and Bob began to share their common experience, the incident that had brought them together, the course of their lives since then.

"The formal greetings, the somewhat reserved conversation, were now over between us," says Bell. "Karl and I were able to discuss seriously our mutual experiences and probe each other for details."

Degener-Böning responded favorably and generously to Bell's intense, rapid-fire inquiries. As he observed his host's reaction, Bell recognized in Degener-Böning a man deeply moved by and sensitive to the hardships endured by those who had suffered because of submarine attacks.

"He was especially troubled by the fact that women and children were victimized by warfare," says Bell. "And he made it clear to me that very few German soldiers or sailors had any respect for the Nazi Party. He was a loyal German, through and through, but he hated Hitler and the swastika."

The next day, Monday, September 28, Bob Bell awoke knowing that he had arrived at a momentous point in his life. After visiting the broadcast facilities of Westdeutschen Rundfunks, the West German radio and television system, where Karl Degener-Böning worked as a sound engineer, the men went to a theater to view the current hit movie throughout all Germany, *Das Boot*. Bell had some limited understanding of what life aboard a submarine might be. In 1979 he had gone to Chicago's Museum of Science and Industry, where *U-505*, the only German U-boat captured during World War II, is on display for guided tours. But watching the movie with a veteran submariner gave the spectator a different perspective.

"Karl translated the dialogue for me," says Bell, "whenever necessary. Many times he laughed at the contrived situations in the movie. His one concern expressed to me was that anyone might think that everything happening in the film was typical of every sub patrol."

"It wasn't that dramatic most of the time," Karl told Bob. "Often it was simply very boring."

That evening offered a dramatic encounter far more realistic. At 8:05 P.M. the door opened to the house at 17 Nachtigallenweg, in the city of Detmold. There stood Dr. Friedrich Markworth, former commander of *U-66*. Bob Bell stood quivering.

"I was nervous, curious, anxious, excited all at once," he says. "I wasn't exactly afraid, but I was concerned about making a slip, misreading something, blundering in this awkward social situation."

But Markworth put Bob Bell immediately at ease. "All my anxieties were instantly erased upon meeting the man. His loud, deep voice welcomed us with greetings in both German and flawless English. In the gallant manner of Europeans, he kissed Ruth's hand. We were ushered into the parlor, furnished tastefully with antiques."

Because his wife was not at home that evening, Markworth performed all the duties of a host. Bell remembers particularly the genuine interest Markworth demonstrated in his American guests.

"Dr. Markworth's presence is compelling," says Bell. "His speech to us that evening consisted of words carefully chosen, and not just because he was speaking to us in English rather than German. I had the impression of a man thoughtful and precise about anything he utters — a man of exceptional intellect and articulate expression."

Bell also noticed that Markworth's eye contact magnetized his audience. "All in all," says Ruth Bell, "he is one of the most charming, completely captivating men I've ever seen. Growing up, I was infatuated with Gregory Peck, the movie star. Now, standing in the same room was a man equally handsome. At seventy-one years of age, he had not a gray hair. So youthful, so vibrant!

The former commander expressed his fascination with Bell's quest to know the other participants in his story. Markworth himself had no further details about the sinking of the *West Lashaway,* but he arched his eyebrows when Bell told him about the freighter's secret cargo of Free French gold.

"Ah, Degener-Böning," Markworth addressed his one-time *Oberfunkmaat,* "if only we had known!"

The two German Navy veterans laughed over the lost treasure.

"Yes, Commander, that would have been worth a deep dive!"

Markworth rose and went to his desk. He had prepared two copies of his personal map tracing the course of *U-66*'s several patrols. He now gave both Karl and Bob a map, with his compliments.

Commander Markworth had been a motion-picture photographer for many years. His Leica 16-mm camera had been packed as part of his gear on every submarine patrol. Because of heavy bombing attacks on his hometown, Markworth's property had largely been destroyed. He had managed, however, to salvage three reels, which he had subsequently reprocessed into a single super 8-mm film.

"He narrated the film for us as it flickered across the screen," says Bob Bell. "It showed him as young lieutenant on *U-103,* under the Commander Victor Schütze; then in command of his own boat, *U-66.* We watched the sinking of a freighter—I believe it was the *Rosewie*—followed by the submarine's efforts to assist survivors and capture the captain."

From time to time throughout that evening Bell slipped into phases in which he had to convince himself that this was not just a dream. Markworth's home movies affected him most deeply of all; yet he could not bring himself to ask the retired naval commander the pertinent question: Why had *U-66* offered no assistance to the *West Lashaway's* victims? Awestruck, dazed by the surrealism of emotion mixed with fact, intimidated by hospitality, Bob Bell could not force the issue. Instead, sitting in this pleasant company, Bell realized a truth of history, known only by those who survive its senseless wars: The hostility of nations makes needless enemies of otherwise decent men. But now, the war was long over, its terror behind him. Bob Bell and his family had survived without Markworth's aid at that time. Markworth, too, had suffered and survived. Together these two men could at last bury their common catastrophe.

Now Bell was ready to meet the rest of the submarine crew. On Wednesday, September 30—just eleven months short of forty years later—Bob Bell had his climactic reunion with *U-66*. "The day began quietly," he recalls, "and ended with a roar!" From the Degener-Bönings' home in Bielefeld, Karl drove 150 kilometers south toward Schmittlotheim, a rural village near the Edersee. There Hans Hoffmann, formerly a fireman on *U-66*, now owns a resort hotel, where the reunion would convene.

"At once and in quick order," Bell says, "I met twelve other officers and seamen from *U-66*. My mind was in a whirl!"

Firm handshakes, strong expressions of greeting, formal yet friendly, passed between the Germans and their American guests. Initially, some seemed cautious, some reserved, watching their comrade Degener-Böning. But his delight in having actually achieved this remarkable link-up of foe-become-friend seemed so genuine, so infectious, the other veterans soon entered fully into the spirit intended for the occasion.

For several hours these men exchanged stories. Of course, all the Germans listened intently as Bell narrated his adventures. They seemed astonished at his utter lack of hostile feelings toward them or their cause. "I simply reassured them that—as I'd stated in my introductory letters to each man—I have no lasting animosity, whether national or personal," Bell affirms. "I also used this opportunity to speak about God's forgiveness and His power enabling us to forgive others."

From the National Archives, Bell had obtained official transcripts recounting the sinking of *U-66* and the capture of its surviving crewmen. This twenty-four-page record, dated May 16, 1944, the German submariners found especially interesting. Pages eleven and twelve listed the name, rank, and age of the thirty-six men who lived through the May 6 ramming by the destroyer USS *Buckley* and incarceration onboard the aircraft carrier USS *Block Island;* another twenty-four names, including that of the commanding officer who had succeeded Markworth, Oberleutnant Gerhard Seehausen, were also listed as casualties.

"How young we were then!" said Hans Hoffmann, checking the list. "You, Leonhard," pointing to Leonhard Bürian, former seamen second-class, "and you, Helmut Illing, and you also, Vinzenz Nosch, were only twenty-two years old. And I was all of nineteen!"

"Infants!" scoffed Georg Olschewski, who, at age thirty-five, had been the oldest on *U-66*.

"Yes," Degener-Böning noted, "but look at what the

Americans say about our esteemed comrade Fröhlich!"
Pointing to the intelligence report, Karl read in his most
mock-formal tones, "The old sea dog, Stabsobersteur-
mann Werner Frölich!"

The veterans guffawed in glee.

"Old sea dog!"

"But I was only thirty years old at that time!" protested
the former helmsman and chief quartermaster.

"Ah, but you'd been around a long time, Frölich!"

"Old sea dog, indeed!"

Among his papers, Bell had a letter from the father of
the American pilot, Lieutenant Jimmie J. Sellars, USN,
who had first sighted *U-66*, then hovered overhead, firing his 45-caliber pistol, while the *Buckley* sped toward
the submarine. The father, J.H. Sellars, had written from
his home in Binger, Oklahoma, to complete that phase
of the story.

> *Jim circled over the sub to keep the location, and
> they shot at him; so he used his 45 and shot back.
> He was in radio contact with the carrier, and Jim
> told them he was shooting back at the sub. When
> the* Buckley *arrived, it came on so fast it cut the
> sub in two. Then when Jim returned to his carrier,
> he was asked all about it by the admiral, and the
> admiral told Jim it would make naval history—the
> first sub sunk by a 45! Jim was too bashful to do
> radio broadcasts and such when he got into port
> in New York. He did receive a Distinguished Fly-
> ing Cross for this action.*

The father's letter went on to tell that, in 1951, while
flying as a test pilot for the Navy, Sellar's plane malfunc-

tioned. Ordered to bail out, Sellars decided not to endanger the Maryland town by abandoning his plane. Before he could steer away to open space, the plane exploded.

All this information excited the German veterans to tell their own stories about the demise of *U-66,* their capture, their subsequent internment, first, in Casablanca, then at various POW camps in America.

"I was briefly at Norfolk, Virginia," said Helmut Illing, "then sent to Fort Meade, near Washington, D.C. From there, I was sent to Camp McCain, near Indianola, in Mississippi."

"Ah, Mississippi!" Karl Degener-Böning exclaimed with ironic nostalgia. "An oven in the summer, an igloo in the winter!"

"Were you well treated as prisoners of war?" Bell asked.

All agreed that they had received humane care from the American authorities.

"Excellent food," said Werner Frölich.

"And excellent treatment," added Vinzenz Nosch. "I was at Camp Shanks near New York City—"

"Camp Shanks! I lived at Nyack, just over the mountain from Camp Shanks!" said Bob Bell.

As a teenager, he told them, he and his friends often hiked in those wooded hills, testing each other's courage with reports of escaped German POW's lurking behind every tree!

"How long after V-E Day were you kept as prisoners?"

"Excuse me, Bob," Degener-Böning interrupted, "but in Germany we don't know the expression 'V-E Day.' We speak of the capitulation."

"Forgive me. How long?"

"I was back in Germany by June 1946," said Nosch.

"It was 1947 for me," said Frölich. "Karl and I came home by way of England."

"Ah, the English!" said Karl. "In March 1946 we left New York — about three thousand of us POWs — bound for Antwerp and home, or so we thought. But at Antwerp, we were turned over to the English, who also wanted a hand in our repatriation. But first, they decided to show us the beauties of the English countryside.

"And also the efficient methods of English farming," Frölich added sarcastically. "They taught us all about growing crops. . . . "

"Tending to carrots and wheat and potatoes," Karl said.

"Were the British vindictive?" Bell asked innocently.

"Let's just say that between England and Germany runs a long history, a long memory."

"We were paying back reparations, in a manner of speaking."

"I got back home in September 1947," said Karl.

"And that was early!" commented Paul Breyer, who had left *U-66* in March 1942, assigned to *U-541*. "My boat surfaced near Gibraltar at the time of capitulation. Three years later, in May 1948, the English finally allowed me to return home!"

Just before the evening meal, Georg Olschewski and Werner Fröhlich called the group's attention.

"Silence on the ship!" barked the old sea dog.

"Mr. Bell," Olschewski addressed him, "we have corresponded for three and one half years. We want to present you with a remembrance for your wife and you. Fortunately, now we are friends and forget the former enmity; we hope we will be friends forever.

"I don't want to make a big political talk," he went on. "We only want you to know how glad we are that you made the long trip to see us and to spend a day with us at our reunion."

Olschewski held out a metal commemorative plate bearing the insignia of the Second Flotilla and the number *U-66*.

"Please take this plate, which is given by the crew of *U-66* as a memento. I hope you will hold us in good memory."

Immediately after dinner, Edmund Wilshusen began to play his accordian, announcing the beginning of hour upon hour of singing. Navy songs, beer-hall songs, popular German songs poured like the endless German brew. Throughout the evening the veterans and their wives spoke affectionately with Ruth and Bob, toasting their visit and its significance.

"May God please stop any further slaughter of his people," said Hans Voigt, a former first mate in the diesel room, "and may no one be subjected to such suffering again as we all have known!"

Another fireman from *U-66*, Georg Grölz, spoke with fervor. "Like you, I hope that our countries will never again be involved in a war, so that we and our children can live in peace."

While her husband, Edmund, played the accordion, Wilma Wilshusen moved closer to Ruth Bell. In halting English she said, "Does your husband know that my husband go *boom-boom?*"

For an instant Ruth looked in puzzlement. Then she understood, and other women seated nearby confirmed, that Edmund Wilshusen had been the torpedoman on *U-66* in 1942. Now he led a group of happy singers, including one whom, years ago, he had thrown upon the mercies of God.

In July 1982 Bob and Ruth Bell welcomed Karl and Hilde Degener-Böning to their home in Stony Brook, New York. This time, Karl's journey to America was voluntary, as a free man. For Bob, the occasion offered more than just a chance to reciprocate the hospitality of Bielefeld; it also provided him an opportunity to bring together his sister Mary and his strong protector on the raft, Joe Greenwell, to meet his new friend.

As a gift, Karl brought with him a copy of a book, *60 Jahre Deutsch U-Boote 1906-1966* (60 Years of German U-boats) by Bodo Herzog. On its flyleaf he had inscribed his sentiments, in both German and English:

Meinem Freund Robert W. Bell . . .

My friend Robert W. Bell,
for your untiring work for understanding and
friendship between former enemies.
Thank you so much, Bob!

Your friend, Karl Degener-Böning.

The quest had been fulfilled.

EPILOGUE

This book ends with the sentence: "The quest had been fulfilled." So Bob Bell believed in 1984, when the book was first published. But, as E.J. Kahn, Jr., briskly noted in his 1988 feature article in *The New Yorker* magazine, "not quite." Bell soon discovered that his epic first reunion with the submariners in 1981, and Karl Degener-Böning's return visit in 1982, merely whetted his appetite to learn more about the men and their vessels who had altered his life that summer's day so long ago.

In July 1985, Bob and Ruth Bell returned to Germany, this time as tourists and guests in the homes of several crewmembers of the *U-66*. A month later, in Pulaski, Tennessee, Bell met with five other survivors from the raft: sister Mary, George Marano, Joe Greenwell, Richard Shaw—and his sister Carol, now Donna Hobson Taylor, from Conway, Arkansas. The date was August 30, exactly forty-three years after the first torpedo struck.

Donna had written to Bell the year before. The woman known to Bell as Carol Shaw explained how the circumstances of her life had combined to supress the significance of her experience as a seven-year-old orphan. "I don't remember the fear, cold, heat, hunger, pain, or any of that. I remember eating raw fish and liking it, I remember the pea coat a sailor gave me for protection, but I'm afraid that's about it."

But Donna Hobson Taylor ended her letter on this triumphant note: "Let me share that the shipwreck experience was only the beginning of being taught about the sovereignty of God. He has been teaching me that all of my life! And it is so comforting to know that there is no place I can go, nothing I can do that is not in His permissive will for my life."

That reunion, Bob Bell recalls, "was just as though we had not been separated for all those years. We were conscious of how closely knit we were. Our families could feel it, too. There were many laughs and many anecdotes to share."

Other reunions followed. Bell became almost an honorary shipmate of such varied crews as the USS *Buckley,* which sank *U-66* and captured its crew in May 1944, and the USS *Block Island,* the aircraft carrier to which the prisoners of war were transferred for their formal incarceration. In July 1987, and again in July 1988, survivors from the raft redezvoused with *U-66* crewmen, including Degener-Böning, at the USS *Buckley*'s reunion.

American naval veterans became interested in Bell's odyssey through history and began sending him bits and pieces of their own puzzle for him to fit in place. Cadet Midshipman Jim Fischer had served on the USS *Cherry Valley,* one of the few ships attacked by Markworth's *U-66* that survived; he sent information about that incident in 1943. Captain James MacDonald of the United States Coast Guard owned an oil painting of the *West Lashaway* and sent a print to Bell. Robert Johnson sent a copy of an official letter of condolence from the War Shipping Administration, received by his grandmother, the widow of Axel Anton Johnson, an engineer lost when the *West Lashaway* went down. From Lieutenant Commander Harold J. O'Leary, an officer on the USS *Barney,* DD149, Bell learned the name of that phantom ship, which on Monday, September 14, 1942, had tacked to and fro in futile search for shipwreck surviors.

So the quest remains unfulfilled because, so long as there are stories to be told and retold, comrades-in-arms or respected former enemies will eagerly rehearse their tales for any willing listener to enjoy. And Bob Bell will go on telling how his mother's faith in the providence of God sustained a raft of shipwrecked souls in peril on the sea.

Other Living Books® Best-sellers

THE ANGEL OF HIS PRESENCE by Grace Livingston Hill. This book captures the romance of John Wentworth Stanley and a beautiful young woman whose influence causes John to reevaluate his well-laid plans for the future. 07-0047 $2.95.

ANSWERS by Josh McDowell and Don Stewart. In a question-and-answer format, the authors tackle sixty-five of the most-asked questions about the Bible, God, Jesus Christ, miracles, other religions, and creation. 07-0021 $3.95.

THE BEST CHRISTMAS PAGEANT EVER by Barbara Robinson. A delightfully wild and funny story about what happens to a Christmas program when the "Horrible Herdman" brothers and sisters are miscast in the roles of the biblical Christmas story characters. 07-0137 $2.50.

BUILDING YOUR SELF-IMAGE by Josh McDowell. Here are practical answers to help you overcome your fears, anxieties, and lack of self-confidence. Learn how God's higher image of who you are can take root in your heart and mind. 07-1395 $3.95.

THE CHILD WITHIN by Mari Hanes. The author shares insights she gained from God's Word during her own pregnancy. She identifies areas of stress, offers concrete data about the birth process, and points to God's sure promises that he will "gently lead those that are with young." 07-0219 $2.95.

COME BEFORE WINTER AND SHARE MY HOPE by Charles R. Swindoll. A collection of brief vignettes offering hope and the assurance that adversity and despair are temporary setbacks we can overcome! 07-0477 $5.95.

DARE TO DISCIPLINE by James Dobson. A straightforward, plainly written discussion about building and maintaining parent/child relationships based upon love, respect, authority, and ultimate loyalty to God. 07-0522 $3.50.

DAVID AND BATHSHEBA by Roberta Kells Dorr. This novel combines solid biblical and historical research with suspenseful storytelling about men and women locked in the eternal struggle for power, governed by appetites they wrestle to control. 07-0618 $4.95.

FOR MEN ONLY edited by J. Allan Petersen. This book deals with topics of concern to every man: the business world, marriage, fathering, spiritual goals, and problems of living as a Christian in a secular world. 07-0892 $3.95.

FOR WOMEN ONLY by Evelyn and J. Allan Petersen. Balanced, entertaining, diversified treatment of all the aspects of womanhood. 07-0897 $4.95.

400 WAYS TO SAY I LOVE YOU by Alice Chapin. Perhaps the flame of love has almost died in your marriage. Maybe you have a good marriage that just needs a little "spark." Here is a book especially for the woman who wants to rekindle the flame of romance in her marriage; who wants creative, practical, useful ideas to show the man in her life that she cares. 07-0919 $2.95.

Other Living Books® Best-sellers

GIVERS, TAKERS, AND OTHER KINDS OF LOVERS by Josh McDowell and Paul Lewis. This book bypasses vague generalities about love and sex and gets right to the basic questions: Whatever happened to sexual freedom? What's true love like? Do men respond differently than women? If you're looking for straight answers about God's plan for love and sexuality, this book was written for you. 07-1031 $2.95.

HINDS' FEET ON HIGH PLACES by Hannah Hurnard. A classic allegory of a journey toward faith that has sold more than a million copies! 07-1429 $3.95.

HOW TO BE HAPPY THOUGH MARRIED by Tim LaHaye. One of America's most successful marriage counselors gives practical, proven advice for marital happiness. 07-1499 $3.50.

JOHN, SON OF THUNDER by Ellen Gunderson Traylor. In this saga of adventure, romance, and discovery, travel with John—the disciple whom Jesus loved—down desert paths, through the courts of the Holy City, to the foot of the cross. Journey with him from his luxury as a privileged son of Israel to the bitter hardship of his exile on Patmos. 07-1903 $4.95.

LIFE IS TREMENDOUS! by Charlie "Tremendous" Jones. Believing that enthusiasm makes the difference, Jones shows how anyone can be happy, involved, relevant, productive, healthy, and secure in the midst of a high-pressure, commercialized society. 07-2184 $2.95.

LOOKING FOR LOVE IN ALL THE WRONG PLACES by Joe White. Using wisdom gained from many talks with young people, White steers teens in the right direction to find love and fulfillment in a personal relationship with God. 07-3825 $3.95.

LORD, COULD YOU HURRY A LITTLE? by Ruth Harms Calkin. These prayer-poems from the heart of a godly woman trace the inner workings of the heart, following the rhythms of the day and the seasons of the year with expectation and love. 07-3816 $2.95.

LORD, I KEEP RUNNING BACK TO YOU by Ruth Harms Calkin. In prayer-poems tinged with wonder, joy, humanness, and questioning, the author speaks for all of us who are groping and learning together what it means to be God's child. 07-3819 $3.50.

MORE THAN A CARPENTER by Josh McDowell. A hard-hitting book for people who are skeptical about Jesus' deity, his resurrection, and his claims on their lives. 07-4552 $2.95.

MOUNTAINS OF SPICES by Hannah Hurnard. Here is an allegory comparing the nine spices mentioned in the Song of Solomon to the nine fruits of the Spirit. A story of the glory of surrender by the author of *HINDS' FEET ON HIGH PLACES*. 07-4611 $3.95.

NOW IS YOUR TIME TO WIN by Dave Dean. In this true-life story, Dean shares how he locked into seven principles that enabled him to bounce back from failure to success. Read about successful men and women—from sports and entertainment celebrities to the ordinary people next door—and discover how you too can bounce back from failure to success! 07-4727 $2.95.

Other Living Books® Best-sellers

THE POSITIVE POWER OF JESUS CHRIST by Norman Vincent Peale. All his life the author has been leading men and women to Jesus Christ. In this book he tells of his boyhood encounters with Jesus and of his spiritual growth as he attended seminary and began his world-renowned ministry. 07-4914 $4.50.

REASONS by Josh McDowell and Don Stewart. In a convenient question-and-answer format, the authors address many of the commonly asked questions about the Bible and evolution. 07-5287 $3.95.

ROCK by Bob Larson. A well-researched and penetrating look at today's rock music and rock performers, their lyrics, and their life-styles. 07-5686 $3.50.

THE STORY FROM THE BOOK. The full sweep of *The Book*'s content in abridged, chronological form, giving the reader the "big picture" of the Bible. 07-6677 $4.95.

SUCCESS: THE GLENN BLAND METHOD by Glenn Bland. The author shows how to set goals and make plans that really work. His ingredients of success include spiritual, financial, educational, and recreational balances. 07-6689 $3.50.

TELL ME AGAIN, LORD, I FORGET by Ruth Harms Calkin. You will easily identify with the author in this collection of prayer-poems about the challenges, peaks, and quiet moments of each day. 07-6990 $3.50.

THROUGH GATES OF SPLENDOR by Elisabeth Elliot. This unforgettable story of five men who braved the Auca Indians has become one of the most famous missionary books of all times. 07-7151 $3.95.

WAY BACK IN THE HILLS by James C. Hefley. The story of Hefley's colorful childhood in the Ozarks makes reflective reading for those who like a nostalgic journey into the past. 07-7821 $4.50.

WHAT WIVES WISH THEIR HUSBANDS KNEW ABOUT WOMEN by James Dobson. The best-selling author of *DARE TO DISCIPLINE* and *THE STRONG-WILLED CHILD* brings us this vital book that speaks to the unique emotional needs and aspirations of today's woman. An immensely practical, interesting guide. 07-7896 $3.50.

The books listed are available at your bookstore. If unavailable, send check with order to cover retail price plus $1.00 per book for postage and handling to:

Tyndale DMS
Box 80
Wheaton, Illinois 60189

Prices and availability subject to change without notice. Allow 4–6 weeks for delivery.